D0461363

RADICAL

RADICAL

My Journey out of Islamist Extremism

MAAJID NAWAZ
WITH TOM BROMLEY

LYONS PRESS
Guilford, Connecticut
An imprint of Globe Pequot Press

To buy books in quantity for corporate use
or incentives, call **(800) 962-0973**
or e-mail **premiums@GlobePequot.com**.

Lyons Press is an imprint of Globe Pequot Press.

Project editor: Meredith Dias
Layout artist: Melissa Evarts

Library of Congress Cataloging-in-Publication Data

Nawaz, Maajid.
  Radical : my journey out of Islamist extremism / Maajid Nawaz ; with Tom Bromley.
    pages cm
  ISBN 978-0-7627-9136-1
  1. Nawaz, Maajid. 2. Muslims—Great Britain—Biography. 3. Extremists—Great Britain—Biography. 4. Islamic fundamentalism—Great Britain. I. Title.
  BP166.14.F85N38 2013
  297.092—dc23
  [B]
                                                                              2013017848

Printed in the United States of America

10 9 8 7 6 5 4 3 2 1

For my family, my son, and for all my friends.
And for those with whom I started a movement.

The moving finger writes, and having written moves on.
Nor all thy piety nor all thy wit, can cancel half a line of it.
—OMAR KHAYYAM, *RUBA'IYAT*

Being American

If there is one identity today that is as misunderstood as being Muslim, let that be the American identity. And just as few religions are as mischaracterized by Americans today as Islam, few other groups mischaracterize America today as much as the world's Muslims. Matters, to put it quite simply, have come to a head. *Radical,* as well as being a factual and candid account of my life thus far, is an act of diplomacy dressed in the disguise of storytelling.

The story in this book is one of a Western-born Muslim who first found his voice of rebellion through a heady diet of American hip-hop, graffiti, and dance. The first part of *Radical* tracks my conversion from B-boy to Islamist—the gradual yet complete ideological transformation of a disillusioned young British teenager to a hardened Islamist recruiter. I came to live—and was prepared to die—to counter what I saw as American hegemony on a global scale.

In righteous indignation I traveled to four different countries to seed my divisive Islamist message, casting America as the enemy of "my people." Fusing faith with fury, I dedicated my entire youth to awakening what we called "the sleeping giant"—rousing the world's 1.5 billion Muslims against the USA. My charge was halted only upon my 2002 incarceration in Egypt for inciting Egyptians against Hosni Mubarak's US-allied dictatorial regime. I'd never wanted vengeance more than during those first few days following our arrest. I'd never felt more violent than those few days immediately after our torture. But mine was exactly the sort of mind, or more accurately the sort of heart, that America needs to hear from now. *Radical* addresses the reader in the voice of that young man, bringing the reader as close to his heart—across time and distance—as is possible through the medium of prose.

Despite my aggressively "anti-West" stance, it was, ironically, American subculture (through hip-hop) that first lent me a voice, first taught me to rebel, and first inspired in me a sense of self-worth. While this was totally lost on me at the time, I owe my very political awakening to America. It was American subculture that laid the foundations for me to reject "the West" entirely—and this too was done through an entirely Western discourse.

In this way, I have come to believe that a strange fetish exists between the hater and the hated. It is a relationship that the hater will do everything in vain to deny, yet one he cannot quite shed. It is also a relationship that the object of hate will act incredulous to, yet cannot quite help but to douse with fuel on occasion. And what was lost upon us all was that by defining ourselves against something, we were in fact defining ourselves *by* it.

The ideology of Islamism could have benefited greatly from this insight—that it was born, and flourished, in this hatred of "the other." During my time in Cairo's Mazrah Tora prison, I happened to share a cell block with the current global leader of the Muslim Brotherhood, Dr. Muhammad Badee'. In a poetic twist of fate reminiscent of Joseph's rise to power after his own imprisonment in Egypt, the Muslim Brotherhood now rules Egypt while the former dictator Hosni Mubarak is held in that very same prison.

During our prison years Dr. Badee' and I struck up a friendship. He told me that it was he who had originally smuggled Sayyid Qutb's Islamist manifesto—*Milestones*—out from that very prison to the wider public in the early 1960s. Qutb was the founding father of modern-day, militant Islamism, otherwise known as Jihadism. Qutb was eventually executed by Egyptian president Gamal Abd al-Nasser in 1966, but the Islamist ideology of *Milestones* outlasted the legacy of Nasser's Pan-Arabism, going on to inspire hundreds of thousands of Islamists the world over. It directly inspired bin Laden and Ayman al-Zawahiri, who used *Milestones* to form the philosophical foundations of al-Qaeda.

Qutb's journey toward a more aggressive, anti-American dogma in fact began after his two-year sabbatical to 1940s America. How ironic, the history of Islamist vitriol was inextricably linked to the object of our

CONTENTS

CONTENTS

Part Three: Radical

hate—the USA. Some of the most influential figures in our ideological journey had defined themselves against America. It was as if she were a fraternal twin, one whom we hated yet had no choice but to acknowledge. In this way, America has a curious history with Muslim extremism. From the reverse racism of Malcolm X's early days in the Nation of Islam (a movement that—through Public Enemy—inspired me during my teenage years) to Qutb and Islamism, America had inadvertently bred her own worst enemies, her strongest codependents.

Qutb was so disillusioned by his own inability to integrate with 1940s America, and presumably hurt by the common assumption that he was African American, that it seems to have inspired within him deep shame and embarrassment, provoking in him the crudest of prejudice. After this trip, which included time at Stanford University, Qutb returned to Egypt and published *The America that I Saw*, an exercise in blind bigotry the likes of which would make even today's most committed Islamists cringe:

> *The American appears to be so primitive in his outlook on life and its humanitarian aspects that it is puzzling to the observer . . . a primitiveness that reminds one of the days when man lived in jungles and caves.*

It's astonishing to read this from someone with an otherwise keen mind. Qutb vented against the racism he experienced in 1940s America without it occurring to him once that he was playing into this very same, and rather ignoble, racial stereotyping:

> *The American is primitive in his artistic taste, both in what he enjoys as art and in his own artistic works. "Jazz" music is his music of choice. This is that music that the Negroes invented to satisfy their primitive inclinations, as well as their desire to be noisy on the one hand and to excite bestial tendencies on the other. The American's intoxication by "jazz" music does not reach its full completion until the music is accompanied by singing that is just as coarse and obnoxious as the music itself.*

The book was a bigoted tour de force on everything from American men's hairstyles and their proclivity for developing "oxen" arm muscles, to the nature of American women:

> [T]he American girl is well acquainted with her body's seductive capacity. She knows it lies in the face, and in expressive eyes, and thirsty lips. She knows seductiveness lies in the round breasts, the full buttocks, and in the shapely thighs, sleek legs—and she shows all this and does not hide it.

Inspired by the prejudice he felt, Qutb's remedy was only more prejudice. This would be laughable, if it were not so consequential and so dangerous: his observations went on to directly inspire modern-day jihadist terrorism. And here is the ugly truth of the matter: al-Qaeda's quest to fell the Twin Towers had its intellectual genesis in this man's two-year sabbatical at Stanford University in the 1940s.

—~◦~—

I feel for American Muslims who are often stuck between a rock and a hard place: "America or Islam," "the West or the Muslim World." The fact is that the opposite of America is simply not Islam, nor is it the so-called Muslim World.

Even in geographical terms, in this age of citizenship and freedom of religion it is no longer relevant—if indeed it ever was—to perpetuate this simplistic binary. It's steeped in a medieval legacy that the "Christian West" and the "Islamic East" are irrevocably opposed. In the "East" there are many Christians—20 percent of Egypt's population, in fact—as well as other religions. It follows that Egypt is not a "Muslim Country" but a republic, a country for all Egyptians. Likewise, there are more Muslims in China, Russia, India, and Europe than there are in a number of Middle-Eastern countries. In contemporary times there is more freedom of worship and economic opportunity for Muslims born and raised as Western citizens than there exists for their counterparts in many Muslim-majority countries.

The "Islamic World" is not some geographic bloc "over there." Like all other religions, Islam is now as at home in the globalized West as anywhere else. There is no homogenous "Islamic World." There is only, if we must use a religious descriptor at all, Muslim-majority and Muslim-minority countries. In introducing themselves, Muslims would not lead with the fact that they are Muslim. Just as being Christian—or Jewish, or any religious marker—is not what others would lead with. There is no monolithic "Muslim culture." Despite this, and for ideological reasons, extremists on both sides seek to perpetuate an illusionary dichotomy; they falsely juxtapose a highly charged and politicized Muslim religious identity with an incomparable Western one. *What better way to create an Islamist superstate than to exclusively define Muslims against everyone else?*

I have been both victim to, and the propagator of, the crudest of these stereotypes. And it is no longer the case that such narratives are confined to the extremes. Just as anti-Muslim hatred has risen of late across the world, anti-American prejudice has rocketed, too. Fueled by a cocktail of unfortunate policy decisions, an ill-informed use of language (such as Bush's use of the word "crusade" to launch his war after 9/11), Hollywood and right-wing myths, and Islamist groups grinding their ideological axes, America's reputation over Middle East policy is at an all-time low.

Hatred of "the other" thrives on myths and stereotypes. The sad reality is that Americans and Muslims mutually spread some of the crudest of these stereotypes, about each other and among each other. And even though the America-or-Islam juxtaposition is false, the peddlers of prejudice have no chance of gaining power unless they succeed in pushing it. It only benefits them to encourage this dichotomy.

During the course of my efforts to challenge Islamist extremism among Muslims, I have been told that Americans are Islamophobic, ignorant, arrogant, loud, lazy, wasteful, selfish, godless, fundamentalist, promiscuous, racist, isolationist, and imperialist. Muslims often overlook the fact that these very pejoratives are used to describe them, too. It is further lost on them that by excluding Islam as one element of being American, they dis-empower their fellow American Muslims whom they purport to care so much about.

America and Islam are both so much more complex than this. Alas, these days it takes a radical to state such things openly.

I played my part in creating and spreading such prejudice. As an antidote of sorts I present *Radical*, an effort to recount the disenchantment that formed my early years and to retrace the steps I took to spread the very prejudice I claimed I was fighting. By following my voice as it develops, you will feel the pain and confusion as I grew into a committed Islamist revolutionary—in some cases you will even feel the anger. I think it's important to feel, not merely know, why young Muslims like me—and there will be many more—choose this collision path. It is the only way that we can fumble our way forward. But the third part of my story is even more important—how I pulled away from extremist thought. I hope reading *Radical* will help the retreat from this downward spiral of antagonism and enmity.

Having served in the same prison that originally held Qutb, and having broken bread with the man who smuggled out his jihadist manifesto, I had come to feel a connection with Qutb and his journey to America. It was with this in mind that after my very own journey to America, having been invited to testify on extremism before the US Senate, I posted an online video in direct response to Qutb's message.[*]

My message was also called "The America that I Saw," and its aim was to highlight some of the basic inconsistencies in Qutb's observations of American society. I noted that it was these same personal freedoms he so despised that allowed Muslims to build their own places of worship in the United States. I also noted that the disgust so often aroused in fundamentalists by what they consider "sexually permissive" practices is really disgust at what is aroused in themselves; and the fight to stamp out such behavior is, in fact, a fight against their own passions.

Radical is a longer, fuller effort made by me to break down such generalizations on both sides. Through the course of this story, the reader will find me on either side of this false juxtaposition. I have defended Islam as essentially a religion of peace in New York against Islam critic and women's rights commentator Ayan Hirsi Ali[**], yet when asked to choose a side for an Oxford Union debate about the American dream, I decided

---

[*] www.youtube.com/watch?v=Q0qdURg4Qz0.

[**] www.intelligencesquaredus.org/debates/past-debates/item/573-islam-is-a-religion-of-peace.

to stand among a predictably anti-American European crowd in order to defend America.[*]

I did so despite having once despised America and wanting to see her brought low. I did so despite having fought against and then fallen prey to Bush's War on Terror. I did so because I knew that no matter how far we had drifted from noble intentions and lofty principles, the abuse of principle is not sufficient to render the "dream" itself as flawed. I had no choice but to state clearly that we must not hold the American Dream hostage to neo-conservative foreign policy blunders, just as I had previously argued that terrorism by Muslims should not reflect badly on the faith of Islam itself. Standing there in the prestigious and historic Oxford chamber, I found myself once more inextricably linked to the fate of both Islam and America. I had no choice but to argue for consistency. After all, it was this very ability to distinguish practice from principle that had helped me on my own journey away from Islamist extremism.

Amidst this protracted affair between Islamists and America, my personal life seems a curious case in point, mirroring the rest of the narrative. During those early days I had been married to—and then divorced by—a member of my former Islamist group that was bent on destroying American hegemony. Sadly, our relationship lasted as long as my belief in my ideology. It took me a good few years to overcome the trauma of the mother of my child leaving me for deeply personal and ideological reasons. I had become an enemy of the cause, a "defender of the West"—whatever that means. I was devastated, and I played my devastation out in an unflattering array of actions. I did not fully trust in relationships nor myself.

After years of rediscovery and rehumanization, what I call my re-identity crisis, my heart eventually found solace in the arms of someone I felt finally understood me as I had come to be. And so I proposed to her. She happened to be an American. It had taken me a couple of years to actually believe that I could make this leap, from being married to Rabia—then a committed Islamist raised in Britain yet born in Pakistan—to joining hands with Rachel, a liberal born in Tennessee who

---

[*] www.youtube.com/watch?v=VWCKHGcvFVk.

came of age in New York. From Rabia to Rachel, the contrast teased out an observation that brought me a level of uneasy solace; after everything that had happened, maybe I had not really changed.

During those early years, the "love for my cause" was indistinguishable from the "love of my life." And now, as I raised my head arguing for political pluralism and reconciliation, perhaps my heart had once again followed the same pattern in my personal life. In her sentient, serene, and even musical gentleness, Rachel embodied the antithesis of the violence that had once forged me. Her comfort in the abstract, among the arts, her subtlety and tenderness being the very traits I needed to rely on to soften my combative instincts, to anchor my weathered soul. Perhaps I was only really able to love what I believed in, and would be destined to seek out the person who came to personify those beliefs.

But it was deeper than that; accepting myself and embracing a hybrid array of identities meant that I was now truly free to love someone who relished this complexity. And here it is that one can discover the real hope in my writing *Radical*; for we can all try to understand "the other" in times of conflict, and though sometimes we will succeed, other times we are destined to fail. But it is not so much in understanding this "other" that brings lasting reconciliation; rather, it is in understanding ourselves. It took me years in prison to finally realize that my hatred was against myself, and that my Islamist rebellion was informed by, and constructed from, the most Western of political ideas and methods. In short I was being American; I just hadn't realized it yet.

Maajid Nawaz
London
April 2013

FOREWORD

This is a book about change and transformation. Maajid Nawaz's extraordinary account of his life—from young childhood in Southend through teen years embroiled in street violence and induction into Islamism—makes it relatively easy to understand how political and ideological radicalism occurs. His description of the violent prejudice he experienced in his youth is a salutary lesson in what can happen when institutional racism is allowed to flourish. He makes it very clear how and why he became desensitized to violence and shows how racist aggression created a fertile recruiting ground for Islamist extremism. He writes powerfully about his gradual detachment and inability to feel empathy for others; such was his experience of immersion in radical ideology. But what is most fascinating to me is the evidence that radical extremists can change; it is possible. Maajid describes his awe at the compassion of ordinary human beings who, after his arrest, unfair trial, ill treatment, and imprisonment in Egypt, put aside their own dislike of his politics, stood up for the universality of human rights, and campaigned for his release. Chief among them was Amnesty member John Cornwall. Not only did he prompt Amnesty International to adopt Maajid as a Prisoner of Conscience, but he also wrote letter after letter of friendship to Maajid himself.

I am moved beyond measure to read of the transformative effects of these letters on Maajid. It reminds me again of why I am proud to work for Amnesty International UK, whose members' actions were so instrumental in enabling Maajid to reconnect with life and humanity. In essence, human rights, compassion, and kindness helped to save his humanity. This book is the account of his redemptive journey—through innocence, bigotry, hard-line radicalism, and beyond—to a passionate advocacy of human rights and all that this can mean.

Kate Allen, Director, Amnesty International UK

Prologue

SOUTHEND, 1992

Slamer: that's my tag when I'm out bombing, plastering the streets with graffiti. I write it without a second "m"—"Slamer"—because it's quicker that way, and speed counts if you don't want to get caught by the cops. I'm a hip-hop B-boy, into Public Enemy and N.W.A tracks like "Rebel Without a Pause," "Fear of a Black Planet," "Fuck tha Police"—their lyrics are deep. I'm in a "click" suit, baggy corduroys with pin tucks at the bottom, rocking Adidas trainers. My hair's a grade zero up to the top—when not in a red bandana it stands up in a box-cut, with a mad design trimmed up the back. My crew all wear the same clothes, blast the same tunes. Like E.P.M.D., we look the *Business*.

I'm fifteen years old, and I live in Southend in Essex, Southeast England. This summer, like every summer, the fair is here, in the park across the way from my house. When I was young, I used to go to the fair with my folks. Back in those days it was all about the rides: the dodgems, the Egg-Roller, the Carpet Roll. These days I go with my boys, and at night, not during the day. Now I go to chill and check out the skins on show, the local female talent.

As Ice Cube once rapped, "it was a good day"—or at least it had been. The sky is full of blurred lights against the blackness: there's a backdrop of girls' screams and thumping tracks from the rides; that sweet and sour fairground smell of candy floss and fried onions. We're bowling around, on the prowl, when out of the crowd comes a face I recognize. It's my friend Chill—real name, Tsiluwa. Chill and I are tight. Born in Zimbabwe, he came to Britain a few years ago. He's pelting towards us, crisscrossing through all the people, and I can see straight away that he's relieved he's found us.

"Yo, Chill. Whassup, bro?"

"We've got beef, boys," he says.

Chill turns around and I follow his gaze to where, and whom, he's been running from. Barging through the crowd is a group of white boys in green bomber jackets, and they're stepping to us big time. When they see

Chill has friends, they stop in their tracks. The crowd between us starts to thin, and I can feel my heart racing. The leader, a well-known local thug called Mickey, scopes us as he raises his right hand in a fascist salute. Then his friends are all at it, swearing and giving Nazi salutes, calling us "niggers" and "Pakis" and telling us to "fuck off back to where we came from."

It's good to know that in situations like this my boys've got my back. Mickey's threats are clear. I've been here before, but it's not something I'm about to get used to. Especially when it's more than all mouth: I know from experience that they'll be packing knives. If we get caught, we'll get sliced to pieces. The longer our stand-off lasts, the more the crowd melts away, and the hustle and bustle of the fair gives way to an ominous ring of space. No one wants to know.

We split. I'm running between the stalls, weaving in and out of people, running so hard I can hear my breath thumping against the screams from the rides. I know the park well, know where to go. That means I can give these skinheads the slip, and I realize with relief that the shouts of "Paki!" are drifting further and further away as I make my way to the gate. Then I'm over the road, heading for home. Straight in and up the stairs, up to my room and under the bed where I keep it: my favorite hunting knife. Taking three stairs at a time, *bish-bash-bosh*, I'm down and back out of the door before my parents can ask what's going on.

Now's not the time to cower and hope the shit blows over. Now's the time to stand with my boys, to back them up. No racist is gonna run us off our own streets.

The group reassembles at one of our prearranged meeting points when we get split up like this. It takes awhile, but once we're sure it's safe, we gather on the corner of Chalkwell Avenue and London Road. We're not looking for trouble, but we sure as hell aren't backing down either. We're not gonna be run down by Mickey and his goons.

As we walk back up London Road, a white van suddenly pulls up behind us. Back doors open, and out climb a group of nasty-looking skinheads.

Shit, here we go.

I've heard stories of "Paki-bashing" before. Tales of groups of men driving around in search of unsuspecting victims to stab. But this is the first time I've been the "Paki" in question. We've been set up. Mickey and his bomber-jacket crew, for all their front, are just local youths like us. These skinheads are in a different league: big men, built like brick shit-houses, in their twenties, tooled up and ready for action. There's a glint of a blade in the street lights as they climb out of the van. Some are carrying clubs with nails hammered in the ends. If they catch us . . .

My friends all have the same idea as me: we need to move fast. *My blade!* I think, as I hear them tearing down the street. *I've gotta ditch my blade!* If they find me with it, they'll think I'm up for a fight. My only chance is if I can prove I'm not strapped, try my luck, see if they'll let me be. I dive into a side alley, duck down, and hide the knife behind a bush. Then I'm out, pelting up the street, in the panic of the moment not sure which way to turn, and—oh *shit*—I'm surrounded. There's five, six of them, around me on all sides. Knives, brass knuckles, clubs. There's the Hitler salute again, pierced by more swearing: *Fucking Paki! Fuck off back to where you came from!*

I can feel my fear rising, my adrenaline pumping. The look on these men's faces can only mean one thing; they know there's no escape for me now, and so do I. This is it, *"that's the way the ball bounces."* I've had my skins, blasted my tunes, and enjoyed the good times. Now, I guess I'm just gonna get *got* . . .

EGYPT, 2002

Am I being driven to my martyrdom, my *shahadah?* I'm bound and blind-folded with filthy rags, packed between other frightened, hapless crea-tures, sweltering beneath an unforgiving desert sun. Heat and salt. Heat and salt. It's all I can taste. The sour, putrid smell of fear is thick in the back of the van, reeking from the sweat of those I'm trussed up against, and I'm certain I smell the same to them. Someone to my right is mur-muring incomprehensibly: a prayer, a whimper, or just gibberish. The rest are silent but for the sound of their ragged, labored breaths, waiting, wait-ing for what lies ahead.

It seems like four hours since I awoke, maybe five. There's no way to tell. The searing heat could be Cairo, but then again it could be anywhere in Egypt. *Allahu a'lam*—God only knows. Maybe it will be a bullet in the back of my head. The state security, Aman al-Dawlah, has been known to bus people out to deserted areas to do just that. What a mercy that would be. Quick and easy. Just time enough to read my testimony of faith, the *Kalimatain*, before I go. Yes, the Qur'an, I must remember the Qur'an. Chapter *Ya-Seen* will surely calm my nerves. I try recalling the words with all the focus I can muster, but nothing penetrates through the asphyxiating haze.

And then I hear it, announced with relish as a policeman, *a shaweesh*, jostles us out of the van and down steps we can't see: al-Gihaz. The Apparatus. Headquarters of Aman al-Dawlah, notorious in all Egypt for what has been whispered about its dark, underground cells. Many have come out crazed, unable to speak of what they encountered inside; others never come out at all.

In here I have lost my name. I am now a number. Forty-two—*itnain wa arba'een*—is what I must remember, and what I must answer to every time it is called. *Itnain wa arba'een, itnain wa arba'een, itnain wa arba'een.* Everything else is uncertain. I don't know if I will get down these steps without falling, I don't know when I'll be beaten. I have been stripped of defense; my blindfold means I cannot see it coming. Clenching my body in anticipation of the blows is exhausting, but it's all I can do. The muscles in my stomach and the back of my neck ache with the effort.

The change in the air tells me I am being shoved below ground. The space becomes constricted; dank, invisible walls start closing in. As I'm pushed through a corridor, the smell hits me like a blow to the gut; the stench of human waste left stewing too long. It cuts through the agony and the fatigue, leaving me gagging for air, begging soundlessly for respite. I feel movement on both sides, the restless stirring of confined bodies. Packed holding cells to my right and left.

With no room to spare, I am made to lie on top of others already lying on the soiled floor of the corridor; we are like human dominoes. I can feel a strange body crushed beneath mine. *Ya akhi*—my brother, forgive me for what my weight must be doing to you. I want to speak, but our orders are to maintain absolute silence, or be silenced. Hour after hour, new bodies pile up around me. In the solitary world of the blindfold, I have no way of distinguishing one living corpse from the next.

And so it begins, the long sleepless vigil of al-Gihaz. No rest, no communication, no movement. Shivering and sweltering between carefully orchestrated extremes of temperature, we must be ready at all times to answer the hourly roll call of our assigned numbers. *Itnain wa arba'een, itnain wa arba'een, itnain wa arba'een.* I must not forget. Failing to answer or falling asleep means a vicious boot to my face.

In moments of lucidity I remember that no one, not the wife and child I left behind screaming after me in the middle of the night, or the parents who fretted about my move to Egypt, know where I am. Panic rises like bile in my throat as I struggle to regain control. Allah have mercy. *Hasbi Allah wa ni'mal wakeel*—you are sufficient and the best of protectors. Ever since I dedicated myself to the reestablishment of our Caliphate, I have spent years knowing that this moment would come. Pharaohs were never defeated without blood and sacrifice, and the victories of the righteous have always extracted a heavy price. But help me through this ordeal, my Lord, as I am scared and alone. *Ya Seen, wal Qur'an ll-Hakim* . . .

Days, nights, I can no longer tell the difference. But I recognize with a shudder when the roll call stops and the "questioning" begins. A brother somewhere down a corridor nearby—assigned the number one— is yanked to his feet.

Raqam wahid!

Scuffling amid muted cries, he treads his way between the rows of prisoners to a room down the corridor. The door is left open like a warning to the rest of us. Shouts. Thuds. Pleas. And then a noise that turns my stomach. The sharp, unmistakable crackle of electricity, followed by a bloodcurdling scream. *A'uzu billah*—I seek refuge in God! It is hard to imagine the impact of such a howl until you actually hear it. A chorus of murmuring engulfs my corridor as all the brothers pray under their breaths. We all know that our own numbers will be called soon enough. Think! I tell myself. Recite the Qur'an! But my lips are quivering, my throat is dry, and my mind is shot with exhaustion and fear.

There are fewer footsteps as the brother is brought back to his place. His limp body is dumped against a wall with a sickening thud of finality. And then:

Raqam itnain!

It's on to number two. With time the threats and shouts of the guard and wailing of the nameless brothers blend into an endless stream of screaming sound. With brutal regularity the numbers are called, growing ever nearer to my own—drawing ever closer.

Itnain wa arba'een, itnain wa arba'een, itnain wa arba'een.

I must not forget.

TEXAS, 2011

Spring is giving way to summer in Dallas, and I've already decided it's too warm here. My suit collar chafes against my neck as I gaze out of the car that has collected me from my hotel; the neighborhoods are getting visibly grander as we near our destination. Unsurprising really, given where I am headed.

Dallas has just launched the Presidential Center for Democracy, and I have just spoken at its inaugural conference. I was invited to discuss the role of social media in the recent uprisings in the Middle East— mass protests that set the region alight and shook decades of tyranny and repression. Naturally, the rest of the world is paying very close attention. On the panel with me was Oscar Morales, a friend and fellow activist. Oscar is the man credited with organizing the largest demonstration against terrorism ever recorded—twelve million people responded to his viral campaign by taking to the streets to protest against the Colombian terrorist group FARC. Together, Oscar and I addressed an audience of global activists on how online platforms can be harnessed to mobilize and feed into traditional media. Surreal. Two years earlier I had not heard of Twitter. Now I was using my account to inform television programs about an uprising in Egypt.

The formalities over, I'm on my way to lunch with the sponsor of the event. I reach a large, imposing house, and at the door I am greeted by a butler who tells me that guests are to "go casual" for this one—lose our jackets and ties. Uncomfortable with shedding my jacket, I make my way through the patio doors to a huge, immaculately kept lawn, where the other invited guests are mingling and a buffet-style lunch has been laid out.

As enticing as the smell of a Texan barbecue is, the guests are more so. I spot former national security advisor Stephen Hadley and former secretary of state Condoleezza Rice chatting in a corner. While I'm standing in line for barbecue, a man comes over and introduces himself as Michael Meece, former chief of staff. He informs me that I have been invited to join our host at his table. Following Meece, I find myself among familiar faces: American activist and campaigner Stephanie Rudat, and various Egyptian and Syrian revolutionary activists. And there, ushering me to an empty seat next to him is the host: former president of the United States, George W. Bush.

I keep my expression neutral as I look into that familiar face; so much rushes through my mind. I return the handshake he extends and take my seat. Lunch with Bush: this is something I didn't see coming. Half-remembered memories of television appearances, the public persona, the caricatures, all flash through my mind as I recall his "War on Terror"—his war on me.

A discussion is already under way at the table, and I tune in to catch up on the debate. Bush listens intently to each person, interrupting frequently to ask questions and seek clarification. It's Egypt's future that's being deliberated; the Egyptians are advocating passionately for swift justice for the ousted dictator, Hosni Mubarak. For them, his trial and incarceration will herald a new dawn for Egypt.

But I beg to differ, and feel I must give voice to my concerns. I try to explain why this single-minded focus on "justice" might be detrimental to Egypt's long-term interests. "What is needed first and foremost is a constitution, followed by an election process, after which justice against Mubarak can be sought. If Egypt fails to define a constitution for itself at the outset, the first party to win an election will mold it in their own image. Justice cannot be arbitrary; it must be set in law." I argue this not from detached interest but from a deeply personal place; the suspension of constitutional rights following the assassination of Egyptian president Anwar Sadat in 1981 impacted my life in a way I cannot begin to explain. I have learned what Emergency Law and the overriding of individual liberties really mean. I have witnessed what Mubarak's regime has been capable of: the paralyzing fear, the routine humiliations, the torture . . .

"Stop," Bush sharply interrupts. He has now turned his full attention to me. "How do you define torture?"

I pause. *Has George W. Bush just asked me for my definition of torture?* I know immediately his interest isn't merely academic—during his time in office, the question of what did and did not constitute torture was a vital component to the "War on Terror." In 2002 Bush's Office of Legal Counsel wrote a notorious memorandum on the subject of "waterboarding," an interrogation technique involving the simulation of drowning by pouring water over the prisoner's cellophaned face. The memorandum famously, and highly controversially, concluded that waterboarding was not torture but instead an "enhanced" interrogation technique, and thereby admissible by US law.

Where do I begin? Should I say how I feel about the overly militarized aspect of the "War on Terror" and what it has cost the world in terms of human rights violations, reinforcing the terrorist narrative, and widespread damage to countries? Should I bring up Iraq? I've been on record talking about these issues, but how do you respond when the leader of the "War on Terror" asks you for your opinion over a barbecued lunch in his own backyard?

I decide to deal directly with the question asked. "How do I define torture? What about electrocution?" I look back at Bush and wait to be asked about waterboarding. Instead, he nods and agrees solemnly. "Yes, that *is* torture," and with a wave of a hand, "Please carry on."

PART ONE

B-BOY

Notice to all passengers, please do not run on the platforms or concourses. Especially if you are carrying a rucksack, wearing a big coat, or look a bit foreign.

—ANONYMOUS GRAFFITI IN THE LONDON UNDERGROUND,
AFTER POLICE KILLED AN UNARMED BRAZILIAN,
JEAN CHARLES DE MENEZES, AT STOCKWELL STATION
WITH SEVEN SHOTS TO THE HEAD, JULY 22, 2005

CHAPTER ONE

Memories of the Ghost Train

I was born in the late seventies, the same time hip-hop was busting its first moves in New York. The B-boys in the Bronx started it all, poppin' and lockin' to the original loops. Afrika Bambaataa, he was there at the beginning. So were the Sugarhill Gang, sampling Chic and hitting the mainstream with "Rapper's Delight." Then there was Grandmaster Flash and the Furious Five; Melle Mel gave voice to their fury in "The Message." A dozen years later, I'd find inspiration in this scene, discover my voice in its rhythms. Until then, I'd grow up in isolation on the other side of the Atlantic, my own fledgling years mirroring hip-hop's early development.

Even so, my own beginnings could not have been more different from those of hip-hop. The Southend of my childhood was not at all like New York—it wasn't, and still isn't, a place of ethnic diversity. Of its present-day population of 160,000, 96 percent are white. When I was growing up, that percentage was even higher. There were few Asian families in Southend—literally a few hundred people, no more than 0.1 percent of the population. At that time if you saw a Pakistani, Indian, or Bangladeshi face in Southend, you would usually know their parents, where they had vacationed last year, and the latest domestic scandal in their family.

Growing up in such a minority community has an effect on you. It was a completely different experience from being brought up in a large Pakistani community. It meant that we had no choice but to engage with the wider community, and as a result, I grew up feeling far more equipped to deal with cultural differences.

Such communities are big enough for people to live their whole lives within them, never to venture out. For many people the only interaction they have with white kids is in a fight. And the only time they come into contact with white women is when they are chatting them up in the hope of a quick one-night stand. That has a corrosive effect on how each community perceives the other.

My family originally hails from Gujrat. This isn't to be confused with Gujarat in India, which gives its name to the more prominent Gujarati community in the UK. There is another Gujrat, in Pakistan. It's a district and a city in the province of the Punjab, in the northwest of the country, toward the border with Kashmir. It is near Islamabad, though given the bad roads, it is still a good two-and-a-half-hour drive away from the capital, and equally far from Lahore. Gujrat lies on the banks of the River Chenab, and my family is said to have settled in the area from the eighth century, coming to the subcontinent with the Arab armies of Muhammad bin Qasim.

Gujrat is a city with a disproportionate influence over Pakistani politics. The Chaudhrys are a local dynasty that has long held sway within the army, and the city has produced prime ministers and powerful political factions. Gujrat is also fabled for its clan, or *biraadari*-based gangsters, and beautiful women. In folklore, the tragic ancient love story of *Sohni Mahiwal* takes place in Gujrat. Sohni, a Punjabi word for "beautiful," is said to have drowned in the River Chenab as she desperately tried to reach her forbidden lover Mahiwal. Infatuated by her beauty, Mahiwal jumped in to save her, and he too drowned alongside his lost love. This story has in turn inspired numerous poems, paintings, songs, and even two Bollywood movies. Family legend has it that my *Nana Abu*, my maternal grandfather, spent his childhood during the British Raj in close association with an English doctor, who resided on the hospital grounds with his family. Having grown extremely close to *Nana Abu*'s father, the doctor often invited his family over to share meals, festivals, and holidays. As a boy, *Nana Abu*, named Ghulam-Nabi, or servant of the Prophet, developed a deep fascination with this English doctor. Keenly impressed by his culture, education, and generosity, *Nana Abu* decided that when he was married and had children of his own, he would raise them all to be doctors, and run a hospital just like this one. This was to become his guiding dream.

A medical education wasn't immediately available to *Nana Abu*. With a heavy heart he joined the army of the British Raj in the hope that this would give him the opportunity to follow his ambition. He pursued a demanding slate of extracurricular courses alongside his day-to-day routine in the army. He quickly succeeded in qualifying as an accountant and was appointed to manage the military accounts for food stocks. With his dream still seemingly attainable, *Nana Abu* got married. My *Nani Ammi* was a beautiful woman from Gujrat named Suraya, which means a constellation of stars. Newly wed and full of hope, *Nana Abu* took *Nani Ammi* across India to Lucknow for their honeymoon. That same week in India, history was about to take place.

In 1947 the British decided to create two countries: India, which would have a majority of Hindus; and Pakistan—at that time West Pakistan and East Pakistan (now Bangladesh)—in which the majority would be Muslim. This meant that vast numbers of people had to leave their homes and move across the new border to live: Hindus to India and Muslims to Pakistan. There was chaos and pandemonium. The great human exodus unfolded right before my grandparents' eyes—on their *honeymoon* no less. In a panic they rushed to catch a train back to Gujrat, which was suddenly on the Pakistani side of partitioned Punjab. But it was too late. Mob violence and mass murder ruled on the trains. Bloodthirsty hordes, hell-bent on revenge, were boarding the carriages and indiscriminately killing all Pakistan-bound commuters. Train after train would pull into the station in Pakistan, everyone on board dead. These were the ghost trains.

Nana Abu was on one such ghost train. The mob had cut his train in two. The front carriage, where *Nani Ammi* and all the women sat, had been separated and taken off into the distance. The back portion, containing *Nana Abu* and all the men, was held captive to be massacred. By what can only be described as the grace of Allah, somehow *Nana Abu* escaped the massacre that followed. In that chaos, desperately seeking his new bride, *Nana Abu* ran from platform to platform, avoiding rampaging mobs while searching for his wife. He stumbled across her, frantically waiting for him at another station. Together, the traumatized newlyweds fled India, now a foreign country, back into Pakistan, now a new country.

Things changed so rapidly for *Nana Abu* after the Partition. Having been raised in a multiethnic and multifaith united India, he lost many of his childhood friends. Those who now belonged to the "wrong" faith were forced to immigrate to India; others left for England. Disturbed by memories of the ghost train, and having been torn from many of his friends, he became restless.

The British education system was seen as something unparalleled, and *Nana Abu* wanted his children to have that opportunity. In those early days, he often instructed his children, "Be not as strangers to the goodness and kindness of others. We must adopt as our own piety, truth, and goodness wherever it comes from."

And so he took advantage of his right to live in the UK. Immigration, at that time, simply wasn't an issue. It was Southend where they—we—ended up: a seaside town with no family links, no halal meat shops, no mosques, and no community. *Nana Abu* and his friends set all of this up. They created the first mosque in the town and organized space for Muslim burials in the town cemetery. Due to his education, good temperament, and thoughtful nature, *Nana Abu* quickly became a leader for his community.

Nana Abu was a traditional Muslim, which in those days meant being conservative, not extremist or fundamentalist. He expected his children to accept arranged marriages to other Muslims. Pakistan, like most of South Asian culture, was historically non-dogmatic. That comes from the way in which mysticism became entrenched across the Indian subcontinent. My grandfather was typical of that mind-set, liberal when he was young and more religious as he got older. That was a very Pakistani thing to do. I say "was" because of the rise of extremism among so many young Pakistanis today.

My mother was the third of nine children and was roughly nine years old when the family moved to Southend. They started off in a rented property for two to three months, then bought their own home. Despite being an accountant back home, *Nana Abu* found that his qualifications weren't easily recognized in England. Undeterred, with dreams of the hospital spurring him on, he supported the family by getting a job as a bus driver, and drilled into his children the need to study, work hard, and make the most of themselves. He typified the stereotype of the hardworking immigrant and was determined to give his children the best chance; he made sure that they grabbed it with both hands.

The result was that his children excelled at school. They started off in some of the worst schools but ended up going on to universities. Every one of that generation in my family is an engineer or a doctor of some kind, apart from those, like my mother, who were married off before they could go to university. But *Nana Abu*, for all his forward thinking, still believed in arranging husbands for his daughters.

Before he could ever build his beloved hospital, *Nana Abu* collapsed and died from a double stroke. He was only fifty-eight years old. I was nine at the time, and I still remember how much I cried on that day.

My mother had been born and brought up in the UK and has always been very liberal and progressive in her outlook. Most Pakistanis in the UK had parents who grew up in Pakistan and then came over here. It was unusual, therefore, for me to have a mother who had been brought up in England, speaking in an English accent. It meant that her experience was similar to mine. I was brought up calling her *Baji*—a title for an older sister—and it was easy to relate to her. Until, that is, I became interested in political Islamism: almost immediately, she became representative of everything liberal and Western that I began campaigning against. How such an estrangement could occur is the rest of this story.

One way in which my mother—known endearingly to all as Abi—enlightened her children was through literature. She encouraged me to read from an early age, and I have many memories of the sort of books that I read at the time. Roald Dahl was a particular favorite: *Charlie and the Chocolate Factory, James and the Giant Peach, George's Marvelous Medicine,* and so on. C.S. Lewis was someone else I read, though I had no idea about the religious connotations of *The Chronicles of Narnia* until much later. I also used to love those Fighting Fantasy books, *The Warlock of Firetop Mountain* and so on, where you'd read a page and be given a choice as to what you wanted to happen next. The idea of being able to create my own story always appealed to me.

All of this was quite different from the old Pakistani tradition of storytelling. The old tradition was oral, most obviously represented to me by my *Tai Ammi*, my dad's brother's wife. When she visited, she would tell us stories at bedtime in Urdu, such as *Ali Baba and the Forty Thieves*. My brother Osman and I would love hearing them because there was something magical in their telling, in the inflection of the story voice and the emotion each line would portray. Rather than putting us to sleep, they would awaken our senses to imagine a far-away land of flying carpets and genies, or *jinn*. We never told *Tai Ammi* that her stories woke us up rather than helped us sleep. There's a lot of skill within that oral tradition: it's all about telling stories in a way that is intriguing and suspenseful. *Tai Ammi* was very good at that: we'd sit on the edge of our seats, wanting to know what happened next.

But as wonderful as this oral storytelling tradition can be, it doesn't necessarily encourage children to read themselves; even today reading in Pakistan is not as widespread as it should be. How expressive a child could be if parents were to combine these two methods, the old and the new. I believe that it was precisely this combination within myself that gave me passion during the most difficult times.

One book that particularly tested my mother's liberalism, and my own changing views as a teenager, was Salman Rushdie's *The Satanic Verses*. When this was published in 1988, it caused a huge furor among many Muslims around the world. Its depiction of the Prophet Mohammed, upon whom be peace, was deemed blasphemous, and the author was forced into hiding after the Ayatollah Khomeini issued his now infamous fatwa. True to her fiercely independent spirit, Abi bought the book and read it to make up her own mind.

By then, my belief that she was dangerously on the wrong side needed no more confirmation. Abi's response had been a classically liberal one: "Let him write his book. If you don't like it, go and write your own book against him." That is Abi through and through.

My father was affectionately known to all as Mo. From an early age he grew up with a lot of responsibility. Both his father and elder brother died when he was young, which left him as head of the family before he was married. In the old days in Pakistan, when a man died, his wife would often return to her parents' family. The absence of a welfare state left only blood relatives as the safety net. But my father wanted to do things differently. He asked *Tai Ammi*, his brother's widow, to stay with him so that they could bring up his two orphaned nieces, Nargis and Farrah, as his own daughters. This ensured that *Tai Ammi* did not have to remarry again merely for convenience. Over forty years later, *Tai Ammi* remains a widow out of love for her late husband.

My father started out working for Pakistan's navy and trained as an electrical engineer. Unfortunately he contracted tuberculosis and was honorably discharged on medical grounds. The navy paid for his treatment and wanted him to return to work. However, he didn't respond to conventional treatment and the navy lost hope. My father then went to see a *hakeem*—an herbalist trained in ancient natural remedies—and he provided a number of powders. Curiously, these worked where modern medicine failed, and I suppose I owe my life to an obscure herbalist who has probably long died somewhere in the Land of the Five Rivers.

My father resumed life as an electrical engineer: he laid a lot of the electrical foundations in what is now the Pakistani capital, Islamabad. He laid down political foundations too, and it is this proud defiant streak in him that has rubbed off on me. He had been doing some work for the Dawood Group—a powerful industrial group in Pakistan. The company was immensely powerful politically, and unions were prohibited. At this time Pakistani workers, heady with Soviet socialism, became aware of their organizing power. Upset with working conditions and knowing that employers would never concede rights unless forced to, my father set up the first trade union in his industry.

Dawood's response was to try to shut them down. My father and his fledgling organization were taken to court. This was real David and Goliath stuff, and my father's eventual victory was a huge coup at the time. Dawood was forced to allow the trade union to operate.

My father married Abi in an arranged marriage when he was thirty-four and Abi just eighteen. He moved to the UK and used his experience as an engineer to get a job with the Oasis Oil Company in Libya, where he worked until his retirement, and where we were to visit him later on.

Because of this, I had an awareness of Gaddafi's tyranny long before it became common knowledge. My first memory of trouble in Libya harks back to the late eighties. I asked my father why the name of his company had changed from Oasis to *Waha*. My father explained that Colonel Gaddafi had nationalized the company and kicked out all Westerners in revenge for American airstrikes that had killed his son.

"But why are you still there, then?" I naively asked.

"Because Libyans like Pakistanis," he assured me.

I didn't understand this. As an ex-pat he was very well paid for the time, and we eventually moved into a large six-bedroom house as a result. Why didn't Gaddafi consider him British? What I didn't know then was that in 1974 Gaddafi had gone to Lahore and publicly supported Pakistan's right to pursue nuclear weapons. In turn, Pakistan named Lahore's main sports stadium after Gaddafi. I had no idea how this pursuit of nuclear weapons would go on one day to affect my own life so profoundly.

My father went in for the whole oil look. This was the era of *Dallas* with J.R. and Bobby Ewing. We all loved to watch *Dallas*; in fact, I still catch myself sometimes humming its catchy theme song. Typical of charming, worldly-wise Pakistani men of his day, my father didn't shy away from flaunting his style. He'd wear a Stetson, cowboy boots, a big belt buckle with his name embossed into the leather at the back, and an expensive diamond-encrusted gold watch; these days you'd call that *bling*. Like any child growing up, I didn't rate my father's fashion sense, but I did inherit his love for cultivating an individual style.

My father's job gave me something of a polarized childhood. He would alternate between spending a month in Libya, and then having three to four weeks at home. When he was away, Abi would be in charge, and her more liberal outlook would prevail. When my father was back, we lived under stricter, more traditional house rules. This created conflict between my parents—a clash of backgrounds, really, as well as a generational difference. My father was socially liberal but with traditional family values. Abi was fiercely independent and free-spirited, always the first to dance at weddings and the last to sit down.

Though work was the focus of my father's life, politics was the way in which he socialized with friends at home. This was a typically Pakistani and typically Muslim way of going about things. His stance toward the pressing questions of his day was essentially a "plague on both your houses"; he was very much anti-colonial, but having lived and worked under Gaddafi, he was also anti–Arab dictators. Importantly, and unlike many of the "old" European left, he wasn't pro–Arab tyrants just because they stood up to Western imperialism. He was well aware of Gaddafi's record of torture long before it became public knowledge in the West. He knew of the hatred that everyday Libyans bore their leader.

It's hard not to look at *Nana Abu*, Abi, and my father without thinking that something from each of them has rubbed off on me. Although they are very different characters, what unites them is the way they have gone against the grain: *Nana Abu* leaving a newly independent Pakistan for Southend to pursue a dream; Abi's liberal views challenging those of her community; my father taking on a leading corporation to set up the company's first trade union. Apart from all the other traits that I have been lucky enough to inherit from them, it is this instinct to rattle the status quo that strikes me as their most significant influence.

CHAPTER TWO

This Game's Not for Pakis

I first encountered and became properly aware of racism at around eight years old. I was having lunch at my primary school, Earl's Hall, and as usual I was lining up with my tray to get my food from the dinner lady. This particular day, it was sausages on the menu. Now, I knew I wasn't meant to have sausages. I wasn't quite sure why, but I was aware that my father didn't want me to eat them. When my brother Osman and I had started at the school, Dad realized that the food served there might be a problem. So to avoid it becoming an issue he'd said to us, "Eat anything you want, even if it is not halal. The main thing is, keep from eating pork. So no sausages."

The dinner lady put my lunch down on my plate.

"What is this?" I asked.

"Sausages," she said.

"I'm sorry," I said politely, handing the plate back. "I'm not allowed to eat them." At this stage I was still very much a timid little boy.

"What do you mean, you're not allowed to eat them?" the dinner lady snapped back.

"I'm . . . I'm not allowed to eat them," I repeated nervously, but stood my ground. "My dad told me I wasn't allowed sausages."

"Why on earth not?"

"I don't know," I replied, quivering. "All I know is that I'm not allowed to eat them."

At this point, I remember being very scared, not just as a small child standing up to an adult, but also over why I wasn't allowed to eat the sausages. I didn't really know what they were, but my dad had been so insistent that I thought I might have some reaction if I ate them. I could feel everyone in the canteen looking at me.

"Stop being so *fussy!*" the dinner lady shouted, shoving the plate back at me, so I had to take it. "This is your lunch, and you're going to eat it."

The dinner lady came out from behind the counter to where I was sitting and insisted that I ate them in front of her. Now I was crying. I felt the eyes of everyone staring, as if I was some sort of freak. I didn't know what to do.

"What a fussy little boy," she snapped again. "You *will* eat your sausages."

With fear rising up like a lump inside my throat, caught between parental and school authority, I addressed the immediate threat and put a piece of sausage in my mouth. At which point, fear took its revenge and pushed out the offending morsel, along with everything else in my stomach. I vomited all over my plate. As I continued to cry, the dinner lady's stance changed.

"Oh goodness me," she said. "You're *allergic* to sausages. That's why you can't eat them."

I shook my head, tried to tell her otherwise, but she was convinced. "You should have said," she continued. "You should have said you have an allergy." And she escorted me off to the medical office, where despite my protestations I spent the rest of the afternoon lying down until Abi came to pick me up after school.

Things have changed in the last twenty or thirty years. I don't think the dinner lady was being deliberately racist: I suspect her attitude was well-meaning in an "eat your vegetables" way, but there was a lazy cultural ignorance behind it that said much about attitudes of the time. It did not even cross her mind that there might be a religious reason behind my refusal to eat pork.

Earl's Hall was almost universally white: the only other non-white child I remember was a Sikh called Satnam. For the first few years I was there, I was generally happy. There was an annual art competition at school, and I won first prize for several years consecutively. I remember a picture I did when I was eleven, which I copied from a photograph of a boy on a drum barrel, writing and sticking his tongue out. My picture was then printed in sepia for a school exhibition, and it made me hugely proud. I acted in the school plays, including one about refugees during the Second World War. I even had a little girlfriend named Sarah. We mostly just held hands, and I think I kissed her once on the cheek. I would go to her parents' house, and her family was always incredibly hospitable. Later on, on our first day of secondary school, I would leave Sarah, telling her "there are too many new girls here to choose from." I was eleven. She cried and I felt pangs of guilt, believing her lovely parents would hate me.

Maybe because I had managed to make many friends, I became too "prominent" for some kids. My mother's attempts to integrate us into British culture all felt quite natural until that point. I even joined the Cub Scouts and really enjoyed it. But when I was about ten or eleven, the atmosphere at Earl's Hall suddenly changed. Almost overnight, the color of my skin defined me to friends who had previously seen only a happy, sociable boy. When a child sees the world, he doesn't see his own face, only everything else around him. It's often all too easy for children to imagine that others don't see their faces either. The mid-eighties permanently changed this for me. Concern about AIDS had risen sharply in the public imagination. For all the government education films about the disease, its rise led to all sorts of rumors and accusations in the playground about its origins. One day, a big lad called Tony, who had been a good friend for years, suddenly turned on me.

"AIDS is your fault," he told me. "It's people like you that caused the disease."

At the time, there were stories going around saying how the disease originated in Africa. Not that I was African, but I wasn't white, and as far as this boy's knowledge went, that was close enough. For the first time since the incident with the dinner lady, I felt like all eyes were on me. The kids had started whispering about me behind my back. Children were scared to touch me.

"You lot have sex with monkeys," he continued. "That's how AIDS started."

The accusations would have been laughable, had it not been for the anger in his eyes.

"That's rubbish," I said.

"It's true," the boy sneered. "My dad told me."

I tried to reason with him: this was a boy who'd been my friend, whom I'd been playing with normally just the day before. But he wasn't having any of it. "My dad told me I am not allowed to speak to you any more. Now get lost, bugger off, and don't talk to me again."

Not long after, my friend Patrick was playing football* at lunch break, and I went over to join in.

"Can I play?" I asked. What usually happened is that you'd turn up wanting to take part, and those already playing would assign you to one or other team, depending on which was short of players. On this occasion everyone was ignoring me. So I went over to Patrick and asked him what was going on. He suddenly turned around and punched me hard in the stomach. I doubled over in agony, unable to breathe. The inability to draw breath totally petrified me, as I had never experienced such a sensation before.

"This game's not for Pakis!" he shouted. "Don't ask to play again." He wandered off back to his team, leaving me confused and gasping for breath, as I used the railings to support myself from falling to the ground. Once I caught my breath again, I looked up and saw that I was truly standing alone. My friends were all playing football. It was this feeling of being completely alone, rather than the pain, that hurt the most. As I fought back the tears with all my willpower, I resolved there and then that when I grew up I would never stand alone.

It was this incident more than anything else that destroyed my childhood innocence. Standing in a playground with secret tears rolling down my cheeks, I decided that the world is like an obstacle course, to climb and sit on top of. A child is often judged in the playground by how well he can play, and a social pecking order based on the game quickly arises. After that incident I never took part in football again. The kids at primary school wouldn't let me. By the time I got to secondary school I was embarrassed that I couldn't play; the rejection rang in my ears and I didn't even try to join in. I would have to work doubly hard to climb that obstacle course without the advantage of playing football.

---

* Soccer.

My parents' response was to turn the other cheek. There was a feeling among previous generations that they did not have a right to fight back, because they were visitors, immigrants.

"So what if they call you a Paki?" they'd tell me. "Just say you are a Paki and you are proud of it, and walk away." Now, that's confusing advice for a child. Children have a very strong sense of right and wrong at that age: here was something that was manifestly unfair, yet I was being told to accept it. Even though the names and accusations were unacceptable, was I really expected just to take the abuse and walk away?

The fact that my skin color hadn't been an issue for those early years of schooling says everything about where racism originates: it is a cultural issue, a societal and familial problem that children soak up as they become more aware of the world. But while my generation began by following the stance of their parents, there was one very noticeable difference that separated those coming of age in the late eighties from earlier times: the level of violence that we faced.

What had changed, particularly in places like Southend, was the rise of the skinhead revival culture. Some skinheads adopted an exclusively white, aggressively racist line. By the mid-eighties, these violently racist skinheads were the ones who had taken over, and they dominated the football clubs.

In Southend the shin-high Doc Marten boots of the skinheads stomped with authority. Their green bomber jackets acted as their visible insignia, a uniform for hate, which was truly on the march. The casual racism of my primary school years had suddenly gained a sharper and more sinister edge. Those children began to believe that football was "no game for Pakis." The compromise choice of earlier generations was no longer available to us; turning the other cheek was no longer an option. It was either time to retreat within the community, to keep off the streets and cower out of sight, or it was time to stand in the path of these thugs, with dignity and honor.

CHAPTER THREE

The Doctor Who Said "Fuck tha Police"

It was my Uncle Nasir, Abi's brother, of all people, who got me into hip-hop. By the early 1990s he was a doctor in Newcastle. Nasir had ended up marrying my cousin from my dad's side, Farrah, the daughter of *Tai Ammi*, who told the fascinating bedtime stories. Nasir was my favorite uncle, a soft-spoken, deeply intelligent, and insightful man. His marriage to Farrah, someone I consider a sister, made this family my special relatives to visit, and their kids Raheem, Alia, and Habiba became my closest cousins.

In his mannerisms, dress, career, and proper English, Nasir is the opposite of the street culture I eventually embraced. But what was so impressive about him is that he had empathy for those who were less fortunate. I remember how he would always go out and talk to the roughest neighborhood kids, who were otherwise stealing cars and picking fights. I asked him once why he did this, and he replied: "My surgery's located here; the majority of my patients are from this estate. If I don't speak to them, who will?" I loved him even more for that, and so did these dangerous youths. His car never got stolen, and I learned a valuable lesson.

In the summer of 1989 we went up to Newcastle to visit, and Nasir decided that he would play Osman and me a type of music that we had never heard before. With a glint of mischief in his eyes, he put on a track called "Fuck tha Police" by N.W.A (Niggaz With Attitude), and pumped up the volume. A year earlier N.W.A had released *Straight Outta Compton*, their debut album, on which Ice Cube, Dr. Dre, Eazy-E, DJ Yella, and MC Ren had laid the foundations for what would later become known as "gangsta rap." By introducing this one rap track to us, and without realizing what he had just unleashed, Dr. Nasir helped his two young nephews find their voice.

"Fuck tha Police" is a statement as much as it is a record. It gives it to the police for treating black communities like dirt, targeting them and lazily assuming that anyone with a car or a bit of money must be a drug dealer. It slams them for their prejudice and for their violence, and N.W.A promises to mete out its revenge, fantasizing about "takin' out a cop or two." All of this is delivered by the various MCs with an aggression, a passion that grabs hold of the listener, a raw, seething anger coming from one of LA's roughest ghettos, Compton. It's a history lesson with a booming drum track and packed into five minutes.

I was never the same again. The track quite simply blew me away. It was the attitude and confidence that I took to immediately. This was definitely *not* the sound of someone turning the other cheek: this was the sound of a community finding its voice, and using it to say that they weren't simply going to lie down and take it. They were saying *you treat us like that, and we're going to take the fight straight back to you.*

My uncle was of the same generation as my mother, who'd grown up by giving way and stepping back when confrontation arose. This doctor's love for N.W.A and the fact that he was sharing it with me spoke volumes; it must have given vent to all his frustrations growing up. He could turn up "Fuck tha Police" and even now as a respected doctor, he could find strength in their stand. For me, the N.W.A attitude had more practical connotations: unlike my uncle, whose job had taken him away from having to face such situations, I had my teenage years ahead of me. The experiences of racism at primary school had scarred me, and the thought of having to accept more years of the same was a frightening one. Listening to N.W.A, I realized that I didn't have to. Others were fighting back, and so could I.

The fact that rap lyrics rubbed everyone the wrong way made me love such groups all the more. People's offense at the expletives helped make the band feel cool. I remember listening to "Fuck tha Police" in the car, on a cassette player, and my parents being completely shocked. "What the hell is this?" my dad asked, as Eazy-E rapped about his "bitches" providing him with sexual favors, while Dad tried to concentrate on the road. New music is often popular for the very fact that earlier generations find it shocking: this was "our" music, misunderstood by others.

What most people heard was just a load of shouting and swearing; they thought the music appealed because of its shock value. They couldn't have been more wrong. These rappers were bright, street smart, and articulate. Their rhymes encapsulated the experience of being young, male, and black in a way that simply didn't exist elsewhere in the media. This was a time when banana skins were still being thrown at black players at football matches, when Nelson Mandela was still in prison, and when the beating of Rodney King by LAPD officers was about to send shockwaves around the world. The sense of disenfranchisement, that you couldn't rely on the state for help, was very real.

The odd thing is that up until that summer, Osman and I would bicker like most young siblings over almost anything. There was only a year and a half between us, and where he was undoubtedly the bigger one, I liked to think I was the sharper one. I would try to use my wit against his power, which led to many clashes and parental intervention. But when Nasir got us both into rap, we found a common cause, a common purpose. It was like we were suddenly on the same side against the rest. Our bickering stopped and we began sharing music, going out to the same parties, and sharing friends. We began to feel like a team with a cause. Our cause was rebellion against the status quo.

If it was my uncle who introduced me to N.W.A, it was Osman who first got me into Public Enemy. "Rebel Without a Pause" was the first single of theirs that I heard, and it still sticks with me now. Here was a group who didn't just have the attitude, but the *political insight* to go with it. There was always a thought-out philosophy to Chuck D and Professor Griff's rhymes—this was a band sampling Malcolm X and bringing the Black Nationalist message into teenagers' living rooms. Professor Griff had his security team, the S1Ws—the Security of the First World—and an interest in the Nation of Islam. They were fearless. The more I listened to the records, the more the lyrics and influences began to seep into me. I had never really heard of people like Malcolm X before. Now I had a real thirst to find out all about him.

The fact that Professor Griff was an advocate for Islam made an impression, too. Considering myself an agnostic, I had never been a religious person: it hadn't been a big issue growing up. The few times I'd been to the mosque it had been a disaster. The imam didn't speak any English and got his message across with the use of a stick. I told my parents I wasn't going back because he used to hit children and that was it; they didn't make me go again.

Professor Griff made something I had considered old-fashioned feel vibrant and interesting. He wasn't the only one: in 1993 Brand Nubian used the Muslim call to prayer "Allahu akbar" as a sample for one of their songs in their second album, *In God We Trust*. I absolutely loved it. I had little understanding at the time that most of these Black Nationalist rappers belonged to racist sects of Islam such as Farrakhan's Nation of Islam and the Five Percenters. What mattered was that these sorts of endorsements from young, streetwise rappers made me rethink my identity. The faith I had inherited was no longer some backward village religion to be ashamed of or apologetic about. It had been re-branded as a form of *resistance*, as a self-affirming *defiant* identity. On the back of such groups, the black conversion rate to Islam was going through the roof. Even members of the nascent British hip-hop band Cash Crew ended up converting. All of a sudden, it was cool to be a Muslim.

That September, in 1989, I enrolled at Cecil Jones High School, at precisely the time that hip-hop was starting to really kick off. If rap was the form, hip-hop was the culture. Dr. Nasir's little "Fuck tha Police" intervention couldn't have been better timed. I had left primary school intent on never letting anyone pick on me again. At Cecil Jones I changed my dress style, wearing a baggy uniform with my sweater tied round my waist. I also changed my hair, closely clipping it to a "grade one" on the sides while leaving it long on top, and I got my ear pierced.

On my first day at school, age eleven, I remember consciously talking myself up to people as someone you didn't want to mess with. In fact, I got so carried away that someone even tried to call my bluff and I nearly got hit again. A very crude ranking system operates in school playgrounds, the "hardest" kids are known, and a pecking order is quickly but firmly established as kids jockey for position in the first few weeks of the term.

I soon realized that merely talking myself up would not be sufficient. I needed the right friends, the right "crew," and I ruthlessly began to seek them out.

The fact that I was one of the first kids from my year to get into hip-hop made my task of building a crew easier than expected. White kids were lining up to talk to me, not just about rap music but the whole hip-hop scene. Hip-hop was something that could more than compensate for my absence from football games. My skin color was suddenly something that kids *wanted* to be associated with. Very quickly, Aron and Martyn, respectively the first and second toughest kids in our school year, had become my closest friends. I was to be their very own trendsetter, teaching them the ways of the B-boy, or someone living a hip-hop lifestyle.

It instantly bonded me with all the popular kids in the older classes, too. In my school year there were no black kids, and only two other Pakistanis, one being my cousin Faisal. But in the year above was a boy called Michael, whom we all called Moe. He was Kenyan British and had a group of friends in his year, including Faisal's older brother Yasser. There was a kid called Mark, who was West Indian and equally respected, and friends with Osman. In those early days, we were a small community and hip-hop was our way of life. We had a certain style of dress, spoke in a specific slang, and we clipped our hair very short on the sides, sometimes carving patterns into it, and then left it standing long on top. We believed that we had discovered "cool" where all others had failed, and we quickly bonded with each other over the music.

I've never been one to do things by halves, and once I got into hip-hop, I bought into the scene big time: not just the music but also the look, the clothes, everything. I'd wear what we called "Click" or "Extreme" suits, named after the brands. These were a pair of matching jackets and trousers, the trousers being as baggy as you can imagine—almost Aladdin genie-type—and we would fold them in at the bottom with what we called "pin-tucks." The top would be baggy too and come complete with a hood. The trainers would be Adidas, big and fat to match. Wearing the right labels was everything, and we'd travel up to London to buy the gear.

Word went around that we were connected with the scene in London. If you messed with us, we could make a few calls and bring down heavy B-boys from the big city. We saw the benefits of this sort of hype, but back then it was all about survival. These London connections, knowing the hard knocks two school years above me, and having my own crew meant that in Cecil Jones no one dared mess with me again. Gone forever was the boy who cried alone in a school playground because he wasn't allowed to play football.

It was almost like having bodyguards. Aron and Martyn looked up to me for my knowledge of hip-hop dress, style, and sounds. They developed a loyalty to me, especially the bigger of them, Martyn, whom we called Sav. If anyone said so much as a rude word to me, Sav would stand ready to defend me. But I never forgot what it was like to be victimized, which pushed me sometimes to stop my best friends from getting too rough with other kids. Though other times, in my twelve-year-old mind, I felt that kids "deserved" it, like if they had said something racist. In such circumstances I would not intervene, believing in a playground sense of justice.

At primary school, I'd won prizes for my artwork. Now I used my talents to write graffiti. I chose "Slamer" as my tag. With my friends I would go round "tagging," writing my name and "bombing," plastering a wall with tags. I'd use Polka Pens, which were these big, fat permanent markers with nubs as thick as your thumb. You would have to give the marker a shake to keep the ink fresh, and whenever we got the chance, we'd tag up any wall with them. Alongside my tag, I'd write different words and captions—"fight the power," things like that. I'd draw bode, too: these were little characters, strange-looking duck figures that'd stand by the side of your work. I'd also sketch "pieces," which were basically pencil sketches of graffiti on pieces of paper, which you'd then use as a stencil for a larger, sprayed picture.

There was an area in Southend that the police left specifically for graffiti called The Yard. It was a derelict area left alone in the hope that by letting us tag there, we wouldn't graffiti elsewhere. A lot of kids hung about there taking drugs, and that's where I started. Pretty soon I graduated to the streets, because that was where you'd get your work seen. I'd always have my pen with me, and if I saw a wall I liked, and the coast was clear, I would tag it. When we went bombing, it was a bit more planned: a group of us would target somewhere and blast the whole area in a specific raid. The whole cat and mouse thing with the police just added to the buzz I got from doing it. I was chased a number of times by the police, but always gave them the slip. I was smart enough to never get caught, and smart enough not to get into the spray-painting side of things. That was a far bigger process: to spray-paint a high street wall involved covering an area five times the size; to do that, and do it properly, you could be sitting there for an hour or so. The chances of getting caught were that much higher, and if they did catch you, they'd really throw the book at you.

Graffiti is a culture where if you're shit, everyone is quick to tell you. The mark of respect for a graffiti artist is how long your "piece" and tag stay up on a wall. Out of raw respect, other artists will not paint over something they think is good, and anyone who does paint over it better be prepared for a beat-down. However, if your stuff is no good, or if you are seen as an amateur, you'll quickly find the word "lame" written over your work. The offending person would then leave their own tag at the side as a direct challenge. The only way to get even was to be good.

In the days before the mainstreaming of hip-hop culture and the appreciation of artists like Banksy, this was classic counterculture stuff. No one, apart from my friends and I, knew who "Slamer" was, though his name was scrawled all over Southend. It was two fingers to the police and law and order: we were challenging their authority, and there was nothing they could do about it. That gave us the edge, credibility among those in the know, and we felt we had a way to fight back.

I also got into dancing to the tracks and MC-ing (live rapping) at nightclubs. We'd go to these under-eighteen nights at clubs down by the seafront, or "The Front" as we called it. We would jump around to the sounds of Onyx and House of Pain, then we'd get up onstage for a lyrical excursion over an instrumental. My MC name was "Black Magic." The white kids didn't know what to do and couldn't really move to these strange new beats, so they looked to us for direction.

Our B-boy sub-community just kept growing; we would meet kids on the streets and just bond because they were into the same scene. It's like we instantly knew how to relate to each other. That's how I met people like Marc, and Chill, or Tsiluwa. Marc was a white kid, and a great rapper who was able to freestyle on the spot; his skills made him the right friends. Chill had recently moved from Zimbabwe. He was walking in the wrong direction one night after a particularly violent racist incident, an attack involving a hammer to the head of a friend—a preferred style of attack by Essex-based racists. I saw Chill walking in the direction we were running from, told him what had happened, and asked him to stick with us if he wanted to be safe. This kicked off an instant brotherhood between us, and together we got up to a great deal of mischief.

On one occasion Chill and I, both fifteen, decided to see if we could get into an over-eighteens nightclub. If anyone looked at us, at our builds and lack of facial hair, it was obvious that we were much younger. To get in we cut off some hair from our heads, and glued it with Pritt Stick to our chins. We laughed at how ridiculous we looked—Chill, who had Afro hair, looked like he had a pad of Velcro stuck to his chin—but we put our blazers on and got in. We went straight to the bathroom and washed it all off. After that, the bouncers would let us in every time.

All of this—the music, the clothes, the graffiti, the MC-ing—the hip-hop lifestyle—meant that none of us had any problems with girls. They were almost like groupies, white middle-class girls, who were into hip-hop and wanted to be a part of it. This was a time when mixed relationships became extremely fashionable, especially on the female side: there was a whole group of girls, many from nice girls-only schools, who wanted to be in mixed relationships. They'd talk to us about how mixed-race babies looked so cute. Such talk would make us laugh, and we thrived on the attention. We were just out to have a good time, and were buzzing on a sound, an identity, that we could finally claim as our own.

CHAPTER FOUR

The Stranger Stabbed for Me

While life in school was improving, the situation outside was escalating into something far more serious. Although my generation was being exposed to—and becoming interested in—music emanating from black culture, older generations remained unmoved by hip-hop and threatened by its associated culture. This was a generation who still had the mind-set of the father of the boy at primary school who had filled his son with all that rubbish about AIDS. It was these older, violently aggressive groups of white youths we had to be wary of.

The result was that when we went out, we made sure that we never walked anywhere alone. If we were out in the town, we'd be in groups of five, six, or seven to be on the safe side. We were an overwhelmingly non-white group of B-boys, and as we got deeper into the hip-hop culture, a lot of our white friends began peeling away from us. This was either from fear of attack or through feeling out of place. But Sav, the biggest boy in my school, always remained loyal to me, and was prepared to stand by my side till the end. I'd seen him take blows to his head from iron bars, yet still get back up, brush off his clothes, and walk on. It was hard to find a tougher man than Sav. The rest of our circle eventually narrowed to either West Indians or Pakistanis. We were united by the threat we all faced when the neo-Nazi skinhead group Combat 18 came into being in the early 1990s. And the guy with connections to Combat 18 was Mickey. Whenever and wherever Mickey or his crew saw us, they would draw their knives and hunt us down like animals.

How could we stand up to these guys, men really—they were much older than us—who were dangerously tooled up? It got to the point that from the age of fourteen on I began carrying a knife every time I went out. In those days, you could buy a knife as a kid without any questions asked. Crazy, really. It was a big hunting knife, six-inch steel blade and grip handle with a holder that you could strap to your back. That was very effective in concealing it—I once spent time in a police cell without them ever knowing what was hidden under my shirt. What I particularly liked about this knife was that within the design of the main blade, there was a second, hidden knife. I'd attach this one to a string around my wrist, so if the bigger knife ever slipped from my hand I'd still have the second one ready as a backup.

I bought the knife for protection, pure and simple, not to look for trouble. I'd practice getting it out, make sure I was up to speed, could unclip it and whip it out at a second's notice—the sort of moment where a fumbling could make the difference between getting stabbed and your attacker backing away. I'd sharpen it constantly, make sure the blade was in perfect nick, and learned how best to hold it in a fight. I was fully prepared to use it, but thankfully (and due to pure luck rather than good judgment) I never had to. In those days I trusted that thing more than God, and so we formed a kind of perverse bond. I would look over it from time to time, running my finger along its blade, and wonder whether it would save me or get me killed. I still keep it in a drawer next to my bed to remind me of those difficult times. I'm still not sure whether I love the thing or hate it.

In my parents' time, things were different; if you got threatened, it was all about fistfights, maybe the odd kick—it wasn't nice, but there wasn't the same level of threat of serious injury. That all changed with the skinheads and the arrival of Combat 18: knives went from being the exception to suddenly being the norm. Their favored form of attack was with hammers or screwdrivers, but they also carried clubs and butchers' knives. That started a bit of a local arms race, with everyone tooling up in response to everyone else. Suddenly everyone in Essex was carrying, in a way people hadn't been fifteen years before. Good friends of mine got badly hurt—Moe had his head smashed with a hammer and was lucky to survive. That was the climate non-whites faced in Southend, and that was why we carried knives. We were being hunted down for sport in our own streets by C18. They even had a name for it: Paki-bashing. Friends were being randomly stabbed, hammered, and clubbed just because of the color of their skin. I defy anyone to convince a teenager that he has no right to defend himself in such circumstances. If tooling up could deter such attacks, then for all the risks involved, we believed it was bloody well worth doing.

That day in the park, Chill ran to us for help, and I had ended up surrounded by skinheads. Uselessly outnumbered, I dumped my own knife in a desperate attempt to convince the skinheads that I was no enemy. Whom was I fooling? For C18, my skin color alone was a sufficient crime. Finally surrounded by them, their mouths frothing with frenzy, their eyes glazed with bloodlust, I knew that my time was up. These men had come from hell, in their white van, to Paki-bash this fifteen-year-old *kidult*. To submit to death is a strange sensation; one can only do it by finding hopelessness attractive. The mind searches for ways to console the heart, telling it: "It's OK, when you're dead you'll feel no more pain."

And that's all I wanted really, for it to be done without much pain. But I didn't die. In fact, the strangest thing happened. It was, and remains, rather surreal. A passerby, a respectable-looking, studious type of white guy, saw my plight and entered the fray between the skinheads and me. Despite the panic of the situation, I think he managed to tell me his name was Matt. I cannot be certain about this, but I feel an urge to humanize him, so I'll call him Matt anyway.

"Don't worry," Matt said, "I'm with you."

I remember thinking, *What the heck? Who are you?* Instead, I cautiously thanked him.

Matt didn't look like a fighter at all. Perhaps he was one of them, I thought, undercover and trying to lull me into a false sense of security. Perhaps he was secretly tooled up and ready to scare them all off. "Maybe I won't die here after all," I began to think. Maybe this guy is some sort of Bruce Lee; he'll be able to take them all on and extract us both from this mob. *Why else would he jump into the middle of a knife fight?*

Matt turned to the skinheads. "Guys! Guys!" he said, causing them to turn around in surprise. Being white and having managed to get close enough to their circle, they had assumed he was with them. Who would be crazy enough to put themselves in the path of hammers, clubs, and knives for an unknown teenage Paki?

"Come on, leave it out, yeah?" he said, trying to pacify the situation. "Leave this kid alone."

The skinheads looked at Matt. His intervention seemed to infuriate them even more.

"He's a fuckin' Paki," one snarled at him, "and you're a fuckin' Paki lover!"

"Guys," Matt said, slightly more nervous this time, yet still trying to mediate. "Come on, let's not do anything stupid here. He's just a kid, yeah?"

Perhaps it was the fact that he wasn't part of our world that made him feel he could talk the situation down. Perhaps where he came from, an honest request and a bit of gentle reasoning were enough to resolve any situation. This was my world, though, not his. As they came charging forward, from all sides, I knew they would ignore him and stab me anyway. "Thanks, Matt," I thought, "at least you tried, mate." An honorable thing to do for someone you don't know. And so I prepared to meet my end.

What happened next will haunt me till my dying day. In sudden horror, mixed with a perverse relief, I watched as the skinheads swiveled their attention away from me—and toward Matt. Like famished hyenas they descended upon him, plunging their knives deep into his torso, beating on his head with their clubs and knuckledusters.

"You fucking Paki lover!" they screamed.

The Paki was left by their side untouched. Matt's arms were up, flailing, shielding his head with all the strength he could muster, collapsing under the sheer brutality of their vicious assault.

With penetrating shame I instantly realized that Matt was no Bruce Lee. Matt had no weapon. Matt had no plan. He was just doing for me what I was now failing to do for him. He stood up for me, and he was being beaten to a pulp for doing so while I was forced to watch. I knew that if I joined him I would probably die. My sense of honor urged me to fight. This was my fight, goddamnit, not his! But my common sense scolded me in return: I would have no effect, I was an unarmed boy! All that would be achieved by me joining in would be both our murders. So, I watched, frozen, as the C18 thugs clubbed him, stabbed him, and kicked at his head while he lay on the floor. And not one punch, and not one kick was turned my way. In the distance, police sirens were ringing out. Thank God someone was finally coming! Come, save us! The C18 thugs heard the sirens too, gleefully appraised the damage, and ran off without so much as looking at me again. It was as if I didn't exist. And as I looked at Matt, all bones and blood on the floor, I felt like I didn't deserve to exist. C18 had left me totally untouched while a white stranger lay bleeding profusely on the floor after taking *my* beating.

As the police and ambulance approached, Matt miraculously staggered up off the floor, walking in the direction of C18 and defiantly shouting back at them. As if to say, "Here I am, I'm still standing. You did not defeat me!"

I learned later that as well as the multiple stab wounds, he suffered a punctured lung. Somehow, he still found the resolve to wave his fist and shout after them until the effort was too much, and then he collapsed again. The paramedics surrounded him instantly in a fierce effort to save his life.

The police, meanwhile, were at their worst. They looked at the white guy lying in a heap of blood on the floor, heard shouts coming from the C18 lynch mob standing off at a distance, and decided to question the fifteen-year-old Pakistani B-boy. I was still locked in my place, my feet refusing to move. The police radioed in my identity code. I wondered why they always managed to classify me as an IC 2.3, the police code for mixed white-Mediterranean and Afro-Caribbean.

"No, you're speaking to the wrong guy . . ." I tried to explain.

"I'm not going to ask you again," the officer insisted. "I want you to tell me what your gang was doing to that man."

I snapped out of my dazed state and quickly turned nasty on the policeman, shouting and swearing at him at the top of my voice.

"What're you asking *me* questions for, you fucking pig? They're right over there, the guys who stabbed him up! You can *hear* them laughing, you can *see* them, why aren't you going over to arrest them before they leg it?"

"I'll arrest you if you don't calm down," the police officer responded.

So I checked myself. My main concern was to convince them to arrest the guys who jumped Matt. I suffered the interrogation in the hope that it would speed up their work. It didn't. The officer eventually saw that I was innocent, but by that time the skinheads were long gone in their white van, and the ambulance was carrying Matt to the hospital.

They left me standing right there in the street, confused, exposed, alone, and angry. I wondered if an angel had just descended to save my life. *Was Matt real or had he been sent by God to shield me from murder?* I half expected the skinheads to come back and finish the job. After failing to fight alongside Matt, I now believed that I deserved it. I had been unarmed, but so was he. Yes, I was outsized and outnumbered, but so was Matt; it didn't stop him. Since that first day at Cecil Jones, I had always thought myself brave; now I was just full of shame. I found myself wandering back to recover my knife I had so foolishly hidden. If I hadn't dumped it, maybe I could have helped him.

I never got the chance to thank Matt for intervening. I knew he hadn't died, because it would have been all over the local papers, but I didn't know his surname or how to get ahold of him. He'd just walked into my life, taken a stabbing for me, and then disappeared. The bungled police reaction may have made me more anti-establishment, but my own guilt drove me further away from my white friends.

~~~

By this point, our posse of B-boys was almost exclusively an ethnic group. Because there was only one and a half years between us, Osman and I began merging our two groups of friends. From my lot, the younger crew, there was Chill, Moe, and Andre from Southend, Ricky, Paul, Ade, and Yusuf from Pitsea. Ricky's older brother Rowan headed the older lot. Rowan rolled with Will and Aaron, and Osman would join them when he could. Rowan was renowned throughout Essex. He was dangerous, and people knew his name. Our bonds of friendship were particularly close, forged through a common love of hip-hop, mad times at parties, and standing up for each other in armed confrontations against racists. The younger ones, my crew, felt like my true brothers, and we believed nothing could ever divide us. Most of the wider posse was Afro-Caribbean, but Osman and I had introduced a couple of other South Asians, like our cousin Yasser and our Bangladeshi friend Ronnie.

I was out late one evening with Osman and Ronnie, playing pool. Earlier that day, like many sixteen-year-old boys, Osman had been messing around with a plastic BB gun. Playing in open view, he hadn't thought to conceal what he was doing. In those days terrorism was mainly associated with the IRA. But someone had called the police, convinced that he was going to commit an armed robbery. The police took this accusation seriously and mounted an all-day surveillance operation. So by the time I joined Osman and Ron later on, we were already being secretly staked out by a host of armed officers. We finished playing pool about two in the morning and got into Ron's car to drive home. Our stereo was, as usual, testing the frame of Ron's old car with the heavy bass line.

"That's weird, man," I quipped from my backseat. "I guess pigs can fly after all!" Police helicopters were hovering above us.

"Someone must be in deep shit, man," Ron laughed. "I guess they're lookin' for some real heavyweights."

"Yeah, man, someone's not gonna get much sleep tonight," I laughed back.

"Look! It's goin' down," Osman interjected as police cars sped past us at top speed with their sirens on.

But were we in for a surprise!

Suddenly the police cars up ahead skidded to a halt, horizontally blocking the road in front of us. More cars had appeared from behind, blocking our escape. Ron slammed the brakes on.

"What the ffff . . .?" he muttered in disbelief as armed officers carrying submachine guns appeared from nowhere on either side of the car "Stop the car!"

"Do not move your hands, do not move your hands!"

"Stay absolutely still! Do not move!"

We sat deathly still and in absolute silence. None of us found this even slightly funny anymore. As the helicopter spotlight lit us up, the armed officers rushed to the car doors and pulled Ron and Osman out of their seats, through their still-attached seatbelts, slammed them on the ground, and then held them in locked positions. As I watched police putting a gun to my brother's head, my mind again focused on tangential details. The car was rolling forward slightly. *That's strange, why was it doing that?*

"The brake!" I thought to myself. "Well done, Ron, you haven't pulled your parking brake up!"

Just then a hand grabbed my collar and lifted me out of my seat and down onto the ground with a violent thud and another gun greeted me. Of course, it was to Ron's credit that he didn't reach down for the parking brake; they would have thought he was reaching for a gun, and he would probably have been shot dead.

None of this was making any sense to me. I hadn't been with Osman in the daytime and didn't know he had been playing with his plastic BB gun. But there was no time for thought, and certainly no time for questions.

"You," the officer shouted in my ear, "are under arrest for suspicion of armed robbery."

"Huh, wha . . .?" It wasn't registering in my brain.

"In other words, you're nicked, mate. Get 'im in the car."

I was fifteen years old. I had no criminal record. They threw us all in the cells for the night while they inspected the "evidence." Because I was under sixteen, they had to call and wake Abi up at 3 a.m., and tell her that both her sons had been arrested on suspicion of armed robbery. Crazy. In the morning, after all that, they handed Osman back his pellet gun in a plastic bag and let us go. On the way out, furious at being profiled, I decided to ask one last question, "Is there anything, anything at all that we did wrong?"

"No, you did nothing wrong. It was a misunderstanding. Sorry about that." And that was it.

This mixture of police incompetence and ignorance made us both hate them and simultaneously fear their powers. The one time I did attempt to take things further with the police it blew back in my face. I went in to positively identify a suspect who had stabbed a friend of mine. I pointed out the right guy, but they had to let him go, apparently because of a "procedural error." Worse, I was now exposed as the person who had made the positive identification. I have lost count of the number of knife attacks we were subjected to by racists, many of my friends had been stabbed, but the police rarely managed to make any arrests and hardly ever pressed charges. The gangs would always boast about "contacts" in the police. I have no idea if this was true, but the bottom line is we were not protected. And in the absence of any incentive to change our mantra, we kept singing it loud: "Fuck tha Police."

Not trusting the police to protect us meant that we had to rely on our own protection, which we found among our crew and through fighting back. As our numbers increased and our confidence grew, the levels of violence we faced got worse. We'd be set upon suddenly, like once down on the seafront when pool balls were flying past our heads like cannonballs. Or when another white friend, Dan, was knifed, or that time at Southend Central Bus Station when Aaron got stabbed in the side, and Rowan fought off two men armed with kebab knives, using nothing but a crutch he'd "borrowed" from an old lady waiting for her bus. (Once they ran away, Rowan politely handed the crutch back to the startled old woman.) One of us once resorted to using a metal-tipped umbrella as a weapon, spearing a skinhead who had come down from London and decided to march up and down our high street shouting, "We hate Pakis!" He ended up on the floor in agony with a fractured skull. There was the time Ricky, Paul, Chill, and I had been hounded by a white mob chanting about not wanting "niggers" in their area "stealing their women." Our entire crew returned in three cars the next week to bum rush the house of their ringleader. We were learning how to fight back, and the message was spreading.

One day, I happened to come across Patrick—the same Patrick who at eleven had punched me in the stomach because I dared to ask to play football. With that one act he had changed the little boy that I was; he made me see in color when before I saw only human beings. It felt like an eternity since my days at Earl's Hall.

I was walking down the high street in my full B-boy gear: a red bandana, my Redskins baseball cap—because they used Red Indians as their logo—my Click suit and big trainers, the lot. And there, I saw him. That punch was something I had never forgotten. The moment he saw me coming he turned the other way; I could see that he also remembered what he'd done. This sparked the residues of anger within me, and I headed straight for him. I wasn't with my crew on this occasion; I'd left them somewhere nearby. It was just Patrick and me again. I had my knife on my back as usual. Patrick, for all his cocky confidence back at primary school, was not a street kid in the way I'd become. He saw me, he saw the look in my eyes, and he began to cower.

"Please don't hit me. Maajid, please don't hit me."

I hadn't even said anything, and the kid was begging me not to do anything.

"I'm sorry," he continued, starting to cry. "I'm sorry, just don't . . ." It was the strangest sight—as if he were shriveling up in front of me.

Patrick wouldn't dare repeat his comments now. Largely due to the reputation of us B-boys, it was no longer acceptable to be racist in the way it had been even just a few years earlier. The ball had bounced back, the power dynamic had shifted. I saw that, he saw that, and strangely that was enough for me. Despite all the violence I'd been involved in, I had always had a justification for it in my teenage mind; it was all a form of escalating self-defense. I'd never bullied or picked a fight with a defense-less, unarmed person, and I wasn't about to start now.

"You're a chump!" I shouted at him. "Get the fuck out of my sight."

Patrick turned and skulked away. I didn't need to attack him: it was enough to see his reaction when he saw me. I felt good about myself, pleased that I'd not become as bad as the racists. But there was something more there, too: a sense of satisfaction and vindication. I was on the right path. The incident that had begun my spiral of abuse had finally ended. I had won.

CHAPTER FIVE

The Green Backpack with No Bomb

If you haven't felt the fear and helplessness that violent, organized racism makes you feel, it's difficult to understand. Due to the color of your skin, your entire body is a moving target. And you cannot leave your skin behind, or pretend it doesn't exist. At any moment, hammer-wielding hooligans could use you for target practice. In such extreme circumstances, self defense must be a sacred right; the "turn the other cheek" philosophy would have gotten our skulls crushed. The sad reality is that it's difficult for different ethnic groups to rub along with each other. I'm not saying that my *kidult* way of dealing with the situation was the answer, but it was *an* answer. At the time, it felt like the only option open to us.

Without support from the police or society at large, it felt as though it was the best way to respond—to stand up and take the fight to the racists, in the hope that they'd leave us alone. There's a sort of brutal logic to that position, but once again it's one that doesn't go to the crux of the problem. It's a kind of "Cold War" thinking, where an uneasy peace is created from the knowledge of what damage the other side could mete out.

To be fair, the police force did change. It wasn't an overnight thing—cultural shifts don't work like that—but the general attitudes of the police have undoubtedly improved from where they were twenty years ago. Of course more can still be done, as the shooting by the police of innocent Jean Charles de Menezes on the London Underground in 2005 highlighted. This is partly because the police force is no longer exclusively white. Even one of my old family friends from a Pakistani background, Atif, is now a policeman with Essex Police.

Another form of identity politics was also lurking in the shadows, eventually to emerge as an even more intransigent challenge. Most young Britons of the Muslim faith were of South Asian origin, born and raised in crowded single-ethnicity British ghettos. Though tensions with non-Muslim communities did occur in these areas, part of the problem was a lack of contact with "the other." As race began to take a backseat, and Afro-Caribbean communities began to enter the mainstream through popular music and culture, into these ghettos came war-torn Muslim North Africans, Arabs, and Somalis. A new generation of youth born in the ashes of conflict quickly found that they had one identity shared among them all: Islam.

Many British-born Muslims simply did not consider themselves part of the mainstream race debate. The Ayatollah/*Satanic Verses* affair helped this shift along somewhat. The communities adopted a more isolationist stance, a policy of self-exclusion. For many, the nature of how they identi-fied themselves was changing. So instead of calling themselves "British Asians" as my parents had done, this generation now defined themselves as almost exclusively Muslim. They believed that their allegiance to the global Islamic community, the *ummah,* prevented them from defining themselves as being part of their birth country.

What had caused this shift was a mixture of mutual discrimination and suspicion at home, and a growing awareness of events overseas. Bosnia was particularly crucial in bringing about a shift in identity among Britain's Muslims. In Bosnia, white, blond-haired, blue-eyed indigenous European Muslims were being massacred just because they were Muslim. The slaugh-ter did the opposite of its intended effect. In reaction to these atrocities, Muslims in Europe began reasserting their religious identities even more. It was a natural defense mechanism. But it also exacerbated self-segregation and triggered the shift in our self-identity to *politically* Muslim.

Into this fray jumped groups advocating politicized Islam, the Islamists. No other phenomenon has contributed to the rise of Muslim identity politics as much as these groups. Emerging in a postcolonial Middle East and South Asia, these groups quickly realized that an ideol-ogy that utilized (rather than undermined) the Islamic emotions of the people would be far more potent than Arab socialism. Islamist groups quickly spread and multiplied, arriving in Europe along with Arab asylum seekers and South Asian immigrants.

I would later believe passionately in this approach to politics. But that would be later. Essentially, the rise of Islamist groups was a key factor in shifting Muslims away from their national identities toward a more exclusively Muslim one. It has taken me awhile to resolve many of these pressing challenges posed by identity in our globalized world. Initially, retreating into group identities can be a useful tool for lobbying to overcome legal and institutional discrimination. However, there comes a point when class, economic, and cultural divisions can only be bridged by increasing mutual *integration* and participation among all in society. Instead of mutual integration, however, we witnessed a shift from ethnic communalism, where only a brown person is assumed able to represent brown people and so on, to religious communalism, where only a Muslim is assumed to be able to represent other Muslims. Such entrenched communalism and its advocates, who have abused the original intentions of multiculturalism, have brought nothing but division and the balkanization of Western, and other, societies.

This is where I am now on these issues. But there's a long way to go before I reach this conclusion. First, I need to explain how I became an Islamist in the first place.

———

I was back in the same park with the usual posse. Osman was with me, as was a friend called Nas. Nas's original name was Christian Nathaniel—he was from a Greek Orthodox background. He was into the same music as us, and the fact that his skin was of a Mediterranean complexion was enough for the skinheads to consider him a Paki. If their prejudice wasn't so threatening, their worldview would have been pathetically comic. Under the influence of the times, Nas had converted to Islam and had changed his first name from Christian to Nasir.

Once again we were spotted by Mickey and his crew; there were about half a dozen of them. They were carrying baseball bats, and no doubt were strapping knives. They caught us by total surprise, so we split in different directions. Eventually, once we'd properly tooled up at my house, we reemerged looking for the rest of the posse, and headed back to our rendezvous point on the street corner opposite my house. Osman, Nas, and I were the only ones who made it back; the others must have gone their separate ways.

Then, and I don't know if this was luck or learning, we saw Mickey and his entire crew heading our way. We were completely outnumbered. There were some posts on the side of the road, and they began banging their baseball bats against them, like some sort of war cry. But by now we were battle-hardened. This time, despite being grossly outnumbered, we stood our ground. This was right outside our home; we could see our front door. If we didn't have a right to walk here, then where on God's earth could we walk? I had my knife strapped to my back as usual. Osman had a green backpack on his.

The stand-off continued, and despite their outnumbering us, Mickey began to look nervous. We were only three, yet we were refusing to stand down and this made him doubt himself. Next, to our surprise, Mickey stepped forward and asked to talk. For a moment, Osman and I exchanged confused glances. Mickey had never before uttered a single word to us. It took us a moment to get used to seeing Mickey as anything other than a knife-wielding demon that only knew the word "Paki!" Once we composed ourselves, Osman indicated to Mickey that he should go over the road, while he too crossed over and waited for Mickey to join him. The war cry dimmed, and a worried-looking Mickey walked over to join my brother. What followed was a tense few minutes. My brother and Mickey were deep in conversation. Nas and I were switching between watching them and watching Mickey's mates; Mickey's mates were staring the two of us down. Everyone was poised, hands wrapped around baseball bats or fingers ready to unhook knives, in case it all kicked off.

After about ten minutes, we noticed that the talking had stopped. Mickey and my brother were making their way back across the road. They crossed over, halfway between the two groups and shook hands. This was nuts. I watched in disbelief as Mickey returned to his friends and told them to stand down.

"That's enough, lads," he told them. "No more trouble here."

"Eh?" I asked Osman. "What did you say to him?"

Osman looked at me with a level of confidence in his eyes and told me what had happened: "I told him we're Muslims and we don't fear death. We're like those Palestinian terrorists he sees on the television blowing up planes. We're suicide bombers. We've been taught how to make bombs, and I've got one in my backpack. If you even try to make a move, I'll set mine off. Trust me, I don't give a shit. If we have to take ourselves out to take you out, then that's what we will do."

"Damn, man! What did Mickey say?" I asked.

"He believed me when I told him he was messing with the wrong guys."

Osman's bluff played on Mickey's racism, no question about it. Mickey may or may not have watched the news, but he knew his Combat 18 literature. This depicted Muslims as terrorists, and suggested that we were all murderers given half the chance. So when Osman said he had a bomb in his backpack, and that we had links to suicide bombers, it confirmed every prejudice that Mickey had come to believe about us.

"If we feared death," Osman had told Mickey, "we'd be running away from you. Why would we be standing here when we're completely outnumbered? It's because we have the power to call backup and fight you to the death."

Calling for backup was the sort of language Mickey understood. It's what he'd done previously, and so he figured that this must have been something that we were capable of as well. If he'd even bothered to question the racist propaganda he'd swallowed, Mickey might have seen through this. But this was someone who considered the Greek Orthodox Nas a Paki. In his warped worldview, such statements made sense.

The discussion between Osman and Mickey was the end of our trouble with Mickey's racists. Mickey had decided that we were too dangerous, too connected to take on, and had made his peace with us instead. While Mickey was explaining his climb-down to his crew, there was still one question that played on my mind. Just as I had done that time at the police station, I decided I needed to ask something, to understand.

"Hey, can I ask you a question?" I asked.

"All right," Mickey replied. I saw a different look in his eyes for the first time. The venom had vanished. Now there was wariness, a sliver of fear in his gaze.

"I want to know why you started all this in the first place," I said. "Back in the park that day when you hounded Chill. You seemed to know his name. What happened?"

Mickey paused, for once a little unsure of himself. But his reply was pathetic. "We're tired of all you lot taking our women. We saw your mate Chill pulling all these white girls, and we'd had enough."

It was, frankly, ridiculous. The driving force behind that original attack was as simple as old-fashioned jealousy, with a racist bent. Mickey had seen the way that hip-hop had interested the girls, how they all wanted to get in on the scene.

Osman's successful bluff affected me more profoundly than any other event up to that point. I realized for the first time the futility of relying on men. For all the security that knowing people like Rowan had brought, there was only so far this could go. Rowan was a rock, and I owed him much, but there was no way he could always be around. And while packing knives offered limited protection, it just escalated matters without addressing the root problem.

That problem, put simply, was respect. When I asked Mickey why they had started on us, he looked at me and talked to me in a different way. He was no longer looking down on me. He was, in fact, scared. And that came from the assertive new identity Osman had adopted. *Islamism.* It had done what years of knife fights could not. It had won the psychological war and defeated our enemy. For the first time, I caught a glimpse of its power, and how it was capable of transforming my standing at a stroke. Osman, who by this point had become a committed Islamist, had been banging on about this for a year, but I'd never really taken him seriously. I was still a B-boy: that was my culture and my rule book for climbing the obstacle course that was my life.

The violence I'd been subjected to, the police discrimination, a greater awareness of foreign conflicts such as Bosnia, all made me highly receptive to the Islamist message. I was desperately looking for answers. But it was that afternoon in the park, and the fear in Mickey's eyes, that triggered my decision to take things further.

With a defeated and retreating enemy, I finally understood what my brother had been talking about. I realized Islamism could give me the respect that I'd craved since primary school. Hip-hop had helped us a great deal; it created new friends, but it hadn't been enough to defeat our enemies. It hadn't been enough to provide me with the courage to help Matt. Yet on that day, grossly outnumbered, I stood my ground with Osman, and we won because we invoked Allah. In one conversation, Islamism did what hip-hop couldn't do. It was alive, beating in the hearts of men, and it was prepared to sacrifice everything to regain lost dignity. It wasn't interested in singing "Fuck tha Police." Islamism was shouting from the tops of mountains "Fuck all y'all!"

And I wanted a dose of that courage.

CHAPTER SIX

When Babri Mosque Fell in India

It's important to grasp how Islamism differs from Islam. Islam is a religion, and its *Shari'ah* can be compared to Talmudic or Canon law. As a religion, Islam contains all the usual schisms of any other faith. There are ancient creedal disputes, from which we have the two major denominations of Sunni and Shia, each giving rise to numerous sects within their ranks. From methodological disputes, legal theorists and traditionalists debated whether scripture was best approached through systemized reasoning or oral tradition. From juristic differences, major schools of law emerged. And from a devotional angle, lapsed, traditional, fundamentalist, and extremist Muslims have always existed. Superseding all these religious disagreements, and influencing many of them politically, is the ideology of Islamism. Simply defined, Islamism is *the desire to impose any given interpretation of Islam over society as law*. Understood in this way, Islamism is not another religious schism, but an ideological thought that seeks to develop a coherent political system that can house all these schisms, without necessarily doing away with them. Whereas disputes within Islam deal with a person's approach to religion, Islamism seeks to deal with a person's approach to *society*.

As a political project, Islamism was inspired by the rise of European fascism. Like its European ideological counterparts, Islamism was not safe from its own schisms. Some groups wanted to bring about the "Islamic System" by working alongside the status quo; these were political Islamists, like the Muslim Brotherhood. Others were more revolutionary, wishing to upturn the status quo.

To the untrained eye, such Islamist groups seem "moderate" because they rise above sectarian disputes and tend not to be fundamentalist in devotional matters, focusing more on politics. But though religious fundamentalism may take on social issues, it is Islamism that seeks real power. As with Mussolini's fascists, who were also socially progressive, it is the totalitarian aspect of Islamism that gives rise to major concern. Much later on, Islamism would influence religious fundamentalists, too. This gave rise to a militant strand, Jihadism, and the emergence of groups like al-Qaeda. Jihadism then is the merger of literalist religion with Islamist politics.

My own journey into Islamism resulted in me joining a revolutionary group, known as Hizb al-Tahrir (HT). Sitting between political Islamists and the militants, HT aims to unify all Muslim-majority countries under an "Islamic state," appropriating for it the term Caliphate, or *Khilafah* in Arabic. They hope to attain power by means of a military coup and seek to impose one version of Islam over society. My journey started in 1992 with Osman walking down the high street in Southend and being handed a leaflet. Because Southend was so white, it was normal for us to stop and talk to any brown face we saw. The pamphleteer was a man called Nasim Ghani, a British Bangladeshi Muslim who, like us, had grown up in Southend and was now studying medicine at Barts in London. He was someone we could relate to easily; he was articulate and smart. It felt impressive to us that he was studying medicine because you had to be bright and committed to do that.

The leaflet that Nasim handed Osman was about the Babri Mosque in the northern Indian town of Ayodhya. Built by the first Moghul emperor Babar, the mosque had been there since 1528 and had long been a flashpoint between Hindus and Muslims. Hindus believed that the site was the birthplace of the Hindu deity Lord Ram. Religious violence at the mosque was first reported in the 1850s, and in 1984 Hindus began a campaign to "liberate" the site, replacing the mosque with a temple for Lord Ram. When a court order ruled that the mosque be protected, Hindu supporters decided to take matters into their own hands. A crowd of 200,000 broke through the cordon around the mosque and tore it down, using a mixture of hammers and their bare hands. Eyewitnesses reported that the extra police who had been sent to protect the mosque just stood back. The episode was the trigger for some of the worst violence India had seen for decades. Over 2,000 people died in the riots that followed.

I still remember the rather offensive title of the leaflet: "Hideous Hindus Massacre Muslims." That one leaflet changed the course of my life. It laid bare the behavior of the Hindu extremists in a shocking and inflammatory episode. Osman, spurred on by the likes of Public Enemy's Professor Griff, had taken an interest in politics. He followed the "Intifada" that had been going on against the Israeli occupation of Gaza and the West Bank, and the role of Yasser Arafat's PLO. This struggle for Palestinian liberation, and the crushing Israeli response (with American support), had long been a running sore in international relations. It was undoubtedly a factor that justified the Islamist narrative of victimhood—for a lot of us. The conflict, and the accompanying Western insouciance, came across as manifestly wrong. Identifying with the resistance movement reinforced what we were experiencing on the streets of Southend: it was Muslims who were on the receiving end of things, and the state didn't care. It helped me push my identity away from being British or Pakistani, and toward defining myself as exclusively *politically* Muslim.

The Intifada had been going on since 1987, so by the early 1990s it wasn't anything new. It caught Osman's attention because of the first Gulf War in 1991, when Saddam Hussein invaded Kuwait, and combined United Nations forces removed him. Saddam Hussein, albeit a brutal tyrant, was a champion of the Palestinian cause, and his provocation of Israel (the threat of launching Scud missiles at Israeli towns) kept the issue in the news.

But the Babri Mosque incident in India was something different. The destruction of an ancient Muslim place of worship felt particularly shocking. The number of people killed in the subsequent violence was horrific. It strongly reinforced the message that Nasim's leaflet and Hizb al-Tahrir were pushing. Southend, Gaza, Bosnia, Iraq, India: wherever you went in the world, the story was the same—Muslims were unprotected and under attack, and now was the time to do something about it. After all, we didn't believe in turning the other cheek.

Nasim was everything the mosque imam in Southend was not. Here was someone who was young, slick, and successful, and without a beard. He was studying and living in London, which for us on the edge of Essex felt like a glamorous lifestyle. Osman was exactly the right person, in the right place, at the right time to receive that leaflet. Osman was receptive to such a message, and when Nasim suggested he come to a talk to discuss the idea further, Osman agreed.

Nasim would turn out to be not just any pamphleteer. He was on the path to becoming the leader of HT in the UK and the founder of the organization in Bangladesh. As someone who has gone on to co-found movements myself and has met numerous political leaders of all stripes, I can tell you that Nasim is one of the most committed recruiters I have come across. He is not especially handsome, intelligent, devout, or articulate, yet he combines just the right level of all these traits to give him a dependable-leader quality. I have rarely encountered anyone with such a skill to say the right thing at the right time, in order to convince a person to follow him. He's not someone who leads through sheer force of his personality or authoritarianism. He is pragmatic, rather than dogmatic. An ordinary guy, but extraordinarily good at being one.

Osman started going with Nasim to his talks and study circles, and pretty soon became a changed person. Everything we'd been doing together—going to clubs, chasing women—was now anathema to him. And I thought he was crazy. "What's wrong with you, man?" I'd ask. I'd mock him and laugh at him, but to my surprise he'd just take it. He stopped going out with our group of friends, told women to stop calling for him at our house. Generally, he just retreated.

As much as Osman's change surprised me, it pleased my dad. For many years at home, it had felt as though my brother and I had sided more with our mother and taken advantage of her more liberal views. For the first time, one of my father's sons had taken a serious interest in Islam. At this point, my father didn't understand what Islamism really meant. What he saw was his son taking an interest in religion and behaving more like the traditional Muslim he had always wanted us to become. He approved of that and encouraged it, and that led, inevitably, to a change of mood in the household: the balance of power, as it were, had started to shift. You could see it in Abi's reaction. She didn't know how to respond to Osman's criticisms of her behavior. Later on, when I joined him, she would become even more isolated.

At that point, my impression of *practicing* Islam was still based on my early teenage experience of visiting the mosque. Osman's conversion felt not only as if it had come out of nowhere but also like a retrograde step. To go back to that, to spurn all the girls and partying, just didn't make any sense.

Osman was nothing if not persistent in trying to get me to go along with him. During that year he worked on those friends he thought would be most receptive: Moe, Nas, and myself. We all eventually converted. Although I would dismiss what he said at first, there was no denying his inner confidence when he spoke. As he continued to talk to me, I realized one of the fundamental points about Islamism that so many people fail to understand. The way Osman was speaking wasn't in the orthodox, religious way of the imam with a stick; he was talking about politics, about events that were happening *now*. That's crucial to understanding what Islamism is all about: it isn't a religious movement with political consequences, it is a political movement with religious consequences.

Osman had learned well what the study circles had taught him. Nasim was an excellent teacher, able to expound his theories into a simple, coherent narrative that Osman soaked up. As part of Hizb al-Tahrir training, he had the answers and counterarguments at his fingertips, so any questions I had he could respond to and throw straight back.

Nasim knew that Osman and I were already quite anti-establishment. He knew that he needed to channel our energies from hip-hop and race issues to something more serious, more global. And he had just the thing to achieve this: the Islamist narrative. This was a powerful toxin and it resonated with us. Nasim argued that the suffering we had experienced in Southend, the attacks by Combat 18 and the discrimination we felt from the police, were not isolated incidents but part of a bigger picture. And we were deluded if we thought that it was just a race thing. Yes, race was a factor, but even if we solved that, Western society would never be satisfied with us. *How much whiter could you get than the Muslims of Bosnia, and just look at what was going on there while the rest of Europe stood by and watched?*

And look at our brothers in Palestine, at Kashmir, or at the Muslims killed for defending the honor of the Babri Mosque in India. Why is it that every conflict and war today involves the killing of Muslims? Are you that blinded to believe this is a coincidence? Are you as shallow as the racists to believe it's merely about skin color?

The truth is that there is an international effort to keep Muslims down, he said. They intervene in Kuwait for oil, yet stand by and watch as Muslims get murdered in Bosnia because, truly, they cannot tolerate a Muslim power in the heart of Europe. And if they cannot tolerate white Bosnians, what makes you think they'll ever accept you? We have gone from being the world superpower, the Islamic *Khilafah*, to being the downtrodden minority who get stabbed in the streets of Essex. And we've sunk so low we don't even know how to identify the problem.

The first time Nasim mentioned the concept of "the *Khilafah*," I hadn't even heard of it. That just served his argument.

"Why do you think you have never heard of it?" he asked. "Because it is the West that has written the history books, and decided what they want to teach in schools, even in Muslim lands after they left us their colonial ways.

"In the 'official' version of events, the last bastion of the *Khilafah* was called the 'Ottoman Empire'; they don't even call it by its real name. This *Khilafah* sided with the Germans against the British in the First World War, which is why they don't want to tell you its history. They tell you it was the Turkish Empire that was disbanded because that is what they want you to believe—they don't want you to know what the *Khilafah* really was," he argued. "Do you think the Ottoman *Khilafah* would ever have stood by and allowed Bosnian Muslims to get slaughtered? Muslims stood united and protected under this entity before 1924. The West doesn't want this to happen again, which is why they are working so hard to stop the reunification of Muslims."

This logic led to the curious position of Hizb al-Tahrir endorsing Saddam Hussein's invasion of Kuwait during the first Gulf War. They supported it because it fit in with their narrative of Muslims uniting under a single entity. It also explained the American intervention: the United States didn't want to uphold the principle of national sovereignty, they wanted to stop such an entity beginning to form. It wasn't that HT were fans of Saddam Hussein: far from it. But if Saddam was in charge of two countries, then that was one less tyrant the group needed to overthrow.

Nasim argued that the Western response to repel Saddam was nothing more than a reinforcement of their imperialist past. The British and French had carved up the Middle East in anticipation of the collapse of the Ottoman Caliphate: these were countries with borders drawn quite literally with a ruler at the Sykes–Picot summit in 1916. Look at the right angle that separates Egypt and Sudan: is that a natural, historical boundary? These are the anachronisms of empire, still visible on the maps of today. Kuwait and Iraq were artificial entities. The West intervened to uphold these boundaries to reinforce its own set of colonial rules, not ours.

Everything about the modern Middle East, according to HT, was a product of this colonialism. Even the government of Saudi Arabia, on the face of it a deeply conservative Muslim regime, was an imperialist puppet regime. They allow the Americans to base their troops there and sell them their oil. Saudi Arabia was in fact created as a reward to the House of Saud for their rebellion *against* "the *Khilafah*." Throughout the region, there were agents of the West in charge, torturing the true Muslims to keep them from power: rulers like Mubarak in Egypt, the Shah of Iran before his fall in 1979, even Saddam Hussein had been the beneficiary of Western support for many years. The West talked of democracy and yet pumped millions into propping up these brutal dictators to keep the real force from coming to power: Islam. For HT, none of these regimes had legitimacy: their political authority was based on that of their current, neocolonial masters.

I was sixteen at the time I started hearing all this. When you're that age, already angry and disenfranchised, you're very susceptible to absolutes. This globalization of our grievance was what many would later come to know as the powerful Islamist narrative. It would go on to stir the hearts of thousands of young Muslims around the world, leading to the creation of groups who would commit many atrocities in its name. At that time, before al-Qaeda was ever conceived, all this sounded highly credible to me. I didn't have the political knowledge to come back and challenge what I was being told, and I didn't trust the typical authorities to tell me the truth. I could see the passion with which Osman would lay out his new position, hear Nasim's carefully crafted narratives coming through in what he was saying. I could sense the way it chimed with my own experiences, could smell the atmosphere on the streets. And considering everything my young mind could see around me, it sounded credible.

To begin with, I stuck with what I knew: hip-hop and the counterculture messages the lyrics contained. Even here, though, things were changing. Within Public Enemy, there had always been two competing voices on the mic. The group was first and foremost Chuck D's band—his strident belief in black power, in ensuring the work of Martin Luther King and Malcolm X was brought up to date for a new generation gave PE's message an untainted authority. But equally important for the band's message was Professor Griff. Griff was a member of the Nation of Islam: he didn't drink, didn't smoke, and had his S1Ws, his Security of the First World, dressed up in military gear, carrying imitation machine guns onstage. Griff's politics were more radical and more controversial. He had given an interview to the *Washington Times* in which he claimed that "Jews are wicked . . . [and responsible for] the majority of wickedness that goes on across the globe."* This was on the heels of giving a television interview where he said he didn't wear jewelry because it was named after the Jews, who ran the trade in South Africa. The group's response was to fire Griff for anti-Semitism. For a PE fan like myself, the split was shocking. Public Enemy had politicized me: now there were schisms emanating from the camp. So where hip-hop had once given me strength and identity, its impact was dulled a little from this confusion. I was now facing a split along similar lines at home, between Osman and me, and was desperately trying to work out which way to go.

The culmination was that final meeting with Mickey. The show of strength that I had been part of in Ockendon suddenly felt parochial. The strength that my brother's conviction and politics brought with it seemed to have real power. I'd caught a glimpse of what it could do in Mickey's reaction. I could only begin to imagine its impact if it were replicated on

---

* *Washington Times*, interview with David Mills—May 22, 1989.

a global scale. The fact that my brother succeeded with a green backpack where all my knife fights and shows of strengths had failed, made me think.

I remember something else, too. Whereas, before, his dependable green backpack had PLO graffitied over it, now he had struck out PLO and started to write the name of a group unknown to me: Hamas.

"What's that mean?" I naively asked.

"Forget the PLO sell-outs," he said. "They're not Islamic. This is Hamas, the *Islamic* Resistance Movement. The future belongs to Hamas."

Oh cool, I thought, Professor Griff would like them. I agreed to go to study circles with him, to see what Hizb al-Tahrir was about.

CHAPTER SEVEN

A Land Where Fetuses Are Cut from Wombs

Hizb al-Tahrir study circles took place in people's houses. There would be five to six of us sitting in a circle with the speaker at the center. Nasim or another speaker would talk on a set topic for about an hour and then take questions afterward. The content would be more political than theological, with occasional reference to Islam to back up the point. There was a methodology to these discussions, the framework of which I've continued to use effectively to this day: *always destroy before you build.*

HT was very good at taking apart existing deeply held prejudices, stripping them down to their bare bones, and then rebuilding a new set of reference points. Often it was said, if you try to build on top of existing corrupt concepts, one day your ideas will fall like a stack of cards. In keeping with this, the circles first focused on a thorough critique of ideas such as freedom, human rights, and democracy. Every critique addressed an intellectual, political, and scriptural angle. These discussions were like a thorough, deep cleansing. Such was Nasim's contempt for Western society—it was clear his country of birth was no longer part of his identity. He defined himself directly against this.

There was no link between these study groups and the local mosque. In fact, the study groups were outright critical of the religious classes. This disdain was based on piecemeal history and an element of truth that had been embellished out of all proportion. During the British Raj, there was a theory among some Muslims that the best way to further themselves was to appease their colonial rulers. The Hindus were in the majority, and it was said that if they ruled India they would use their power to oppress the Muslim community. The best way, therefore, to protect Muslims was to keep the British in power—a trade-off between being allowed to pray, fast, and practice rituals, and having to subjugate themselves to foreign rule.

Islamists used this position, which some religious clerics took in India, as evidence against all religious clerics. They had lost their way and turned Islam into Christianity—a meek, spiritual creed that had no effect on life and no control over society. Again, there is some truth to this narrative. Muslim religious leaders had indeed let modernity overtake them, had become politically complacent, and were grossly out of touch. These were the types sending mosque imams, who could not speak English, to teach us in Britain. Rather than admiring the piety of Muslims who quietly went about practicing their faith, Islamists disparaged them for not challenging the neocolonial state they were living in, or the "Westernization" it brought with it.

Secular Islamic heritage, historically strong among traditional Muslims, was taking an Islamist battering. It didn't help that some of the staunchest advocates for this secularism were not democrats but Arab despots. It followed therefore that it was Islamists who were going to liberate the lands and minds of Muslims by teaching them the impact Islam demands to have on life, society, and governance, by overthrowing these despots, rejecting the West and reclaiming their identity, and by establishing the true system for Muslims, "the *Khilafah*." Secular Muslim heritage, caught completely unawares and half asleep, caved in.

Of primary importance was the overall narrative of Islamism: historical facts and theological points were chosen to support this, rather than beginning with the information and postulating a theory from it. So the information and stories chosen were never lies or untruths, but seldom were they the whole truth. The element that supported the story was mentioned; the part that complicated the issue was ignored. That was true of both history and theology: where a reference to Allah was relevant, it would be dropped in.

But there was never a session on how to pray. There was never a session on how to fast. There was never a session on how to read the Qur'an.

We learned how to pray alone; we did because it was considered important to keep up the ritual, and because it was part of the ideology as a
whole. But it was very much only part of the overall scheme. Islamism is
a total theory that encompasses politics, economics, societal affairs, and
personal spiritual ones. For Islamists, the faith element was something
of a given—it was the politics and other issues that were the focus of
attention.

The speaker brought to each meeting that session's leaflet, usually a
single sheet divided into two columns with a heading at the top. This
would be the subject of that day's discussion: a single, straightforward
idea that they wanted the group to adopt.

At one of the first study circles I went to, the leaflet was titled "Born
to be Brown." The basic idea was that skin color is irrelevant, and what
mattered were ideas and narratives. Just because someone is brown doesn't
make them your brother; the person of the same skin color as you can
just as easily be your enemy. What matters is whether you were a Muslim
(by Muslim, they meant an Islamist, which is what they considered to
be a "proper" Muslim). The dividing line did not fall between ethnicities
or nationalities: it was about Islam versus everyone else. That involved a
recalibration of one's identity, to start defining oneself as Muslim against
the rest of the world.

This particular leaflet stuck in my mind because it challenged the
bricks and mortar with which I'd built up my teenage identity. My group
of friends was almost uniformly drawn from the minority communities
of Southend. We'd joined together because of the threats we had faced,
and through a shared interest in hip-hop and black culture. I was told that
what I'd previously found strength in was irrelevant. It was quite a lot to
take in; after all, the racism I'd experienced was part of the pathway for
wanting to join HT in the first place. To stop thinking in terms of racial
lines—and start thinking in terms of Muslims versus the rest—was quite
a shift.

I had very few Pakistani friends. Most of my friends growing up had
been white English non-Muslims and then, when the racism kicked in,
we became part of a West Indian group. I didn't really feel affiliated to
Pakistan or to England, and I knew I was not West Indian. So there was

a real vacuum in my identity, which was the ideal place for someone to be before recruitment to an Islamist organization. They were able to offer me an identity that had previously been absent.

The study circles were supplemented by videos, and most strikingly, those of the conflict in Yugoslavia and the appalling treatment of the Bosnian Muslims by the Serb forces. This was taking place prior to the Internet taking hold: the technology was not yet up to the sort of dissemination of videos we are familiar with today. Back then, it was all about VHS cassettes: copies would be made and meetings would be arranged to watch these tapes. This was footage that wasn't shown on mainstream media; it was shocking, appalling stuff, especially to a raw sixteen-year-old.

The footage reached us because people from the UK had gone to fight in Bosnia. British Muslims went as civilians, trained in camps funded by the Saudis, fought in Bosnia, and came back to recruit more soldiers. This was at a time when, amazingly, going abroad to fight in a war was unlikely to get you stopped and questioned—as long as you were not fighting against your own troops.

In some ways, Bosnia was no different from the situation then in Afghanistan: in both cases, there were Saudi funds available to train and fight. There were training camps all over Bosnia, and a huge growth of Saudi-built mosques that were clearly aimed at funding a religious revival in the country. The major difference with Afghanistan was the proximity. Bosnia was a war taking place on the European mainland, a conflict that was less than a three-hour flight away. When these fighters returned to the UK, they were treated like heroes: with their big beards and talk about Islam, they felt like our very own Che Guevaras.

The videos featured disturbing content. Trays of what appeared to be genitals cut off from Bosnian men by Serbs. Footage of pregnant women with their bellies cut open and their babies ripped out alive. You'd see the dead woman on the floor with the baby lying next to her, the umbilical cord still attached, and the gash down the front of her stomach. There would then be combat footage as well, of trained Muslim fighters defending themselves against the Serbs. The footage was well put together considering the limits of technology. Some scenes were a little grainy, but they'd been edited professionally. I hesitate to use the word "propaganda" because that has negative implications, but that is essentially what they were. There was a genocide going on, and the appalling crimes committed were being used to further an Islamist recruitment drive across Europe. And it worked.

What these videos showed me were two things in particular. First of all, it reinforced the narrative that Nasim had taught me in the "Born to be Brown" discussion. These were individuals whose death had nothing to do with the color of their skin. The fact that they were Muslims was the salient issue, as shown by the fact that all the individuals were white. Second, Britain and other Western governments were doing nothing about it, which reinforced their "blind eye" approach to world politics. When it was Muslims who were under attack, and there was no oil to defend, the West wasn't interested in getting involved. And why should they? These were our people, not theirs. This is why we needed "the *Khilafah*."

These unfolding terrible events served as the perfect recruitment ground for Islamism. These people were being killed simply for being Muslims. Worse, because they were not Muslims with the "proper" understanding, they didn't even understand *why* it was happening to them. But Islamism offered a powerful explanation—this shift in identity politics began to occur both in Bosnia and across Europe. In some ways, you could argue that just as Pakistan's troubles with violent Islamism— Jihadism—were born through Afghanistan, European Jihadism was born through Bosnia.

The first time I saw the videos, it was a shocking, traumatic experience. My immediate response was a desire to go fight in Bosnia myself. I remember Nasim having to take me aside to give me a long talk to calm me down. He told me to stop being emotional, to think about the rational point here instead. No matter what you do, no matter how many people go out there, it's not going to change the long-term game. This is not just happening in Bosnia, it's everywhere. There are fires being lit all over the place. You can get a bucket and try to put one out, or you can step back and look at the root cause of all this. If we had "the *Khilafah*," our armies could stop such atrocities happening. This was the Hizb al-Tahrir message: what we needed was to work efficiently to control the mind-set of the military top brass in Muslim-majority countries in order to eventually establish a state. Simply joining the fight would mean one more soldier lost for the cause. It may save one or two people there but wouldn't change anything in the long run.

Those videos were a powerful recruiting weapon for HT. We would organize viewings for people, and while they sat there stunned by what they saw, we would tell them they were wasting their lives while all this mayhem unfolded. "What are you doing with your life?" we asked. How can you be happy with yourselves, going out for a laugh and a kebab on a Friday or Saturday night when all this is happening on your doorstep? The video and the speech would always have the same, radicalizing effect. Half would want to join HT there and then: but there were others like me who would want to go fight.

The challenge for us, like Nasim had done with me, was to talk these people down. It didn't always work. Omar Sheikh, for example, was a student at the London School of Economics who attended a HT-backed conference at his university about the situation in Bosnia. The leader of HT at the time, Omar Bakri Fostok—who used Mohammad as his surname—was a keynote speaker at this conference. Omar Sheikh's diaries tell of how the conference galvanized him, but that it didn't go far enough. HT offered him a coruscating analysis of the situation but didn't provide any solution. The answer for him was Jihadism. Sheikh went abroad, and is still imprisoned in Pakistan, accused of the murder of *Wall Street Journal* reporter Daniel Pearl.

The war in Bosnia was crucial to Islamism's spread across Europe. From there it spread in the Middle East and Asia: European Muslims were radicalized by events in Bosnia, Egyptians were radicalized by events in Palestine, Pakistanis were radicalized by events in Afghanistan. It was a similar theme all over: grievances, identity crises, charismatic recruiters, and compelling narratives.

For me, the procrastination of Western governments over Bosnia resonated strongly with my own experiences in Essex and the inaction I saw from the police. This was how it was, I reasoned. It was up to Muslims to defend their own community. These days, looking back from a post-9/11 world where Western intervention has been so frequent, we forget that in the early 1990s the world was a different place. The international landscape was still adjusting to the end of the Cold War, where every decision was worked out with regard to what the Soviet response might be. The early 1990s asked new questions about whether interventions within a state for humanitarian reasons were justifiable—Rwanda and Somalia were two other cases.

The consequence of all this was that the Western response to Bosnia was paralysis. Bill Clinton did not want to get the United States involved, seeing it as a European issue. The British response was vacillation. If the West had been more proactive, if they had intervened earlier and harder as when Tony Blair and NATO did so over Kosovo, the situation would have been different, not just for Bosnia, but perhaps also for the spread of Islamism and for HT.

In Bosnia itself, it was left to the new government to sort out the rising Islamist penetration. The Bosnian government began to root out the jihadists who had come to fight there. They recognized the threat from within and the potential for another Afghanistan situation if they did not act. But while Bosnia was successful in doing this, the influence of its fight lingered on for far longer.

Hizb al-Tahrir saw "the *Khilafah*," a Muslim superstate, as the answer to all the injustice meted out to the Muslim populations of the world. It would sweep across all national boundaries; HT's version of Islam would be the ruling philosophy. Apostates, adulterers, and minorities considered abhorrent, like homosexuals, would suffer the death sentence. Criminality would be met with tough justice; thieves would have their hands cut off. Rights such as free speech would be curtailed, because "God's law" must trump all.

It was surprising to some people how easy it felt to switch my mindset to this new political viewpoint. I'd felt I'd found my connection with hip-hop culture, but it fell away with little argument, likely due to my particular set of circumstances and upbringing. The message of Islamism was almost tailor-made for someone like me: intellectually curious and brought up in a Western environment. I didn't have the family or religious background to counterbalance what Nasim was telling me. The HT way of analyzing things was, ironically enough, a modern, European, sociopolitical interpretation of religion. That was the way I'd been educated at school, so I understood the reasoning from the start.

Secondly, there was Nasim himself, an intellectually charismatic guy. The authority and confidence with which he spoke on any number of subjects made a huge impression on me at an age when I was easily influenced. And the subjects he talked about related directly to my life, something my father or the imam had been unable to do. He knew about politics, philosophy, theology—all the issues that bands like Public Enemy had raised—and took them further. The way he tied these different issues together was intellectually intoxicating. It felt revolutionary, and that's exactly what it was: advocating a revolution.

Thirdly, the political element of hip-hop was starting to peel away. What had originally excited me was the politics that bands like PE and N.W.A had brought to the table. PE had carried on without Professor Griff, but the whole anti-Semitic episode had dented their popularity. The vanguard of hip-hop was increasingly becoming gangsta rap: the new stars were people like Cypress Hill, and the underlying messages were less about anti-authority anthems and more to do with boasting about drugs, violence, and women.

The way hip-hop was changing reinforced what Nasim was telling me in the study circles. You related to their music, I was told, because you have been through similar experiences of racism and discrimination. "But Chuck D is not a Muslim. Flavor Flav is not a Muslim. Ice Cube is not a Muslim. They do not know the solution to the problems they rap about because the message has simply not reached them." That is where Hizb al-Tahrir and Islamism came in. It seemed perfectly natural for hip-hop to go one way, and my thinking to go another. I stopped listening to the music and started listening to HT instead.

PART TWO

ISLAMIST

To live is to war with trolls in heart and soul.
To write is to sit in judgment on oneself.
— HENRIK IBSEN, *PEER GYNT*

CHAPTER EIGHT

An Islamist Takeover

At sixteen, recruited to HT's cause and now full of the zeal of the converted, I wanted to move to London to be where the action was. I told my parents that I wanted to attend Barking College in East London to do a specialist graphic design course. At this point they were unaware of the nature of my Islamist beliefs. My father, in particular, saw a son who had calmed down from the B-boy excesses of his earlier teens and appeared to be settling into the life of a traditional, hardworking Muslim. And so it was that I moved out of the family home to study.

Of course the graphic design course was just a front. HT was far bigger in the capital than in Southend, and I desperately wanted to be part of it. By this time Nasim was in charge of HT's activities in East London, and with his help I got a room in a flat there. This was known as the *da'wah*—or mission—house, a flat dedicated to planning HT and occupied solely by supporters. By now I was an HT *daris*—student—the stage before membership. This meant that I was committed to attending HT events and partaking in official activities. My roommates, all HT *dariseen*, were recruited at the university. They included a student called Saleem, a former body-builder and all-around friendly guy; Sohail, a student from Milton Keynes in his second year at Guildhall University; Yaseen, an intelligent man who went on to leave HT and became a teacher; Ali, who would pop in to stay occasionally, and whom at the time we revered because he was already a member; and Nas, my Greek friend from Southend who had converted and moved to London with me.

Ours was a student house, with all the mess that entailed, but it was fantastic to be in the thick of the action, surrounded by "brothers." I loved it. From the get-go, the house was used for HT activities. We'd put up stickers and posters, hand out pamphlets and leaflets, and advertise talks. We would spend all night cutting up boxes to create our boards, sticking posters onto the cardboard, punching holes and running the string through them, ready to be tied up. Then we'd load the cargo into someone's car and blitz the local area, tying our posters to lampposts everywhere. People would drop in to the flat from all over London. After the typical town atmosphere of Southend, and the feeling of being part of a fractional minority, I now felt plugged into a far larger community, a thriving London network buzzing with ideas.

This setup accelerated my commitment to HT. Before, I'd been going to study groups once a week. Now I was *living* with other activists and talking about the cause every day. For the first time, I had a real sense of how the movement was a national and global phenomenon. All the major universities had recruitment drives: we were fast taking over. The 1990s in London was the decade of Islamism. As many women as men were joining the movement, and somewhere we were told was probably our future partner waiting to meet us. This movement would shape how my life unfolded.

There was also the fact that I was living in London for the first time. East Ham might not have been that far from Southend, but it felt like a different world. The diverse community of East Ham made racism less of an issue. And the rising strength of Islamism and Jihadism meant for the first time that you didn't mess with Muslims. With that knowledge, I could walk the streets with confidence.

When I arrived, Nasim appointed one of his protégés, Ed Husain, to help me settle in. Ed, a passionate HT *daris*, was studying at Newham College. We quickly became very close. Before term started Ed asked me which college I was enrolled in. Barking College, I told him.

"You don't want to be in Barking *ya akhi*, my brother, all the action's at Newham College. I'm at Newham's East Ham campus. That's where all the Muslims are, and that's where we could really kick things off together."

Ed was in his final year and needed to hand over his HT drive to someone; I was the perfect replacement. Ed was a studious type: at seventeen he wore a blazer and shirt to class. He was a good public speaker and more devout than I had been, or ever would become. I liked his religious devotion, it helped to calm my wilder side, and we developed a deep, lasting friendship. I went to his house, got to know his parents, and spent Ramadan breaking my fasts with his family. It soon became apparent that Ed and I could work together as a strong team. We led a group of four core HT supporters: Sarfraz and Mustafa, two big guys who were dependable types; Shehzad, a sociable guy who knew a lot of people; and Rehan, lovingly called "Mr. Bean" by our adversaries due to his physical stature and his propensity to intellectually fall over himself.

When the opportunity to become president of the Student Union (SU) arose, Ed suggested that I run for the post, and that our HT group should stand on a single slate. Our desire was to become the dominant Muslim group in the college. When I joined, the Islamic Society (ISoc) at Newham was dominated by the Saudi-Salafists, or literalists. In those days, before the merger between some Salafists and Islamism, the Salafists hated HT and everything we stood for. In the UK, a group called JIMAS coordinated all Salafist activities. JIMAS were known rivals. They loathed us more than non-Muslims for what they saw as our twisting of the Islamic message. The Salafist philosophy was far more religious than the HT message: there was no political element to their thinking. They dismissed our views for not being religious enough, and we in turn dismissed them for providing religious cover for the Saudi king and other absolute rulers. The Salafists controlled the college ISoc and, consequently, Friday prayers. This allowed them to bring in big crowds to their events and perpetuate their control.

Before I had gone to Newham, HT had never really been in a position to challenge this hegemony. Now, we felt confident enough to give it a go. If I could become president of the Student Union, then I would be in charge of funding for organizations such as the ISoc. I could then reduce ISoc's money, and their influence, at a stroke. I could even find a way to divert the money toward HT and our own aims.

We put up candidates for all the various posts on the Student Union. The Salafists were completely thrown off by our tactics and soon found themselves adrift in the campaign. We were more people-savvy and culturally aware. I had my B-boy background; the Salafists were wearing traditional Arab robes and strained to be pious. We would be listening to music and wearing jeans, and they did not know how to handle that. For the Salafists, the emphasis of their message was purity. Their manifesto was about sitting in the prayer room, talking about how to fast, and the benefits of leaving the world behind. Their starting point was the scriptures, whereas ours was the real world. We would talk about Afghanistan and Bosnia in a way that made our message sound relevant, whereas theirs just felt out of touch.

The female Muslim vote, in particular, came across to our side, partly because we were seen as trendy young guys, and partly because of the Salafist attitude to women. Salafists would criticize women for not wearing headscarves, to which we'd say, "Do you think the Bosnian Muslim woman was wearing a headscarf when she was raped? How does that make her any less your sister?"

On a more basic level, we were more aggressive in argument. Nasim had taught us to come back at our opponents. I'd learned the answers to their questions and would fire back a response to whatever accusations they made. That's a powerful thing to do when you're debating in front of a crowd. It makes you strong and your ideas coherent. The Salafists didn't really have a response: their only resort was to their religious purity, which didn't have the same resonance with most people's lives. A few years later, this would change: Salafism and Islamism would fuse to form Jihadism, most famously seen in the eventual rise of al-Qaeda.

The election was a runaway success. I didn't only become student president: all the other HT candidates won as well. Overnight we had completely outmaneuvered the Salafists. We were now the most senior students on campus, with authority to override the ISoc, to represent students in front of management, and to control student funds. At the same time, we set up the Debating Society to arrange events and bring in external speakers. On the forms, we claimed to have been inspired by Gladstone and Disraeli, and by parliamentary debates. We managed to hoodwink the management into letting us set up an HT front group. Such takeovers were happening across UK campuses. Islamism was firmly on the rise.

CHAPTER NINE

12,000 Muslims Screaming *"Khilafah"*

The ISoc Salafists were not the only ones incapable of dealing with us. The same was true of the college authorities, who had been caught completely off guard.

The student-affairs manager, Dave Gomer, was the point of contact between the college authorities and students. A friendly, well-meaning guy, his politics were forged in an earlier era, a time when student protests were about sit-ins and strikes and occupying the Student Union. To someone of Dave's generation, student protest was "kids being kids" and a healthy part of someone's political education. We ran circles around him.

We disguised our political demands behind religion and multiculturalism, and deliberately labeled any objection to our demands as racism. Even worse, we did this to the very generation who had been socialist sympathizers in their youth, people sympathetic to charges of racism, who like Dave Gomer were now in middle-career management posts. It is no wonder then that the authorities were unprepared to deal with politicized religion as ideological agitation; they felt racist if they tried to stop us.

The nearest comparison to our plans was, in a curious way, that of communism. The Cold War had not just been a battle between two military superpowers and their satellite states, but between two competing ideological systems. The West understood that communism was a direct threat to its way of doing business—the Soviet Union was both a physical and existential threat. This explains the McCarthy witch-hunt in the 1950s and "reds under the bed" paranoia.

Islamism demanded no less of a root-and-branch overhaul of society. But because it was cloaked in religious garb, no one quite knew what to do with it, and people were desperate not to offend. There was confusion over whether to define our activism as a cultural identity, an ideology, or a faith. To top it off, Islamism went through a decade of being embraced by both the left and right wings. The default liberal position was to embrace the movement as part of multicultural sensitivity: to tell people to stop practicing their faith was imperialism in nineties clothing, a colonial hangover bordering on racism. Instead, we were embraced as a new generation of anti-colonial politicized youth. Curiously, the default position on the right was to embrace us too, because it had been the Afghan Mujahideen, backed by the CIA, who fought the Soviet Union. This was when Hollywood films such as Stallone's *Rambo III* portrayed the Afghan Mujahideen as heroes.

In fact, the only groups who were speaking out against HT at this stage were people like Jeremy Newmark—now of the Jewish Leadership Council—and gay-rights campaigner Peter Tatchell. This was fantastic propaganda for HT: the opposition of pro-Israeli and pro–gay rights voices only reinforced the message we were trying to get across to Muslims. "The most dangerous of the Islamic fundamentalists is Hizb al-Tahrir," Tatchell wrote at the time. His views and warnings were ignored, and we were left laughing at people's ignorance.

In fact, as president of Newham Student Union, I remember an occasion when Ed and I received a press pack from the Union of Jewish Students, warning all unions about HT activities on campus. They had arranged a training and awareness day. As Newham College's Student Union, we decided to attend. That day we learned all they intended to do to thwart us, and we simply returned to Newham to use it against them.

Our victory in the student elections felt as though it was part of a bigger picture. A few months before, HT had held a global "*Khilafah* Conference" at Wembley Arena and it was packed. I was one of 12,000 people attending from across the world. This was an astonishing sight and a huge boost to my belief in the cause. I still remember the roar of the crowd as it reached fever pitch, all 12,000 chanting *Allahu akbar*, God is Great! I recall how the thunder of their stomping feet shook the arena, and the world's media finally paid attention. It was hard not to come away without thinking that the momentum of historical change was behind us.

Becoming Student Union president felt like an extension of this momentum. Newham was the first college where HT had succeeded in gaining control of the union, which meant that the HT leadership noticed us. So I persuaded the UK leader at the time, Omar Bakri Muhammad, to come down to speak at the college—another feather in my cap.

Omar Bakri Muhammad was a Syrian in the UK on political asylum; in those days he was a rather charismatic figure. Under Omar Bakri's leadership HT swept across the UK. This would not have been possible without his group of influential, rhetorically gifted lieutenants. The most outstanding of these was Farid Kasim, a former socialist, who converted back to Islam when he joined HT. Extremely articulate and intellectual, Kasim led the drive to recruit the student population into HT and used his former socialist tactics to do so. Kasim successfully targeted universities and got the organization to the point where it could gather 12,000 supporters for the international conference at Wembley.

However, as well as growing in numbers, the UK section of HT was also growing in notoriety, which alarmed the *qiyadah*, HT's global leadership. Founded in Jerusalem in 1953, HT had chapters in almost every country in the world. Their sole purpose was to use their global presence to reestablish "the *Khilafah*" in a Muslim-majority country. HT in the UK, however, was directly pitching the group's struggle against British society. Under Omar Bakri's leadership, they wrote pamphlets describing how they would conquer the political establishment. Other pamphlets were overtly anti-Semitic. These tactics were provocative and began to get the group noticed. The *qiyadah* didn't like that: it wanted to use the UK as a base for fund-raising, for recruitment, media, and diplomatic cover. It didn't want the British wing of the organization to rock this carefully balanced, money-providing boat.

In Newham, rather than keeping a low profile, we continued to ratchet things up.

Our campaigns became increasingly provocative and difficult to ignore. We put up a series of posters with a picture of a Muslim woman wearing a face veil, an AK-47 by her side. The title of the poster, advertising a talk we were hosting, was "Women of the West—Cover Up or Shut Up." That poster drew a response from both students and staff. It was the first time that people started complaining about the Student Union, and we got called in to see Dave Gomer. We were completely unrepentant, and I justified our stance to the end.

"All I'm asking for is for people to leave us alone," I argued, somewhat disingenuously. "This is how we believe women should dress: if you don't want to dress like this, that's your decision, but don't criticize our women for doing so!"

Into this atmosphere, we arranged for Omar Bakri Muhammad to come and address the students. We wanted to make a good impression on the leadership and spent the week before creating a buzz about his visit. On the day of his talk, the hall was packed; even the Salafists were there. They turned up in the hope of heckling him, but Omar Bakri rebutted them with his usual flair. Here was someone who did have a beard, who spoke Arabic, and who had the theological authority from having studied *shari'ah* (Islamic jurisprudence) at Damascus University. By demonstrating that we could argue not just in terms of politics but also religion, we began to overshadow the Salafists. The talk became a hugely successful coup for us.

Omar Bakri's appearance came amidst rising tension within the college. The conflict between HT and the Salafists was only one of the battles raging across campus. More serious, in some ways, were the racial tensions that had built up between Pakistani students and African students. For a long time the African students had been the dominant, threatening force within the college. They would intimidate the Pakistani students, and were also responsible for a wave of muggings. They demanded that students hand over their money and got into fights over women. They did all this knowing that the Pakistani students were unlikely to fight back.

I saw myself in these Pakistani students, the younger me who'd been punched and kicked in the stomach. I understood instinctively that what these students needed was a cause. There were more of them; if they had a reason to stand up to these bullies, the tables would turn.

I took it upon myself to turn the Pakistani students into a force to be reckoned with. I immediately knew what would inspire the Pakistanis; I needed to re-create that backpack moment between Osman and Mickey right here in the college. I had to inject them with the fever of Muslim jingoism. And so, unannounced, we walked into the student canteen, stood on the tables, and just addressed all the students in full view. We blatantly challenged the non-Muslim Africans in front of everyone. And dared them to step up to the power of Islam, and warned them of Allah's wrath if they messed with Muslims.

We were grossly outnumbered, yet we faced them unflinchingly, with a fire raging in our chests and the sort of conviction that animates one's expression. The African students didn't know what to do. Our brazen confidence threw them, and they just stood there gaping. Ours was a calculated conflation of the HT message and self-defense: galvanizing the students with the HT narrative and getting them interested in the group's activities at the same time.

We'd inspire the students with tales of jihad, assure them of backup through our networks, but most of all, we led by example. In the middle of such confrontations, which would often spill out into the college courtyard, we would suddenly drop into coordinated prayers, right there in the open in front of our adversaries. And after our prayers, we'd stand back up and shout, "*Allahu akbar*," at the tops of our voices in unison, like a war cry. The African students all had knives; some of them were carrying machetes. But after everything I'd been through in Southend, that sort of weaponry didn't faze me. By this point, I'd been going around with my knife strapped to my back for years. It was second nature to me. I was so desensitized to the threat of violence that I could stand up to the African students without thinking twice. Imbued by my Islamist beliefs and the confidence of my election victory, I stoked the acrid atmosphere still further. Our display did the trick: it galvanized the Pakistani youth, and it made them stand as Muslims.

But it was only a matter of time before someone got badly hurt.

CHAPTER TEN

Servant of the Compeller

Hizb al-Tahrir's view on violence was that, while it condemned its members attacking others, it was reasonable to defend oneself. This policy wasn't universally agreed upon among the group's members; some from the more intellectual contingent thought it better not to carry weapons. They argued that it made the group look bad and made it possible for people to conclude that we were terrorists. By not carrying any form of weapon, they argued, the distinction between HT and jihadists would be more clearly defined. For those of us facing groups like the African students, this all seemed somewhat theoretical. In practical terms, we needed to be able to defend ourselves, so I encouraged the Pakistani students in college to get more aggressively "defensive." The Africans quickly realized that something different was happening—for the first time, they understood that things weren't going their way, but they remained unsure of what to do.

One day, while all this was unfolding, a student whom I didn't know approached me.

"Brother Maajid," he said, "there is someone on campus asking for you. He is going round trying to find out where you are."

"What does he look like?"

"Tall," the student said. "A really tall black guy."

My alarm bells immediately started ringing. The Africans must have called for backup to put me in my place. *This is it*, I thought, *it's time*. Everything I'd learned back in Essex taught me to face such danger head on, so I walked around the college looking for this guy. I wanted it to be me who found him, rather than the other way around. And I did.

Adrenaline pumping, I walked straight up him, fully expecting trouble. "You're looking for me?"

"*Assalaamu alaykum, akhi,* are you brother Maajid?" he said with a huge smile and a warm embrace. He smelled of the traditional scented oils, called attar, favored by our Prophet *'alayhi salam* (upon whom be peace), and sold in contemporary Islamic bookshops.

It turned out that the lanky outsider was a jihadist Muslim from South London called Sa'eed Nur. Sa'eed had come to offer his "support" to the now notorious "HT brothers" in Newham College.

"Brother Maajid"—he always addressed me so respectfully—"I heard of the great work you brothers are doing here and I'm here to offer you my support. No one can mess with you while I'm around, that's my promise *insha' Allah*—God willing."

Sa'eed Nur hailed from a nascent jihadist scene that was developing in Brixton, then one of London's roughest areas. He embodied the merger between religious literalism and Islamism. And though I wasn't a jihadist myself, I was relieved to have found his support. I felt confident in my ability to convert him to our cause over time. Sa'eed became, in effect, my bodyguard: he talked of bringing down "fifty gunmen" from Brixton if we needed them, though he wasn't short of weaponry himself. At that first meeting, he reached into his leather jacket and pulled out a sword.

"This," he said, "is Abdul Jabbar."

In Islamic tradition, *Jabbar* is one of the ninety-nine names of Allah: it translates as the Compeller. Putting Abdul in front of it rendered the meaning: Servant of the Compeller. That was the name Sa'eed had chosen to give his sword.

"I've heard you're having some trouble with some nasty *kuffar*—infidels, here in the college. They're pestering our sisters?" Sa'eed asked, looking sincerely disturbed at this thought.

"So any time you need help," he continued, sliding the sword back away, "just give me a call, *akhi*. I'll come down *fee sabeelillah*—in the path of Allah—and sort it out for you." He then handed me his home phone number, and with another embrace sought my leave, ironically, with the words "*assalaamu alaykum*—peace be upon you."

The first time he turned up, Sa'eed Nur felt like a gift from Allah. Here was someone who appeared, as if out of nowhere, to offer us unconditional physical support. The *seerah*—life of our Prophet *'alayhi salam*—seemed to affirm such divine providence. Islamic tradition relates how the Prophet was granted similar *nussra* (support) by the conversion of his warrior uncle Hamza to Islam. By drawing analogies between Sa'eed's appearance and Hamza, we reinforced our belief that ours was the righteous path. The fact that Sa'eed was black was perfect. It reinforced the point I'd been making to the Pakistanis that this wasn't a racial issue: the dividing line was between Muslims and the rest of the world. Whether it was the white Muslims in Bosnia, black Muslims like Sa'eed, or Pakistani Muslims, it was our *deen* (religion) that gave us our identity and united us.

The next time Sa'eed came to campus, with steely determination he asked to see the Africans. I pointed them out to him, and he strode over to speak to their crew. If my standing up to the gang had surprised them, seeing this lanky black man taking our side shook them even more. I'd already warned Sa'eed that they'd be packing knives, but with Abdul Jabbar hidden inside his jacket, and Allah on his side, that didn't worry him much. He walked right into the center of their group, in front of a packed and gaping student common room, and at the top of his voice, offered to take them all on in one clean sweep.

"You dirty *kuffar!* You think you're bad men? I'll have fifty gunmen up in here in no time!" he growled. "We love death more than you love life. Come, all of you, come and taste death if you dare!"

He went around, one by one, asking each of them who felt confident enough to challenge him. None of them stood up to him.

"Right," Sa'eed said, "if you're not man enough to take me on, you stay away from my brothers!"

And there it was—the Muslims of Newham College had just found their backpack moment. This wasn't a private confrontation. Everyone saw it, and word quickly got around. You could almost see it ripple through the student body. They knew now that they had Sa'eed to back them up if things kicked off.

Over a couple of months, the whole atmosphere in the college changed. Sa'eed would come down regularly and wander around the campus with impunity. Security was fairly lax. The authorities never challenged the fact that a man in his mid-twenties was hanging about, and there were no metal detectors to pick up that he carried a sword. Buoyed by his support, we were running campaigns like the "Cover Up or Shut Up" posters. We were inviting Omar Bakri and other high-profile leaders to speak, confident of the reception we'd get. And the Pakistani students were making their presence felt for the first time. Our vision of Islamisizing the college was going according to plan.

The Africans, however, were still adjusting to this shift in power. After the initial shock of being challenged, and watching the Muslim students assert themselves, the hard-core elements of the gang began to regroup. One day, there was a stand-off in the common room. This would all have been fairly typical stuff were it not for one of the African crew, Ayotunde Obanubi, pulling out a penknife and slashing at a Muslim student. No one was hurt, but everyone split, and word of what had happened got around pretty quickly.

I was outraged. The following morning, I organized a show of strength. I got as many Muslim students to gather in the courtyard as I could, to take part in a spontaneous rally. As the African students stood there aghast, we chanted, "*Allahu akbar!*" and marched around the square declaring our presence. Again, we prayed right there on the street in front of the courtyard, supremely confident that the Africans would not dare attack us while we prayed. For us, prayer had become a propaganda tool and a means of intimidation—not the calming spiritual experience it was meant to be.

And then he arrived. I'm not sure who had called Sa'eed—he'd offered his number to everyone—but he was aware of the incident in the common room and his eyes were bloodshot red. If I had known better, or cared to know, I would have recognized the look on his face as bloodlust.

The atmosphere was suddenly speed and adrenaline. Ayotunde was there with his gang. He watched with contempt as we marched and chanted. He'd come prepared and was ready for trouble. Then suddenly Sa'eed approached him. Words were being exchanged. I decided I had to get closer. Ayotunde had already pulled out a pair of butcher's knives: two big, ugly, nasty blades. He was waving them at Sa'eed. He was shouting at

Sa'eed. He was attacking Sa'eed. I am behind Sa'eed. Ayotunde is slashing with his butcher's knives at Sa'eed's leather jacket. He is trying to stab Sa'eed.

What to do? How to react?

I reach for my blade.

I unclip my blade. *What to do?*

But my world slowed down again as soon as Sa'eed's voice resonated across the courtyard. There was an air of absolute calm in him. He was in uncanny, almost hypnotic, control of his emotions. If he felt threatened, he certainly didn't show it. Instead, he looked at Ayotunde and in a measured tone, said: "If you don't put them away right now, I will have to kill you."

That sentence has haunted my soul to this day. Ayotunde didn't heed Sa'eed's warning but continued slashing at his leather jacket with the knives. By this point, I was certain that Ayotunde was going to get hurt. I told myself this was self-defense. We Muslims are a just people, I thought, but we're not pacifists. We don't transgress, but if someone wants to pick a fight, they'd better be prepared to fight to the death. Sa'eed opened his leather jacket and pulled out Abdul Jabbar.

Then, from the corner of my eye, with my hand still on my blade, I noticed Dave Gomer, the student-liaison officer. He was standing right behind Ayotunde. He had come rushing out of the building after all the commotion. I saw him take in the situation, size up Ayotunde brandishing his butcher's knives, Sa'eed with his sword, and me standing behind Sa'eed. Gomer didn't recognize Sa'eed, wasn't particularly aware of who Ayotunde was, but he knew me all right. He looked at me straight in the eye; it was the most arresting glance, one of extreme disappointment, rather than anger. The look was of someone feeling so badly let down. *I trusted you,* I could see him thinking. *I trusted you to keep all this under control.*

Gomer couldn't have known that I had unsheathed my knife, not from where he was standing, because it was still hidden behind my back and beneath my clothes. But I was there, and for him that was enough.

It was one of those moments where my life could have gone one of two ways. Sometimes the smallest of decisions can have the largest consequences. But Dave Gomer's look cut through me. His cold disappointment sliced through the white heat of my adrenaline. It pulled me up sharp, and for a crucial split second I had a flash of realization about what I might be about to do. I slid my knife back into its sheath, clicked it back in place, and pulled back, completely back. No one knew how close I had been. Gomer has absolutely no idea of the effect his look had on me. He probably thinks he failed at that college. But without his presence, my life would have taken an entirely different turn. And for that, I will be forever grateful to him.

The sad truth is that while I was fortunate enough to have Gomer there to check my behavior, there was no one around to check Sa'eed's. No sooner had I slipped my knife back into its sheath, than he was doing precisely the opposite with his sword. In one swift, calm, almost mechanical movement, Sa'eed plunged his monstrous blade, Abdul Jabbar, the Servant of the Compeller, deep into Ayotunde's chest.

That was the signal. As soon as Sa'eed knifed Ayotunde, from all sides young Pakistani kids came piling in; some had weapons like hammers and knives, others were just kicking and punching. It was a vicious, frenzied assault way beyond my control at this stage. Ayotunde, I knew immediately, had no chance.

Gomer was sensible enough not to do anything either. As it became clear that Ayotunde wasn't getting up, everyone involved ran. There was pandemonium: people screaming, onlookers wanting to get out of the way, those with weapons wanting to disappear before the police appeared and found blood all over the floor. As the emergency services arrived, some sort of order was slowly restored. The paramedics went straight to Ayotunde and desperately tried to revive him as his body convulsed in its final death throes. It was to no avail. I stood there and watched Ayotunde Obanubi die.

CHAPTER ELEVEN

The Womb That Bore Me

The college courtyard was now a murder scene, and the police were soon asking questions. I hadn't been involved in the actual attack and felt that I had no reason to run. I also wanted to give the police our side of the story. Ayotunde had attacked first; he'd brought knives to a sword fight and lost. Sa'eed Nur had responded in self-defense.

I was never arrested myself; in fact, the police wanted to see if I could be a prosecution witness. I was introduced to a young lawyer, an up-and-coming HT *daris* named Anjem Choudary. When I had run the events of the day past Anjem, he assured me that there was nothing prejudicial to the defense in what I said. And as we sat together discussing this in a fast-food restaurant, I remember Anjem commenting on how "sharp" I was for a seventeen-year-old.

"This one will make a great *da'i*—activist—one day," he said, turning to his colleague.

Anjem Choudary would later go on to lead one of Britain's most notorious, and eventually banned, Salafi-Jihadist organizations, al-Muhajiroun. (In 2010, I gave Anjem a rude awakening during our now infamous debate on BBC *Newsnight*. He had completely forgotten our meetings.)

Full of a sense of injustice, I recalled my story to the police. I said that Ayotunde had been armed with two knives and had attacked first. I explained how the African students had a long history of bullying the Muslim students, and this incident was the culmination of that. My views never made it to court. I wasn't called by the prosecution because my memories did not suit the conviction and I wasn't called by the defense because it would have looked as though Sa'eed was part of an organized Islamist conspiracy, which wouldn't have helped his defense. One of the other students, Umran Qadir, was convicted for participating in the murder. Sa'eed was put away for life.

The day of the murder, as the crowds began to disperse, Ayotunde's friends passed me and whispered harsh calls for revenge. My instincts kicked in. I knew these guys would need to witness just how doggedly we were prepared to defend ourselves so that they wouldn't retaliate. The initiative had to be seized by us, and speed was everything. That night I was picked up by some of the former Pakistani gang members; they had managed to find out where a few of the African students lived. We reached their address and parked up outside, keeping the car running with its lights on. Our aim was to be seen, and so we waited until someone came to the window and spotted us. Immediately, the curtains were drawn in what was probably fear. We wanted to scare them and send a message—*if you haven't had enough yet, we're still here and have more to offer.* Once they'd seen us, we drove away, job done.

I'm not proud of what I did. And behaving like this certainly wasn't something endorsed by HT. What we did that night, a calculated move to instill terror in the hearts of men just after their friend had been murdered, is probably the lowest I've ever stooped in my life. It is difficult to argue now that going to their house that night was self-defense, but that's what we did. My seventeen-year-old reasoning was that the African students had started it. They'd come tooled up and had lashed out at Sa'eed Nur. We needed to petrify them enough that they backed off. On a crude level, it worked: they stopped.

My deepest condolences go to Ayotunde's family. Such a cold-blooded response to the murder of another individual was part and parcel of the person I'd become. There was a total desensitization from the violence I'd grown up around. My reaction, too, was inextricably bound together with my membership in HT.

It is very difficult to separate who I am now from everything I have been through. I remain cognizant—as brought out so starkly in William Golding's *Lord of the Flies*—that given the right circumstances most ordinary people are capable of descending to despicable depths. I might now actively campaign against the views that HT espouses, but my skills in being able to argue and organize, to rally and inspire, all undoubtedly come from my training in the organization. To ask if I regret joining HT is a difficult question to answer. It would mean I regret who I am now, that I regret my current work, myself—I don't think that can be the case. Some people may not like that answer, but it's the only honest one I have. Sometimes the truth can be like that: harder and harsher, more bitter than people would ever care to admit.

The murder redoubled my commitment to HT. Dave Gomer's intervention seemed to square with the views of the HT leadership, that direct action was not the way. Once you went down that route, you were exposing yourself to the consequences. The HT philosophy was to challenge and to stir things up, but take things no further. The murder reinforced for me that the HT line was the right one to follow.

That was despite the response of the HT leadership to events. It was Ed Husain and I who were responsible for HT at the college. Ed had been nowhere near the incident: he was studying when the murder took place. As I was the one who had been there in the thick of it, I went to see Omar Bakri to explain what had happened. I was smart enough not to mention the former gang members, but told him everything else. As far as I was concerned, I had been following the edict of the group to the letter. I was whipping the place into fervor as per his instructions. Omar Bakri, after all, had visited the college himself the week before, and had offered no criticism of our conduct. Indeed, he'd seemed delighted with what we'd achieved.

Bakri, however, was under pressure from the *qiyadah*. He had been criticized for the way the British wing was bringing heat on the whole organization. On top of this, there were voices within the UK organization that were critical of his tactics: these included the physicist Fouad Abu Mohammed. On two fronts, then, his provocative leadership was under attack. Now that a murder had taken place, the dissenting voices rose to a fever pitch.

Even so, I still expected his support. Omar Bakri sat and listened to everything I said, and then ignored it. He went out and gave media interviews where he denied any HT role in the incident, said the organization had never campaigned on the campus and condemned Sa'eed Nur for the attack. I was deeply saddened by this. Though it was true that HT had no direct role in the murder itself, condemning Sa'eed without condemning ourselves was a step too far for me. Sa'eed had come to the college to help us; we were the ones, under Omar Bakri's guidance, who had whipped up the tension. Now this brother was being thrown under the bus for the sake of political expediency. My support for HT didn't waver, but my belief in Omar Bakri never really recovered. Whereas before I would have unconditionally followed whatever instructions he gave me, I now felt myself doubting his sincerity.

One of the outcomes of the murder was that it saved me from following Omar Bakri. His attempts to shore up his position by distancing the group from the murder were not enough; his leadership deteriorated to the point that, just a few months afterward, he was suspended by the *qiyadah*. Seeking a new niche, Bakri reincarnated himself as even more extreme. He became a Salafi-Jihadist and went on to form the now-banned group al-Muhajiroun, which eventually became the banned Islam4UK. Anjem Choudary, the diminutive but passionate Abdur Rahman from Redbridge College, and some other prominent HT activists followed Omar Bakri in this folly. About a dozen or so of al-Muhajiroun's members have since been convicted for terrorism-related offenses. This new group continued the same aggressive tactics Omar Bakri had employed while leader of HT, most notoriously protesting at Wootton Bassett—the town in Southwest England through which military processions go when the bodies of soldiers are returned from Afghanistan.

Having lost that emotional pull toward Omar Bakri, I found it easier to stay with HT proper and the new policy of drawing back from aggression. It was decided that showing the videos of the atrocities in Bosnia was pumping up emotions to a fervor that was difficult to control: the line between Islamism and Jihadism was in danger of becoming blurred. The new leadership wanted to distance itself from any suggestion of violence: the carrying of knives or other weapons for self-defense was no longer allowed.

In terms of my passion, I was closer to the position of Omar Bakri than this new leadership. But Omar Bakri hadn't backed me up, and they did, so I gave them a chance. Nasim was crucial here. He was rising through HT ranks rapidly and was insistent that I stay in the group. Importantly, he believed my version of what had happened at Newham. That meant a lot, and in return I fell in behind the group's new direction. I stopped carrying my knife around for the first time in years. I'd gotten so used to having it strapped behind my back that to begin with it felt strange not having it there, like something was missing. I could have thrown the knife away, but instead I decided to keep it. It remains in my desk drawer to this day, to remind me of where I've come from.

Having let the situation escalate, Newham College now made up for lost time. Determined to root out the problem, the school expelled the entire Student Union committee. "Your presence," the letter read, "is not conducive to a safe and secure environment in the college." My parents hit the roof. My saving grace was that my expulsion was not for the murder. I had not been arrested or charged for that, and so I could say to my mother that they were overreacting—they were banning me because of my political activism.

Nevertheless, Abi and I had a huge argument about what I should do next. I wanted to start again at another London college: to carry on as before, continuing my HT activities. Abi, though, wanted me back in Southend where she could keep a closer eye on me.

"Why don't you go to the local grammar school?" she argued.

Grammar schools are selective schools where only those students who gain high grades are admitted so they can be taught in an accelerated environment.

"You've got the grades and could do well there."

I was only thinking about HT and insisted on returning to London. Back and forth this discussion went on through the night. Abi said that she wouldn't fund me going back to live in London. I responded that I was going, and I would find the money so I could do so.

That was too much for her. My mother sensed that something had happened at the college. She could tell that there was something about that crowd that she wanted to keep me away from. The argument got more and more heated, until at about four o'clock in the morning, exhausted, she lost hope—but she didn't stop. Totally exasperated by her errant, stubborn son, Abi started to weep and began beating her womb.

"I curse you!" she sobbed between the blows against her stomach. "I curse the womb that gave me such a son: a son who will not listen to his own mother!"

As I watched her in horror, I felt every blow she inflicted on herself. "Stop it!" I implored, forcing down her hands, and I began to cry. I couldn't watch her do that; it was too much for me. What had I reduced my mother to? I stopped arguing and agreed that I would come home, and try to get into the grammar school. It was the best decision I had made in a while.

Soon after, I went for an interview at Westcliff High School for Boys, with then-headmaster Mr. Baker. My grades were nowhere near the grades of the other students. However, I was able to talk Mr. Baker into letting me in.

"I am a lot more mature from my time out," I explained. "I want to study and really believe I could do well."

I didn't tell Mr. Baker that I had been expelled from Newham College. Instead I said that I'd decided to take a year off. Before everything was computerized such maneuvers were so much easier to pull off. In fact, it was not until many years later, when Mr. Baker invited me back to the school to address the student assembly, that I revealed how I had talked him into letting me in without telling him about the expulsion. The students all burst out in approving, roaring laughter, while poor Mr. Baker flushed every shade of red until I thought the man would have a heart attack.

If nothing else, my HT training had taught me how to argue. To Abi's relief, I impressed him, and he offered me an unconditional place. Abi's desperate intervention to force me to stay in Southend saved my academic career. I certainly would not have ended up at university if on that night, in the early hours of the morning, Abi hadn't beaten the womb that bore me.

CHAPTER TWELVE

A Show of Hands to Harden the Heart

Westcliff High School for Boys could not have been more different from Newham College. I'd gone from a secondary school, where I could count the number of black and Asian people in my year on one hand, to a London campus where Muslim students were the majority, back to a boys-only Southend school, where again, almost everyone else was white.

I stood out from the start, and not just because of my skin color. I was unique in having taken a year off. I was a year older than them and more experienced. I had a formidable reputation in the town from my pre-HT days and my own car: a Vauxhall Astra SRI. When I turned up, many of the kids knew who I was. "You're Maajid? *The* Maajid?"

"Yes, I am, and I'm back," I said.

For the first time in a long time, I was not under threat. The other students were intelligent and studious, a little sheltered but well-meaning. By contrast, I probably seemed exciting and dangerous. In the time since I'd joined HT and been away in London, the whole problem of racism in Southend had died down substantially. A younger generation of B-boys—Moe's younger brother, Chill's younger brother, and others—had taken over; Southend would never be the same again. During those two years, I experienced almost no racism whatsoever.

This peacefulness allowed me the time and space needed to really develop intellectually. I'd always been reasonably capable, but had never bothered to apply myself before—I used to rely on "winging it" and would get by without making much effort. Now, feeling settled, I got into my studies. I discovered what I could achieve if I really put my mind to it. This excited and inspired me.

My history teacher was Dr. White—he had a PhD in his subject and really knew his stuff. A number of the students were scared of him because he was strict, but intellectually he was amazing. Mr. Moth and Mr. Skelly, who taught my economics class, were also fantastic. I appreciated the fact that my teachers genuinely seemed to like me, and that I could talk to them one on one.

Mr. Moth was a lovely guy. He was gay and quite relaxed about it, but I failed to pick up on this. Once, some students and I had managed to get on to the topic of homosexuality. I found myself openly making homophobic jokes while waiting for our economics class to begin. (Behind the jokes was the fact that in HT we prescribed death for homosexuals in our "*Khilafah*.") Mr. Moth entered as my childish jokes were in full swing, and I continued, totally oblivious. A kind soul, he went along by hiding under the table and pretending to shake as the class roared with laughter. It was only afterward, to my utter embarrassment, that everyone said to me, "You do know he is gay, right?"

Nevertheless, Mr. Moth continued to treat me not just with respect but also with encouragement. I can credit him as the teacher who made me see for the first time what I might be able to achieve academically. I'd been thinking about getting a law degree, which required three Bs for entry. When the time came to apply to university, Mr. Moth shocked me by setting my official predicted grade as an A in economics—allowing me to study both Arabic and law. I remember asking him in disbelief, "Are you sure?" But he responded with certainty that I could do it.

"I predict that you'll go very far in life, Maajid. You'll become something like an ambassador, or take on a similarly important role."

I thought to myself, "I'd rather be the Caliph's ambassador to Britain."

But still, I was grateful that Mr. Moth held me in such high esteem. This was a moment akin to when Dave Gomer gave me that look just before the murder. I had this overwhelming feeling that I didn't want to let Mr. Moth down. Predicting an A to a former B-boy from a comprehensive school background was a risk for Mr. Moth, but as a mentor he had shown faith in me, and so I worked harder for him.

However well I got on at Westcliff High School, I still couldn't quite shake the sense of feeling different. Part of the history syllabus was British

Imperial history, and so we studied British India. We looked in detail at the Raj. We studied events like the Indian "Mutiny," where even the name of the event is significant. In the Indian subcontinent the event is referred to as "The First War of Independence," rather than a mutiny implying false rebellion. During one lesson, as we were discussing India and the Raj, the teacher asked the class, "How many of you here are proud of our Empire and its achievements?" Everyone put a hand up, except for me. "Is there anyone who isn't?" Everyone looked around as I put mine up. I sat there in class and pondered for a while that "No matter how well I get along with these people, no matter how much I hide my beliefs, they will always see me as belonging to a race they *civilized*." It was just enough to override the individual kindness Mr. Moth had shown me, and for me to interpret his behavior as an exception to this norm.

Although I had left behind Newham, London, and all the other HT activists, my game plan was still very much focused around the group. When Omar Bakri left, he took with him not only the more aggressive tactics but also the more thuggish elements of HT. What remained was the more thoughtful, more serious side of the organization. The emphasis now was on activists focusing on their studies—HT didn't want people getting expelled or ruining their education. They wanted to produce pillars of society who believed in our ideology and who would be of real use in Muslim-majority countries. In an echo of my grandfather moving to Britain to make the most of its schooling for his children, HT stressed how respected the British education system was abroad. To gain qualifications in the UK and then travel to work in places like Egypt, Pakistan, and Jordan would give the activists access to the best jobs. That suited HT's cause: they wanted to control the intellectual life of a nation, to be in such a position of influence that they could hijack the army and instigate a coup. The fact that recruitment was on the rise in British universities gave them an opportunity to do this.

I also gave my weekends to recruiting. Despite the way things had turned out at Newham, the leadership remained impressed with how I'd brought interest and activists to the cause. I was selected as part of a team seeking to create an HT cell at Cambridge University. I'd go up on a Saturday morning and spend most of the weekend there.

We would go to the prayer hall and the mosque, and get talking to the students. We'd befriend them, take them out for food, and engage with them in discussions about Islam and, ultimately, Islamism. There was a student called Arshad, who was reading Arabic at Cambridge and had already expressed an interest in HT. It was up to us to make him properly committed to the cause. During this time, I also recruited a cell back in Southend. The Muslim community there was pleasantly surprised at my and Osman's conversion, and many held me up as an example to their sons, which I took full advantage of.

At the same time, I was thinking about my university choice. I had wanted to study Arabic, and my father wanted me to study law. There was one university that offered a combination of both, and that was SOAS: the School of Oriental and African Studies in London. To my delight, I got the very grades my teachers had predicted, and I was offered a place at SOAS. This pleased my parents enormously: more importantly for me, it also pleased HT. Out of our elite group I was the first one selected to become a full member of the group, a *hizbi*. It wasn't a big ceremony, just one on one with Nasim, by now one of the leaders of the national group. I swore an oath of allegiance to God, the Qur'an, and to obey and follow the instructions of the group's leader, or *amir*. I promised to represent the ideology at all costs, and to be prepared to make sacrifices for the cause. Convinced of the injustice of non-Islam, or *kufr*, I meant every word I uttered with the chilling sincerity of a true believer.

CHAPTER THIRTEEN

The Romanticism of Struggle

If I had thought becoming a full member of Hizb al-Tahrir was going to lead me into an inner sanctum of understanding, I was in for a shock. Within a couple of days of taking my oath, I was instead introduced to a world of in-fighting and ideological division.

It wasn't just the UK division of HT where disagreements over policy erupted; the same was true of the global leadership as well. The leadership had been in the hands of Abdul Qadeem Zalloom, who was from Palestine, where the group had its origins and enormous support. However, some of the more dogmatic and puritanical elements of the group were unhappy with the way he ran things. One of the many disputes, which was absurd, was over the introduction of color into publications.

HT's books had traditionally been white, with a red font on the cover; under Zalloom's leadership, a variety of colors had been introduced into the group's publications. For the purists, this was anathema: they felt the look of the books had always been different and was easily recognizable in bookshops. Now they just looked the same as everyone else's: symbolic, to them, of the way that under Zalloom's leadership the group was losing its distinctive message.

A new grouping was led by Abu Rami, who had previously been a member of the leadership committee. Rami's stance found favor in Europe and in the Far East, whereas Zalloom's support was in the Middle East. The UK was one of the countries unsure which grouping to support.

All this was happening as I became a member. Within a matter of days of my taking my oath, we were receiving delegates from the Middle East, pitching to HT in Britain to take their side. There was a cloak-and-dagger element in all of this. No one was ever quite sure where the global leadership was—they kept their locations hidden for security reasons. Also no one was completely sure which side a delegate was from. Was he from the original leadership or from Abu Rami? Was he pretending to be from the other side in order to check our reaction? It was typical of the way the organization was run that no one was completely sure.

In a member's house in South London, about thirty or so UK members gathered to be told it was up to our own consciences whom we decided to back. I may have been the youngest in the room, but I felt compelled to speak.

"How dare you come here and tell us to choose!" I snapped. "You know that the means to acquire the leadership is done through the electoral college of the *qiyadah*. What you should be saying is that Abu Rami is a *nakith*, an oath breaker, and a *baghi*, a usurper. You have no choice but to consider him and anyone who associates with him as usurpers."

The delegate was taken aback by the ferocity of my argument.

"Brother Maajid," he asked. "How long have you been a member of HT?"

"Two days."

"Well," he said, somewhat patronizingly, "I've been a member for fifteen years."

"I don't care," I came back, now even more riled. "The *haq*—truth, isn't judged by how long you have been a member. What is right is right, and that's the end of it."

By this point, I was certain he was touting for us to join Abu Rami's group.

A couple of days later a second delegate arrived from the Middle East. He was an Algerian, there to argue the case for Abdul Qadeem Zalloom's leadership. For the majority of us this man felt like the real deal, and we were inclined to trust him. Together with another *hizbi*, Irfan, I took the Algerian back to the hotel where he was staying and returned to my student residence.

When Irfan went to pick him up the following morning, there was no reply from his room. After knocking repeatedly and getting no answer, Irfan persuaded the hotel staff to let him in. He discovered the Algerian delegate lying dead on the bathroom floor, his trousers round his ankles. There were no signs of trauma or bullet wounds on his body.

When we'd dropped him off the night before, he hadn't struck me as someone who was about to die. At the same time, there was no shortage of enemies who might have wanted him dead, and the techniques were available to do so. The Israelis, for example, were known for using non-traceable poisons. We knew that because we were attempting the overthrow of certain regimes, it was likely that their intelligence agents were operating against us. It also could have been an internal affair: Algeria was locked in a vicious civil war between its military leaders and the Islamist and jihadist rebels. Then there were rumors that the split in HT had been caused by Jordanian intelligence infiltrating our ranks. There were suggestions that Abu Rami was acting on behalf of Jordanian intelligence, and it was they who had killed the delegate for his support of Zalloom. We never got to the truth.

Then Abu Rami also died. Again, trying to discover exactly what had happened was impossible. Prior to Rami's death, Zalloom had confidently written to all HT chapters around the world, offering an amnesty to any members who had left—they could come back into the fold within a certain time frame. Rami had died just around that time limit. Zalloom then wrote another letter, slamming Rami and his followers: anyone who hadn't rejoined before his death would never be allowed to return.

Even so, my life was moving forward. I was at SOAS, doing a course I wanted to do. I was a full member of HT, one of the most effective recruiters in the organization, responsible for coordinating activities across Central and South London.

But something was missing in my life—a meaningful relationship. I'd already had my share of romantic liaisons, starting way back with Sarah—the girl I'd left on my first day at secondary school because there were "too many girls here." At Cecil Jones girls were a big part of the B-boy scene, and I loved it. Once I joined HT, however, all this changed. The group frowned on such behavior and wanted its followers to focus on their studies. HT wanted you to do things properly. If you were interested in a girl, it had to be serious, and then you could approach her family with a view to marriage. If the family agreed, then you would become engaged.

You would be allowed to see and speak to each other, but you were not allowed to be intimate. You would have to be patient, wait for the marriage arrangements to be made.

Before my expulsion from Newham, there was a tall, beautiful Pakistani girl who attended some of my talks, at the time not in a headscarf, and so not yet as religious as she would go on to become. I did things properly and got my friend Ed Husain to talk to her on my behalf. The girl was flattered, expressed an interest, and even donned the headscarf soon after. We made approaches to both sets of parents, to tell them that we were interested in a betrothal with a view to eventual marriage once we had finished our studies. Our parents met to discuss the matter, but much to my disappointment, her parents opposed our relationship.

It transpired that her father had already fixed her betrothal in Pakistan. Just before I started university she went with her parents to Pakistan, on the assumption they were going there to visit family. While there she was married to her cousin—a pressured and arranged marriage. The girl I had waited two years for was suddenly taken from me without warning. I was angry, and she was heartbroken. She called my number and said that she was prepared to run away to be with me. Abi, delighted at the idea that a girl could potentially calm the wave of anger she could see rising in her son, offered to take her in and protect her.

Ever the righteous ideologue, I failed her miserably. I didn't want to do anything that went against the teachings of HT, or bring the group into disrepute. So I played it by the book and told her that I didn't want to break up anyone's family. I said that the issue was now a religious one, and that she needed to see a religious cleric, a *shaikh*. This *shaikh*, I told her, would be able to rule on the legitimacy of her marriage in Pakistan. They would be able to say whether the marriage was void because it had taken place under duress. If a *shaikh* ruled the marriage illegitimate, then we would be free to pursue our relationship.

The *shaikh* the girl chose to go to was a Salafist. In her innocence, she wasn't in tune with the whole debate: as far as she was concerned, a Muslim was a Muslim. As soon as I heard whom she had gone to, I felt my stomach turn. I knew already what the Salafist's answer would be. The Salafist *shaikh* knew exactly who I was, and when the girl explained the situation, he quickly backed up her parents. Yes, he told her, your marriage is quite legal. You must forget all thoughts of a relationship with Maajid.

The Salafists finally got their revenge. I had won the crowd at Newham, but they made sure that I lost my heart. And so, full of delusions of piety and sacrifice, I said goodbye to my college sweetheart, failing to offer her the support she so clearly needed. In my heart, I would be hard-pressed to say that romanticism was dead. It was more like the romanticism of a cause, of a struggle, had won a decisive battle against the romanticism of love.

Eventually, Osman told me that he'd met a young Pakistani woman he thought might be suitable for me. I met her in public places like cafes, and I quickly realized she was everything my brother had promised. Perhaps most importantly of all, she was a leader for the HT sisters on her campus. Rabia was a biology student raised between Karachi and London. She had a serene, pretty face, a quiet, high voice, and she was an all-round sensible and loyal person.

Once again, I went through the process of approaching her parents about the possibility of marriage to their daughter. This time, my reception was different. The father had been a senior banker with Pakistan's Habib Bank, and all seven of his daughters supported HT and had pressured him to become a follower as well. His response was to become increasingly devout, to the point where he left his job a year before he was due a golden parachute from his bank. He'd come to the conclusion that bank interest was to be classified as usury, prohibited by Islam. He quit his job, didn't take his retirement package, and instead set up an Islamic bookshop in Shepherd's Bush. That is where my discussions with him about his daughter took place. He saw a smart young man, a law student, promising to take care of his daughter in the Islamic way. To my delight, Rabia Ahmed and I got engaged.

I took the second year out from university to get married, which we idealistically did during the month of Ramadan in 1999. We moved into a two-bedroom flat in East London that Osman had previously been living in. It was not a great start to married life—within a week of our moving in, the landlord reclaimed the flat and kicked us out.

We found another one, a nice flat in Wembley that we were just about to take when my HT activities took over. Rabia was about to face the true extent of my attraction to the romanticism of struggle. A communiqué had been issued from the *qiyadah* asking for British Pakistani members to go to Pakistan and help found the group there. With dreams of a coup fit for a caliph, I told Rabia that I wanted to answer the call.

CHAPTER FOURTEEN

Dreams of a Nuclear Caliphate

In 1999 Pakistan successfully tested its first atomic bomb, becoming a member of that small group of countries that could boast nuclear weapons capability. For Hizb al-Tahrir, this meant that if it could infiltrate the Pakistani military and successfully instigate a coup, then "the *Khilafah*" could start as a global heavyweight. Overnight, our dream of a Muslim superstate felt that much closer.

The difficulty was that HT had virtually no representatives in the country. It had never invested time there because of the view that "the *Khilafah*" should emerge from an Arabic-speaking nation, which Pakistan is not. The second problem was that the few HT members who were already there had been abysmally unsuccessful in drumming up recruitment.

Nasim was extremely reluctant for me to travel and felt I would be better off continuing my studies. As part of my course, I was already due to spend a year in Egypt studying Arabic, and could be of better use there. My parents, too, were doubtful. I told them that I wanted to go on a one-year study course to reconnect with my Pakistani roots. Remembering a much more tolerant, diverse, and spiritual Pakistan from her childhood, Abi thought this trip could do my Islamist fervor some good. My father, though, smelled a rat. "I will support you through your degree," he said, "but if you go to Pakistan, I'm afraid I can no longer support you." By now, he had a far clearer idea of my politics and wanted no part of it.

I listened to Nasim's advice and initially agreed to stay on my course. But then a second communiqué from the *qiyadah* came through, more insistent than the first. It implored members to drop everything and move to Pakistan immediately. That second letter decided the matter for me. This time Nasim didn't try to stop me.

As I was preparing to leave, I came across Reza Pankhurst again, one of the students who had led the recruitment drive with me at Cambridge University. By this time he had relocated to Egypt and was back in London tying up some loose ends. I told him what I was doing, and he became fascinated with the idea of moving to Pakistan as well.

Rabia and I packed our things. Rabia, as a member of HT, could understand why I wanted to go and offered me encouragement. My father was true to his word. Dismayed by what his son had become and very critical of HT, he refused to offer me any financial help. He told me not to tell Abi what I was really up to. So I didn't, and because I enrolled in Punjab University for a year, Abi was happy to let me study and experience Pakistan. I also told her that I wanted Rabia to meet our family. Because of this, Abi sent out money behind my father's back and keenly kept in touch. This help from a desperate mother trying to heal her son turned out to be invaluable, as there was no money coming from HT. They paid for our flights to Pakistan, but after that we were on our own.

I remember Osman dropping me off at the airport and how he cried as he hugged me goodbye. He knew the truth about why I was going. *Please look after yourself,* he said.

———

In 1999, twenty-two years old and full of Islamist zeal, I arrived in Lahore determined to help foment a military coup in Pakistan. Although I had visited the country before, it had been when I was a small child, and it took me awhile to adjust to our new surroundings. A Westerner could actually live extremely comfortably for not too much money. You can have—and people do have—huge mansions, with swimming pools, Jacuzzis, and the works. Outside, however, there would probably be a half-built road, unless you were willing to pay for it. There may well not be regular electricity, and you would have to fund your own electricity generator. These were all typical indications of state failure and bad governance. Pakistan was ripe for rebellion.

Contrary to crude stereotypes, Pakistan is a truly diverse, rich, and cultured country. There is no single ethnicity called "Pakistani"; rather the country is made up of various languages and ethnicities, among them Punjabis, Baloch, Sindhis, Pashtuns, and Kashmiris. Many of these ethnicities and languages span neighboring states too, accounting for a rather stunted *Pakistani* identity. Rather than describing Pakistan, the political entity you see on a map, it is more accurate to describe *Pakistans* in the plural. The country not only has deep ethnic and linguistic diversity but also vast political, class, cultural, and delightful culinary differences. One legacy of the postcolonial partition is that entire provinces are split down the middle, half in Pakistan and the other half in India. Many older Pakistanis still have first cousins across the border, and in Karachi a powerful political bloc has emerged seeking to represent the *muhajir*, or those who moved across from India after the Partition.

Therefore what held this country together by its artificial seams— more than any shared heritage—was the dream of its ailing founder, Muhammad Ali Jinnah, along with a collective fear of what could have happened had Muslims remained a minority in India. Jinnah had wanted to create a safe haven for a Muslim minority in a Hindu-dominated sub- continent. In turn, he had envisioned a country that would safeguard other minorities, too.

In 1947 Jinnah succeeded in outmaneuvering almost everybody to gain independence for East and West Pakistan, but died shortly after achieving his dream. Having lost its founder so early on, Pakistan has been locked in unrelenting ethnic, intra-religious, and linguistic sectari- anism ever since. Troubles came to a head when the Bengalis of East Pakistan succeeded in gaining a majority of seats in the national parlia- ment and wished to form a government. The Punjabi-dominated West refused to accept the results. Disaster struck in the form of civil war, and the Bengalis seceded from West Pakistan in 1971 to form modern-day Bangladesh.

After this war, the founding idea that Muslims could look after each other better than Hindus seemed under threat. The army of West Pakistan encouraged the Islamisation of Pakistan, attempting to glue the coun- try together using politicized religion as the national identity. In 1977

General Zia took over in a coup and did exactly this. Pakistan has never been the same since.

Of course, confusing as it is for most outsiders, there are as many Muslims in India as there are in Pakistan, so what exactly should form Pakistan's national identity is a question that vexes the nation to this day. And for all my teenage idealism back at Newham of Muslims bonding exclusively on nothing but Islam, things began to look a great deal more complicated on the ground.

Arriving into this quagmire in 1999, we believed we had all the answers. I knew that I would have to quickly learn Urdu, the one language that can be understood by most Pakistanis. I heard it a great deal growing up, and so was familiar with its basics. We were met by Rabia's uncle at Lahore Airport. A genteel man named Dr. Abdul Qayyum, he had traveled far and was excited to receive us. Uncle Qayyum was a well-established and respected dentist in a town called Raheem Yar Khan, which sits almost directly halfway between Karachi and Lahore. He wasn't a member of HT at this stage but was a deeply religious Salafist, sporting a huge gray beard and a warm smile. After the conversion of his seven nieces to HT, Uncle Qayyum began to explore the Islamist cause more closely.

I had been stationed in Lahore because that was where Imtiaz Malik, the leader of HT in Pakistan, was based. He had failed to get the movement off the ground, and the leadership felt that he needed help. I immediately went to meet him. He was older than me—in his late thirties—but it didn't take long for my respect for his seniority to dissipate. He was a thoroughly unimpressive character, and I could immediately understand why he had failed to recruit people to the cause.

Imtiaz suggested that the best plan was for me to recruit people in the Islamic department of nearby Punjab University. There was a certain logic to this: back in the UK one of the best ways of attracting recruits was to start with the students. Punjab University was the biggest higher education facility in Pakistan, and the fact that I was a student myself would make it easy for me. There was just one flaw to the plan, which Imtiaz should really have known. The university was already a Jamaat-e-Islami stronghold. These were students who knew about Islam, who were studying Islam, and who were going to be difficult to convert. Any of the departments at the university would have been better to enroll in than that one.

The best place to have started was the medical college; the atmosphere was different. I discovered that Arab medical students had been coming to study here for a year, some of whom were already members of HT. When I arrived, I overlapped with a Palestinian HT member who had been running a few study sessions there. He was leaving, and I couldn't help thinking that this non-Pakistani had achieved more in a short time than Imtiaz had done in five years.

Within a few weeks more reinforcements were flown in from the UK. There was Irfan Wahid, who had been my supervisor back in London. Shortly after Irfan arrived, Dr. Abdul Wajid also turned up. Abdul Wajid was one of the HT members who had been behind the original recruitment drive in British universities. He was an experienced speaker and a seasoned recruiter. Irfan didn't have Abdul Wajid's oratory skills, but he was a decent enough organizer and administrator. I was excited about their arrival, and felt that together we could really do things.

I sat down with Irfan and briefed him on my views about Imtiaz—he listened carefully to what I said. But then, to my horror, he went straight to Imtiaz and apparently repeated all my accusations! I couldn't believe it: I'd tried to paint an accurate picture for Irfan because I wanted to help the cause. All Irfan appeared to have done was to use the information to curry favor with Imtiaz, sidelining me in the process.

I'd given up a lot to move to Pakistan—I hadn't told SOAS that I had essentially given up on my degree. I'd put my future career on the line and was now faced with the position of having nothing to show for that sacrifice. That stung. But what really got me was something more fundamental. I was an activist absolutely committed to HT, believing so passionately in the group that I would do anything the leadership told me would further our work. I had left my studies behind, only months after my marriage, because of how blindly committed I was.

Irfan's actions, however, opened my eyes. I saw that rather than everyone in the organization doing things for the good of the cause, it seemed to me there were baser instincts at work too. From now on, whenever I looked at Irfan, whereas previously I had seen a brother, now all I saw was someone who apparently liked to maneuver for position. For an idealist like myself that was a painful thing to recognize. Looking back, it was the end of my political innocence.

It was around this time too that Osman, back in the UK, had decided he could no longer remain a student of the group. He had never been a full member, but he finally broke his ties. HT had become too controlling for him and too inflexible with his inquiring nature. Secretly, I began to empathize with Osman and I decided that I would never give all of myself in the same way; there'd always be part of me that I'd hold back. I'd gladly give myself unconditionally to Allah, but not to HT. The thought process involved in leaving groups such as HT begins first at questioning an individual in authority, then the tactics, then the strategy, then the methodology, and then finally by questioning the ideology itself. This was probably the first, unrecognized seed that would lead to my eventual departure from the whole cause.

Abdul Wajid, the man who had seemed such an able and committed recruiter from a distance, appeared up-close to be power-hungry. He was transparently overbearing in his desire to dominate and in his belief that he is always the most capable in the room. Just as I had lost favor with Imtiaz and Irfan, Abdul Wajid now made it clear that he considered me an intelligence operative trying to cause dissent within HT's Pakistan operation. His stance was certainly scary to me. The certainty with which he had decided this made me ponder the dangers of a lack of accountability at the top of the organization. What if such people succeeded in taking over the country?

The one thing I could do was recruit. Our strategy for Muslim-majority countries such as Pakistan was a long-term one. We knew that since Zia's coup in the 1970s, the process of "Islamisizing" Pakistan's institutions had been going on long enough. Islamist groups by this time were dominant on many campuses and were attracting hundreds of thousands to their rallies. The country's intellectual elite feared Islamist intimidation and continued to make concessions to them. Thanks to the way Islamist groups were able to hijack Jinnah's vision, thanks to the Afghan jihad and the policies of Pakistani's Intelligence Service (ISI) and the CIA, thanks to the rise of the Taliban, thanks to historic concessions made by the progressive governments of Pakistan, and thanks to corruption and incompetent governance, our job of injecting Islamism into Pakistan's masses was already well under way.

However, we knew that the two power blocs that really mattered in Pakistan, the two sectors without which change could not come, were the intelligentsia and the army. Instead of wasting our efforts trying to build a mass movement that already existed, we began targeting the upper-middle classes and the armed forces. These groups formed the bulk of people who actually ran the nation. If we could hijack them, the masses would gladly follow our lead.

There was already a special team, coordinated by British-Pakistani HT member Omar Khan, working within the army, focused on recruiting cadets. Our job was to target the elite English colleges such as Lahore University of Management Sciences (LUMS) and other places that had previously been bastions of liberal thought. We began visiting posh cafes on Mall Road and yuppie youth clubs, speaking in our perfect English, with our college degrees, our arguments well-honed. Nobody had seen the likes of us before. We were Islamists, but we were clean-shaven, young, wealthy, and mobile. We dressed well, were Western-educated, and yet we were calling for "the *Khilafah*." We swept such places clean in no time.

I put my head down and got to work in two areas—aiming to build supporters within Punjab University and setting up the organization in Raheem Yar Khan, the town where Rabia's relatives lived. I was traveling to Raheem Yar Khan on weekends, and in a short space of time I had set up three *halaqahs*. These *halaqahs* weren't full of students, but of older and more influential individuals. There was even a local Salafist mosque imam who joined us. Then there was the ever-smiling Uncle Qayyum, the friendly doctor with the huge gray beard. The beard mattered in the Pakistani context: it showed he was a serious and religious man. And he was genuinely devout, in the good, pious sort of way. He would leave his house at dawn, walk to the mosque to pray, and once he'd closed his surgery in the afternoon, he'd be seen in the streets handing out food to the poor.

"Maajid *bhai*—my brother, we are instructed by our Prophet, *'alayhi salam,* to be kind to our neighbors. A neighbor is defined as everyone on your street," he once told me. "That's why I try to distribute food to my whole road, so I can get the full *sawab*—the blessings."

For his piety, he was loved by his family, friends, and neighbors alike, as he was by me. Uncle Qayyum and I were extremely close; he became the linchpin for all that I was to do for HT in Raheem Yar Khan. I'd recruited his son, his brother, and many of his friends. The people I recruited were all rooted in the local communities; they were exactly the pillars of influence that HT dreamed of bringing on board. With them you could change the culture.

One day, I got a call from an excited Uncle Qayyum: "Maajid, listen, *bhai*, I've been approached by a man whose name is the 'sincere one.' This 'sincere one' has been going around doing *tableegh*—advocacy for our cause, for around twelve years now, all alone, and has finally found us again! He heard about our work through some people he tried to recruit in Raheem Yar Khan, and has just arrived at my surgery. You must come and see him, *jaldi ajau,* come fast; he's a gift from Allah to our cause!" Word was surely spreading, and our cells in Raheem Yar Khan were multiplying.

I asked Abdul Wajid to come to Raheem Yar Khan to see what I was doing and ensure the continuity for his work. He was skeptical at first, but when he finally did come, he was clearly surprised. They might not have trusted me, but Imtiaz and the others could no longer deny my success. It helped that Rabia had relatives there—it gave me credibility. HT began to subsidize my weekend flights to Raheem Yar Khan, in the hope of creating a real stronghold. For me, this was vindication.

Yet leaving was on my mind. In the midst of all this work Rabia had become pregnant. I was overjoyed, but here was something precious that the group would have no part of. I knew that my wife wanted to have our baby back in the UK and to be near her parents for support. That set a clock ticking for our return. I continued to recruit with the knowledge that we were thinking of returning to Britain. I wrote to SOAS and to my relief, it was possible to extend your leave of absence to two years. I could return to continue my course as though nothing had happened.

It was a remarkable time to be living in Pakistan. This was around 1999, when the democratic government of Nawaz Sharif was removed in a military coup, and General Musharraf took over. The next time I returned to Pakistan, almost a decade later, the country would be democratically ruled again, and I would be campaigning to entrench democratic culture within the country. In a strange parallel, Pakistan's story would echo my own.

It is difficult not to see that period now as the run-up to 9/11. Nobody could have foreseen what was coming, but we all felt the strength of the movement: the way that the ideas of Islamism and Jihadism were spreading and taking root. It definitely felt as though we were part of something big, that we were almost on the verge of taking over. The Taliban in Afghanistan, the Sudanese government, these seemed to be just the start of something that the West was yet to pick up on. In those days the Taliban believed Pakistan was an Islamic state already and had no gripe with the country. I remember meeting a senior Taliban commander in Raheem Yar Khan, in an effort to convince him that Pakistan was an illegitimate colonial entity. It didn't take long for the Pakistani Taliban to adopt our more revolutionary mantra.

Lashkar-e-Taiba (LeT), the group that would commit the Mumbai attacks in 2008, was another fledgling organization that was working to garner support. Although they were Salafist in creed and jihadist in their methodology, their ideology was similar to HT's. In fact, LeT was using HT's own literature as part of their recruitment drive. Because all of this was so new, the authorities were slow to recognize the threat we all posed.

In the same way that before the Newham murder, no one took the warnings seriously, so the Pakistani authorities did little to stop the spread of these organizations. For example, in those early days LeT was holding their annual conferences—their *ijtima*—out in the open in their stronghold town of Muridke, which I attended. I remember seeing some of Omar Bakri's followers, from the now-banned al-Muhajiroun, in attendance there too. I think I caught a glimpse of the fiery Abdur Rahman, from the heady Newham days. (Abdur Rahman would later go on to be convicted under the terrorism law for an offense in the UK.) It said everything then that the keynote speaker at the conference was General Hamid Gul, the former head of the ISI, Pakistan's military intelligence.

CHAPTER FIFTEEN

Caliphs in Copenhagen

When I returned to the UK, it was like nothing had changed. I had my place to get my degree back at college. My father was under the impression I'd come to my senses and come back to continue my studies, and so welcomed me upon my return. As for my position in Hizb al-Tahrir, my troubles with Imtiaz followed me. They sent an excoriating report to the UK leadership about the likelihood that I was "an agent" and how I was not to be trusted.

By this time Nasim had gone off to set up HT in Bangladesh, and the new UK leader was a British-Indian called Jalaluddin Patel. Unlike Nasim, Jalaluddin hadn't known me; he hadn't witnessed that passionate sixteen-year-old B-boy transform into a global Islamist recruiter. Jalaluddin had been raised under Abdul Wajid and was shaped in that mold. I was given a local university role and had one of my former *dariseen*, Amir, placed in charge over me with strict instructions not to trust me. I didn't envy Amir; by now my *da'wah* antics were known throughout HT, and here was one of my former students in the embarrassing position of having to pretend to lead me. *No problem*, I thought, *I managed this in Pakistan, and I can manage it here.* Amir, to his credit, was an intelligent brother, and he dealt with me sensibly. It didn't take him long to be expelled from HT for his independence.

The most significant change in my life was the birth of my son, Ammar, which means "the one who will build great things." We named him after the famous companion of the Prophet, loved by the Sunni and Shia—a son to the first martyrs of Islam, Yasir and Sumayyah, who were tortured to death by their slave master. Our son was similarly born to parents who were going to sacrifice everything for the cause, and in turn, that is what I envisioned him doing as well. The original Ammar, a general to the Prophet's cousin and son-in-law, Ali, may Allah honor his countenance, was eventually killed in Islam's first civil war against the rebel forces of Mu'awaiya. Things always return to the romanticism of struggle.

Back in the UK, as Rabia and I settled into our new life, the first cracks in our relationship began to show. As any new parent knows, the experience of looking after a newborn baby is an exhausting one. The endless sleepless nights can take their toll on the best of relationships. It was a period when Rabia really needed me to dig deep and support her. Yet she now perceived how there were three of us in the relationship: me, her, and our ideology. I was so committed to the cause that stepping back to help her cope with bringing up our son would have felt like a dereliction of duty. If anything, to ward off the temptation of staying at home in the comforting embrace of my wife and newly born son, I *increased* my campaign work during this period.

These were cruel, selfish things easy to do under the delusion of self-righteousness; I crushed that woman's dreams pursuing an elusive "*Khilafah.*" Having denied her a honeymoon, I was now denying her my support during her most difficult time. But we were both incredibly young, only just into our twenties, and still full of this heady mixture of self-confidence and ideological certainty. She wanted to settle more into married life, but she knew who I was when I married her. "If I become the person you are asking me to become, then you would not have loved me in the first place," I argued. And with those words I'd leave the house, questioning whether an ideological bond alone was sufficient for a lasting marriage.

My work felt more crucial than ever. Though Salafi-Jihadism tipped over into international prominence in 2001 because of 9/11, the peak of the movement's support and momentum was the year before. I did my best to take advantage of this surge of interest in Islamism. Back at SOAS I found another brother to tag-team on the *da'wah* with: Ashraf ul-Haque. Ashraf told me he had turned down an offer from Oxford to attend SOAS so he could follow in my footsteps. Together we re-created the glory of those early days right there in SOAS, recruiting another three *halaqahs* of followers. As I guided and protected him through HT's machinery, we became inseparable, bonding in our shared disdain for incompetent HT administrators. Although we didn't advocate Jihadism in any of our teachings, we set a number of students on this path through our politics. One of my recruits that year was Zeeshan Siddiqui, who was later arrested and detained in Afghanistan by US forces, having gone there to join the "Jihad."

I was also given the opportunity to help recruit Pakistani soldiers. There was a group of army officers who had been sent over on a scholarship to train at Sandhurst. This was a goldmine for HT: as I said, their method of taking a country was to infiltrate the military and instigate a coup. It turned out that one of these soldiers had links to HT through his relatives. Someone in his family ran the garage I used to take my car to. The garage owner's son, Aftab, was an HT *daris*, and although not a natural recruiter, had managed to raise the interest of this soldier. The officers were about to return to Pakistan, and so I was brought in for an introduction. My task was to give them a final send-off, with encouragement about how they should recruit within Pakistan's army.

I talked to them about HT and explained how they could be central to our plans of taking control there. Rather than them becoming HT members openly, I said their responsibility was to go back to Pakistan and support the group clandestinely and begin building cells inside the army. They should then wait, and prepare to take part in a military coup.

This was a high-stakes plan, with severe consequences if it wasn't successful. In 2003, journalist Ahmed Rashid reported that General Musharraf had led a purge inside Pakistan's army, rooting out what he described as al-Qaeda–sympathizing cells. He was right about the cells, but wrong about the affiliation: these were the same HT supporters I had met in that dingy London flat and incited to rise up. When I heard the news, I felt stricken: the "War on Terror" was in full swing and I knew that these soldiers were tortured in interrogation.[*]

---

[*] A few years later I met their British-Pakistani cell-instructor, Omar Khan. He had been the secret military contact between HT and these soldiers, and had been arrested with them. He'd been beaten and had a gun put to his head during his interrogation before being deported back to the UK. The soldiers who'd remained in Pakistan were not so fortunate.

In 2000 HT would regularly hold rallies, and I quickly became one of the key speakers at these events. We held events outside the US Embassy and in Trafalgar Square, led marches and ran speaker events in Hyde Park. The rallies would regularly attract audiences of around three thousand people. This was a different skill from the careful analysis of leading a *halaqah,* but I loved it. I enjoyed pumping up a crowd, and relished the chance to get our message across to so many people. The size of these gatherings only reinforced our perception that the movement was on the cusp of a major breakthrough.

I also answered the call to kick-start the branch of HT in Denmark. This was like the jet-setting version of my work in Pakistan. I would spend the week in London, doing my studies at SOAS during the day and the *halaqahs* in the evening, and then on a Friday evening, I would fly out to Copenhagen and spend the weekend in Denmark. This made my work for HT a seven-day-a-week affair and created a schedule that put even further strain on my marriage.

The *qiyadah* were desperate to develop Denmark in order to help establish HT's roots on the European continent. For various reasons, the European chapters had not developed as they should have. The original HT chapter in Denmark had come under the authority of the European leadership in Germany and had followed their recruitment strategy of targeting first-generation immigrants, who had gone to the country for economic reasons. The result was that the European branches were almost entirely formed of North African and Turkish people. In the UK, by contrast, the focus had always been on those born and raised there, the angry younger generation: students at the universities and disaffected youth. The German strategy had never included these people, who were considered "slackers." Our brothers in Denmark had now decided to follow the UK model, and HT was fast expanding there. But they were yet to see penetration of the young Danish-Pakistani community, which could have offered the organization another bridge into Pakistan, as we had done from the UK.

Given my background and experience in both universities and abroad, HT felt I was the ideal person to turn this situation around. I quickly made inroads into the community, setting up study circles and even meeting some Pakistani army recruits willing to support the cause.

What was striking about Denmark was how markedly worse it was from the UK in terms of racism. It felt as if I'd stepped back in time to my teenage years in Essex. In Britain, the issue had to some extent died down and society had moved on, whereas everywhere I went in Denmark people complained about racism. The lines on the continent were drawn differently. Third-generation Turks born and raised in Germany were still only classed as guest workers, seriously affecting how they saw themselves.

The response of the minority communities in Denmark to racism had been exactly the same as mine had been in Southend: violence. The potential recruits I met all had stories of serious criminal activity: these were former gangsters, former drug dealers. While Southend had been all about knife culture, here everyone had grown up around guns. I was told many tales of shoot-outs with police, attempted armed robberies, and on more than one occasion a shirt was lifted up and I was proudly shown a bullet wound or two.

Because of my background I was able to relate to these recruits in a way that the other recruiters couldn't. The potential recruits were interested in my journey, and how I'd gone from spewing anger to teaching revolutionary Islamism. I was in Denmark at the height of the Islamist fervor, which certainly made recruiting easier. I succeeded in seeding the growth of the Danish-Pakistani branch; it's sad, but the HT branch in Denmark is known as one of the organization's more extreme chapters to this day. Eventually, the German government would impose a ban on HT activities, and in 2006 the Danish chapter's spokesman, Fadi Abdul Latif, was convicted for hate speech and inciting violence.

Given all this commitment to HT, it is perhaps not surprising that my studies suffered as a result. When the results came in for my exams, I had passed the sections on law but failed my Arabic grammar, which is actually much harder. Without passing Arabic, I couldn't go on to the next part of my course: a year studying Arabic in Egypt's beautiful city of Alexandria.

I re-took the Arabic class at the beginning of September 2001 and passed. I could take up my place at the University of Alexandria, at their College of Literature's Centre for the Study of Arabic Language for Foreigners. Once again, Rabia and I packed our family belongings, by this time quite disillusioned with our relationship; she was again following me to another country.

As our flight left, I watched London disappear beneath our plane, Ammar in my arms, and thought: *Twelve months and I'm back here, I really need to work on my marriage, for little Ammar's sake.* Little did I know that it would be many years before I would set foot on British soil again, and then, as an irreversibly changed man. Or that by the time I arrived in Alexandria, events on the other side of the Atlantic, on four different US passenger flights, were about to irrevocably change the world.

CHAPTER SIXTEEN

The Polemic

You drop bombs on my people while knowing full well that the level of "collateral" damage—we call them innocent Muslims—will far exceed the damage to any "legitimate target." For you, killing our children en masse—and you still call it collateral damage—is an unavoidable consequence of pursuing your policies in our lands. To us, they are simply children. Don't you think we've been crying too, like you are now, for years? Do you think we felt no pain as you raped and plundered our lands and bombed our cities? What lands, what cities, you ask? Your arrogance is only compounded by your ignorance. Look to Iraq. In order to remove Saddam Hussein, after the Kuwait war, you killed over half a million children because you could. Because you could! And because my people were too lost, too defeated, to be able to stop you. These are our children. We cry for them even as you feel absolutely nothing. What of Lesley Stahl's question on 60 Minutes *posed to Secretary of State Madeleine Albright:*

"We have heard that half a million children have died—I mean that is more children than died at Hiroshima and, you know, is the price worth it?"

Albright's callous response is etched in our memories, staining our innocence with her venom:

"I think it is a very hard choice, but we think the price is worth it."

And you wonder why we are so angry? You wonder even now why, after all these years, as we speak these words, we are consumed with rage? The price of killing half a million children with your depleted uranium bombs is worth pursuing, but woe to us if we ever strike back! In your world, Albright's interview was barely mentioned: a Dow Jones search of mainstream news sources after the attack turned up only one reference to the interview in an Orange County newspaper. But in our world, in the hell we live in, this was major news. We will not forget our dead just because you have no feelings.

Is killing civilians justified only for your own foreign policy interests? You claim that, unlike us, you don't target civilians, that your intentions are noble, that you seek only humane concerns. How many deaths of "untargeted" civilians by your hands entitle us to respond? Five, ten, a hundred, half a million? Are three thousand deaths enough to make you feel the pain of each and every mother you "untargeted" with depleted uranium? If not, then know that our intentions in bringing you death can also be noble, we too shroud destruction in humane concerns. You do not have a monopoly on reaping devastation off the back of good intentions, and don't you dare claim such a thing, you arrogant monsters. You can support, fund, and train dictators in our lands who have been torturing our brothers and raping our sisters in their prisons for decades, and yet you invade our countries, claiming to bring democracy? And you cite international law at us, while you willfully ignore Israel's occupation of Palestine, as defined by the UN? We will never forget your friendship with Mubarak and Assad, your unconditional support for an occupying Israel, the way you used us as Mujahideen in Afghanistan only to turn on us once you'd got what you wanted. You chose your side and we have chosen ours.

We have come to know that no amount of civilized pleading, no amount of appealing to your humanity, for your mercy, no amount of playing by your rules in your game, will move you. You are stupefied in ignorant bliss while we bleed and secrete pus from every orifice. There is only one thing you people value and cherish, and that is your own lives, your own happiness, and your own selfish oblivion. If inflicting upon you even an atom's weight of the pain we suffer at your hands wakes you from your stupor and forces you to listen to our cries as we drown, then I'm afraid we have finally decided that though it is "a very hard choice, we think the price is worth it."

This was powerful stuff, and it worked, but my polemic—a reflection of my instinctive response immediately after 9/11—was only half the truth. How easy it is for a victim to construct a narrative out of half-truths and inspire thousands in the name of righteous indignation.

But the other side only saw half the truth too, and that was the problem.

Understanding how I reached such a detached position is the key to grasping the mind-set of an Islamist, living his life on the verge of violence. I was an ideologue—that was the prism through which I saw the world. It was difficult for non-Muslim audiences to really understand where Muslim indignation had come from, but it was a tangible, palpable thing. The American-led invasions of Afghanistan and Iraq after 9/11 only served to cement these attitudes further. *If America could bomb and invade in response to being bombed, why couldn't jihadists do the same? And if the deciding factor was that one party was a state while the other was a loose grouping, surely the state should be the more responsible one?*

And while we in Hizb al-Tahrir disagreed with the tactics that al-Qaeda employed, most of us shared their sense of vengeance. Curiously, my position wasn't entirely detached from humane concerns. Rather, it was too attached to, indeed motivated by, humane concerns—but for Muslims alone, and at the expense of "the other."

My above polemic may have been uncomfortable reading, especially for my friends who survived the 9/11 attacks, and for that I am sorry. The reality is, and it will help us not to pretend otherwise, there are still many people out there who think this way, whether we like it or not. These days I work to build an understanding of the mind-set that can make people so angry that they lose all empathy for others. I work to humanize even those who dehumanize others, so that the process of healing may begin.[*]

Stalin once infamously said that a single death is a tragedy; a million deaths are a statistic. That's what my initial response to 9/11 was. It wasn't about individual people; it was about the overall picture, and by this time I was so consumed by the suffering of "my own people" that I had no empathy left for the suffering of those I accused of causing it. There is a lesson there for the more hawkish elements among Western societies too.

---

[*] I have since visited Ground Zero on a number of occasions and have been honored to speak there upon invitation by the board of the 9/11 Memorial Trust. It was a humbling experience, and I would be a strange person indeed if I had not been deeply moved by visiting the site.

In Egypt, as I digested the events of 9/11, my overriding concern was very narrow and cold: this was going to play badly for HT and for Islamism. I wasn't convinced of the necessity of the attacks, though my objections had little to do with the human cost involved. Back when I was at Newham College, the global HT leadership had been critical of Omar Bakri's aggressive policies, which were bringing heat on the group. That was the fallout of one murder—this was the killing of several thousand in the heart of New York and Washington, not to mention the destruction of iconic American landmarks. The heat on Islamism was going to be turned up for years to come, not just on bin Laden and al-Qaeda, but on all of us.

We had specific concerns too about how the Western response would affect long-cherished HT projects. As it became clear that Afghanistan was going to bear the brunt of the US reaction, HT was about to lose what was considered a key link in the chain to developing "the *Khilafah.*" When I had started a few years earlier, HT had begun to put down serious roots in Pakistan. The same was true in Uzbekistan, where our organization formed the country's largest opposition group, with hundreds of thousands of followers. HT was considered such a threat that the Uzbek president, Islam Karimov, had resorted to extreme torture to halt its spread.

HT's vision was to rise to power on either side of Afghanistan, in Pakistan and Uzbekistan, after which the Taliban would act as the bridge in building the first modern, nuclear-armed Islamist superstate. In 1999 HT even sent a delegation of senior Arab members from Palestine in order to offer the Taliban just such a partnership for our future "nuclear *Khilafah.*" In those days, the Taliban had not yet come to believe that Pakistan was a *kufr,* un-Islamic state, but they politely refused to cooperate with HT.

It didn't take long for our *da'wah* to change the Taliban's view on Pakistan, and by 2009 they had usurped large parts of the country in the north as well. What 9/11 did, by precipitating the NATO occupation of Afghanistan, was destroy this dream of a Central Asian "*Khilafah*" in one stroke. We had always been critical of Jihadism for being the wrong way to go about bringing about an "Islamic state," and now we had been proven right.

A couple of weeks after I had settled in Alexandria and begun my course, I made contact with HT in Egypt. Egypt in the 1970s witnessed the rise of state-sponsored Islamism, as Pakistan had, just as the decade before had witnessed the rise of socialism in both countries. President Anwar Sadat released thousands of Islamists from the jails of his predecessor, Gemal Abdel Nasser, in an attempt to shore up support for his new regime against the "Godless" socialists. He even ennobled himself as *Ra'is al-Muslimeen*, President of the Believers. But Sadat would soon learn the hard way that Islamism was not a beast easily tamed.

Having been founded next door in Palestine, HT had been operating in and out of Egypt since the late 1960s. Taking advantage of Sadat's Islamization policy, HT managed to gain critical mass and planned a coup in Egypt as early as 1974. The failed attempt led to the loss of many lives and the virtual obliteration of HT cells in Egypt. But HT didn't give up, and in the late 1970s a Jordanian member of the group named Salim al-Rahhal took up the task of reviving the group's cell in Alexandria.

Because of the failed coup, HT landed on the radar of Egypt's security establishment. In 1977 al-Rahhal set up a new organization called Tanzim al-Jihad, or the Jihad Organization. By all accounts al-Rahhal was a highly capable and dangerous man. Around eighty of his armed followers were discovered later that year in Alexandria raids. Eventually, considered too dangerous to remain, Salim al-Rahhal was expelled from Egypt. But as we were taught inside HT, ideas are more dangerous than people. Al-Rahhal left his disciple Kamal Habib in charge in Alexandria, while a man named Abdus-Salam Faraj began expanding the Cairo branch of Tanzim al-Jihad.

Still focused on the military strategy, Kamal and Faraj managed to find Abbud al-Zummar, a military intelligence officer who joined Tanzim al-Jihad in 1980. It was this core of Islamist activists at the helm of Tanzim al-Jihad, founded by HT member al-Rahhal, who went on to assassinate Anwar Sadat in 1981. Tanzim al-Jihad went on to split, forming the larger and more prolific al-Gama'a al-Islamiyya and the smaller yet more sinister Jihad al-Islami, led by one Ayman al-Zawahiri. Zawahiri later merged his group with bin Laden to form al-Qaeda, and the rest, as they say, is history. Thus the trail becomes clear: Hizb al-Tahrir is a significant and necessary link in the world of Islamism as we know it today.

In 2001 our job was to revive the original HT organization in Egypt. My contact began with an email, which led to a phone number, which led to instructions to travel to a town called Kafr el-Sheikh. There I met a man named Hisham, and we began studying in a *halaqah*, in the utmost secrecy. After a while, a meeting was arranged for me with Alaa' el-Zanati, the head of HT in Egypt. I met Zanati and discussed my previous experiences in Pakistan, Denmark, and the UK. He was sufficiently impressed to put me in charge of HT activities in Alexandria.

The fact that I was given a central role so quickly, and the fact that seeing Zanati involved so many clandestine contacts, was indicative of what Egyptian society was like and how little penetration HT had by this time. The memory of the failed 1974 coup, and the group's chilling effect on Sadat's assassins, lingered on for Egypt's Intelligence Services; they treated any hint of HT presence in Egypt as a "code red." Because the Egyptian state was so dependent on the military, they were particularly watchful of a group whose aim was to infiltrate the army. The lengths that the state would go to shut down the organization were extreme. Since the assassination of Sadat in 1981, the country had been under Emergency Law, ruled with an iron fist by Sadat's successor, Hosni Mubarak.

These Emergency Laws gave the authorities sweeping powers to arrest and detain civilians indefinitely. (The laws stayed in place until President Mubarak's overthrow during the Arab uprisings of 2011.) These were flagrant human rights abuses that the United States and its allies tolerated in return for the promise of stability in the region. Technically, HT wasn't a banned organization in Egypt. But that was only because the Emergency Law worked the other way around: there was no natural right to association—a group needed the state's permission to do so. While some political parties had a permit to operate, HT had never had any such thing.

In Alexandria, there were two other HT members from the UK who had also arrived in Egypt. Reza Pankhurst I had known for several years by this point, having recruited with him at Cambridge University and having encouraged him to travel to Pakistan to spread the message. Reza was in Cairo along with Ian Nisbet. Ian had converted to HT when he was a student at Westminster University. We all got on well, and Rabia and I would travel up to Cairo to meet their families on a regular basis.

Meanwhile, echoing Salim al-Rahhal in Alexandria all those years before I was born, I began the process of recruitment. Because of Egypt's State Security, the much-feared Aman al-Dawlah, it was all very surreptitious. I did not talk about HT on the phone, in case it was tapped. If contacting people by email, I would write the blandest of messages, like "I am coming over for dinner." I would meet up with people at prearranged places and was initially very careful about bringing HT into the conversation. It was more about befriending and getting to know people, getting a sense of their views.

One such individual was Ahmed Eid, a medical student at the University of Alexandria. Ahmed was very bright, had an almost photographic memory, and was already a very committed Salafist. Ignoring our tried and tested tactic of recruiting people from a secular background, I knew from Pakistan that it was indeed possible to recruit Salafists. What I had overlooked was that Egypt was not Pakistan; whereas Pakistan was only just coming to terms with Islamism, Egypt had already lost a president to it.

It was around December 2001 that things began to get serious. There was another British-Pakistani student on my course named Hassan Rizvi, a young streetwise kid who had come over from the University of Exeter. Like most young British Muslims in those days, Hassan identified with Islamism even if he hadn't joined any group. We clicked immediately. One day we were out in Alexandria—we tried to mix regularly with Egyptians to help us improve our Arabic. Hassan had been in a mosque to pray, and as I met him outside I could see immediately that something was troubling him.

"Hassan bro, what's wrong?" I asked.

"The weirdest thing, man, someone gave me a message for you," he said, looking puzzled. "I was in the mosque, after having finished my prayers, when someone appeared next to me and asked if I was brother Maajid. He said he was a friend of Ahmed Eid's, and that he needed to talk to Maajid urgently. He said that you were in danger, bro."

By now, I felt worried too, and was looking around to see if anyone was watching us.

"He wanted me to take him to you," Hassan said. But Hassan was street-smart enough to know what the score was. "I said no way, bro, I refused. I mean, he could've been Aman al-Dawlah for all I knew. I said I needed to talk to you first. If you wanna speak to him, I've arranged a time and place where we can go together, tomorrow. But I'm coming with you, bro, just so you know I've got your back."

As Hassan was telling me this, something suddenly hit me. It might just have been coincidence, but I hadn't seen Ahmed for a few days. There might have been any number of reasons for that, but I couldn't recall having seen him around. *Had he been picked up?* He was the one person in Alexandria I'd discussed HT with, but our conversations had just been between the two of us. I decided that it was unlikely to have been the secret police who had been talking to Hassan; if they had wanted to find me, it would have been easy enough to have done so.

The next day I turned up at the prearranged meeting place with Hassan. We stood there waiting when a car pulled up and we were told to get in. We were driven around Alexandria for what seemed like an eternity. Then the car pulled up behind another vehicle, and we were told to get out and get in that one instead. Driven around the city again, we switched vehicles a second time. Eventually, we were put in a taxi and driven to the outskirts of the city.

A while later the taxi pulled up and we got out. Ahmed's friend was waiting for us, and he apologized for driving us around.

"We had to be careful," he said. "We had to make sure that you weren't being followed."

By now, my head was rushing. "What's up?" I asked in my newly acquired Arabic. "Where is Ahmed? Is he OK?"

"He is OK now," the friend said. "He was arrested and tortured. He has just been released and wanted me to warn you."

"*Subhan Allah*—Exalted be Allah! What? . . . Why?" I asked, as my heart started to beat fast and my brow broke out in a cold sweat. "What's he been arrested for?" I suspected the answer.

Ahmed's friend looked at me gravely. He must have seen what the

Aman al-Dawlah had done to his friend and knew, as I did, that it was his association with me that caused it. "Ahmed wanted me to tell you that Aman al-Dawlah knows all about you. They know that you are a member of HT, they know your life history. They know about you recruiting in Pakistan and about your desire to establish a *Khilafah* here in Egypt. You need to know that Hizb al-Tahrir is considered by them the most dangerous organization to have ever come to Egypt. They hate you more than they hate the jihadists."

It was the word "Pakistan" that really took me aback. I had discussed HT with Ahmed, but I hadn't gone into my time in Pakistan. That information could only have come from Aman al-Dawlah.

"Ahmed wanted me to tell you," his friend continued, "that they are preparing a major case against you; they will arrest you and put you on trial. That was why he was tortured, to gather information for the case against *you*. He tried to protect you as best he could, *akhi.*" Ahmed's friend emphasized the point about the trial again. "They're not talking about deporting you, but incarcerating you. *Akhi* Maajid, you're from the UK, your jails are not our jails. Do you understand what that means? *Wallahi*—by Allah, Maajid, do you know what might happen if they find you guilty?"

I nodded. At this moment my mind started to drift to minutiae, the way it does when it senses pending danger.

"Where are we, by the way?" I heard myself mutter.

"We're in Abu Keer, on the outskirts of Alexandria; it's an old village famous for its fish." He got back to the point. "Ahmed wanted me to tell you, as a friend, that you should leave Egypt immediately. You should get out while you still have the chance. *Allahu ma'ak*—May Allah be with you."

Ahmed's risk in getting this message to me is what we called in Egypt *Gad'ana*, a very chivalrous thing to do. It touched me deeply: here was a man tortured for information about me, and yet he further risked his safety, and that of his friends and family, to warn me in advance. Such loyalty, such brotherhood, is hard to come by. It was in moments like this that Islamism seemed to be the only bond that could inspire such chivalry in the hearts of men. The easy option would be to get himself free through setting me up, or failing that, to have nothing more to do with me.

I replayed what Ahmed's friend had told me over and over in my head, blood pumping through my temples at a speed I didn't know was possible. The time had finally come. All those years of preparation, the romanticism of struggle, and now it was my time. I knew, too, that I couldn't just pick up the phone and ring Nasim back in London for his advice, or try to make contact with my other HT members in Egypt. There was a strong likelihood my phone was already tapped: there had been clicks on the line ever since I arrived in Alexandria. There was a good possibility I would be followed and lead Aman al-Dawlah to the whereabouts of other activists. Whatever I decided to do, I only had Allah to rely on, *Allahu Musta'an*.

I thought hard about leaving the country. But how would I get past airport security? Surely they would just stop me at the border. As fortune would have it, Rabia and Ammar were already out of the country, having gone back to the UK to see family. I decided it was too dangerous for them to return, and got a message to them, without giving anything away, that they should stay in the UK until further notice. Rabia immediately knew the code for what it was; we had rehearsed this moment over and again, and she spent weeks in prayer worrying for my safety. I decided the best course of action was to lie low. I stopped all HT activity instantly and without notice. I steered clear of my flat and moved around instead, staying with friends until everything had calmed down.

Over the next few weeks, I was living on the edge of my nerves. The fact that I was crashing on different people's couches didn't help—bad nights of sleep punctuated by being woken by every new creak and groan of the floorboards. But as the days turned to weeks, I began to relax. It was the Christmas holidays: I had no classes to attend, Rabia and Ammar were away, and I couldn't do any HT work. It might seem an odd scenario under which to have a break, but for the first time in a long while, that's exactly what I did.

Toward the end of the holidays, about a month or so after the meeting with Ahmed's friend, I felt confident enough about the situation to test the waters. I decided that I would try to leave the country to see what would happen. So Hassan, Hiroshi (my Japanese friend from Arabic class), and I caught a bus from Alexandria to Cairo, and went to catch a ferry, assuming security there might be less rigorous than at the airport. To my huge relief,

I got through border security without a murmur. We took the ferry across the Red Sea to Aqaba, in Jordan, and drove over to Amman. From here we caught a taxi over the Allenby Bridge into Jerusalem, where we stayed in the Old City for a night. We were going on an adventure.

Being in Jerusalem, or al-Quds in Arabic, was like taking a walk through an ancient history book. I remain mesmerized by the sheer majesty of the place. I traced the steps of Jesus *'alayhi salam* through the old city, eyes welled with reverent tears. I was incredibly humbled by the fact that I was walking in the footsteps of prophets. I saw the Mosque of Omar, the Prophet's companion and Second Caliph of Islam, built on the footsteps of a church because Omar refused to enter the church to pray, out of fear that his followers would later convert it into a mosque. So they built the mosque on the footsteps anyway.

And as we entered the Al-Aqsa compound, into Islam's third holiest site for Friday prayers, I became overwhelmed. The sheer significance of where I was, the purity of the place, and the fact that each brick, each slab, was currently suffering due to the conflict, overcame me. We could see bullet holes in the sacred walls. We prayed there, *salat al-Jumu'ah*—our Friday prayers, right there under the green dome of the Al-Aqsa Mosque; right there where the seal of Allah's Prophet Muhammad *'alayhi salam* led all other Prophets in prayer on that night known as *Israa*. Muhammad *'alayhi salam* then ascended to *Jannah*—Paradise, from the very rock beneath the golden dome of the Qubbat al-Sakhra, right there, where I broke down and kissed the floor and begged Allah to forgive my transgressions against Him, my wife, and my son in case I never saw them again. My own group, Hizb al-Tahrir, had been founded in this very mosque in 1953. Filled with an all-encompassing sense of awe, from that day I dedicated my heart to the lands of Palestine.

It felt so good to be away from Egypt. For those couple of days, it felt as though the suspicion and the stress of being watched were falling from my shoulders. It's difficult to describe the experience of living in a police state if you've never lived in one, but because someone might be watching you or listening, because you can never quite be sure, there's an inherent tension in how you go about your life. It's only when you leave the country, and you literally feel this tension disappear, that you realize how wound up you've been. It's hard not to check your actions or feel paranoid, even when you're doing nothing wrong. Ironically, I felt more relaxed in Israeli-controlled al-Quds than I had been in Egypt.

While I was still in Jerusalem, I took the opportunity to reconnect with HT in the Al-Aqsa Mosque. I introduced myself to Issam Amireh, a senior member. I told him about my background, my studies in Egypt, and my HT activities in the UK, Pakistan, and Denmark. He suggested that I should return there after I had finished my year in Alexandria, to study with him for a while. This would have been a huge honor, and I readily agreed. We discussed the situation in Egypt, but not in detail— there was little he could have done to help me with Aman al-Dawlah. For those golden couple of days, I could see my HT career stretch out in front of me: studying in Jerusalem, returning to Pakistan to recruit, and cementing my place in Islamic history by helping to bring about "the *Khilafah*."

I returned to Egypt by the same route. Again, there were no problems at the border. In retrospect, it does seem strange that I got in and out so easily. It might have been because they'd deduced from my return ferry ticket, and that I didn't have any possessions with me, that I was planning to return. Equally, it might have been a mistake on their part. Just because Aman al-Dawlah was ruthless in its actions, it didn't mean that they were competent in everything they did. Theirs was perhaps a more scatter-gun approach to keeping tabs on people.

It might also have been that there was a tightening of security after my return. After all, this was the immediate aftermath of 9/11, and the policy situation was still quite fluid. No British citizens had yet been tortured in a foreign country as part of the War on Terror. I was a member of a group that was perfectly legal in the UK, and it seemed out of the question that I could be arrested without cause and without any blowback.

However, things were starting to change. It is hard to say how far and how deep the intelligence sharing was between countries after 9/11. But the fact that Aman al-Dawlah knew all about me suggests it was happening. The timeline is important here: by early 2002 the Taliban had been defeated, and the focus on military operations was giving way to the interrogation of captured prisoners. For the first time, your citizenship didn't matter. Neither did such niceties as the Geneva Convention. It may have been that, in those weeks after my return from Jerusalem, I became fair game to the authorities. Maybe they'd just gotten the green light that the British government wouldn't intervene.

Whatever the truth, I returned to Egypt less worried than I had been a month or so before. I was relaxed enough to give the all-clear for Rabia and Ammar to return to the country. I was still careful to maintain my distance from other HT members—I didn't go and see Reza, for example, or go back to recruiting. It was as if the situation were back to normal. Little did I know that this calm was an illusion—and a storm was about to come.

CHAPTER SEVENTEEN

Welcome to Egypt: We Do As We Please

APRIL 1, 2002

The banging on my door came at three o'clock in the morning. I was awake, as I'm sure they knew. Thinking about it later, they'd probably followed me all evening. My last night of freedom was spent with Hassan, enjoying the unmistakable quality of Alexandria at night: the intoxicating smells of coffee and shisha smoke, intermingling with the cool crispness of the sea air. I was lucky to have wandered the streets underneath the stars that night: it would serve to give me a shard of civilization to remember in the months and years ahead.

They must have already been there when I said good night to Hassan and made my way back to the flat. I must have walked straight past them, as they gestured to each other and sent a radio message that I had returned.

Did they sense me, as I tiptoed through the dark and sleeping apartment, careful not to wake my son, my wife, or her friend Zahra, who was staying with us?

Did they see me as I stepped out onto the balcony, soaking up one last look at the glistening skyline before bed?

Did they hear my one-year-old son stir before I did, his restlessness and murmuring giving way to needy cries?

I tiptoed over to Ammar's cot and picked him up, held him against my shoulder and rocked him gently. In those days he would wrap his little hand tightly around my index finger as I soothed him with Ayat al-Kursi, the sacred Muslim prayer, *Allahu La ilaaha illa huwa al-Hayyu al-Qayyum . . .*

T. S. Eliot famously wrote that the world would end, not with a bang, but with a whimper. My world ended with both—the whimpering of my son and the banging at the door. It was the sort of noise that rings louder in your soul than in your ears, as the bottom of a police boot kicked at the door, again and again, and the double lock offered some resistance.

Even before I saw the soldiers I knew instinctively what was happening. Even before little Ammar started weeping, clinging to my arms from terror, I knew what had happened. And then . . . *the door*, I thought tangentially, *I must save the door.* I calmly walked over to the door and opened it before they could kick it down. There was nowhere to run to in this high-rise flat, nowhere left to hide. As the soldiers burst into the flat in full armor, protective vests, carrying stun grenades and machine guns, I rushed back to shelter Ammar.

First they secured the area, checking to see if any resistance would meet them, and then they zeroed in on me, all guns trained on father and son as they barked orders in Egyptian Arabic at this young father trying to shelter his crying little boy from the barrels of submachine guns. I stood subdued, not moving, just praying to heal Ammar's fear, chanting God's name in rhythmic tones gently in his ear, *Allahu Allahu Allahu Allah.* In the background, I could hear them approaching the bedrooms. *They will storm in on my sleeping wife,* I thought. *I don't care what they do, I will not let them wake Rabia with their guns.* I lifted a lead-heavy foot and started moving.

"Maagid Nawaz, where are you going?" a voice asked in accented English, with the Egyptian pronunciation of the J as a G. In front of me, the phalanx of machine guns gave way to a smartly dressed man in a suit. He was young, in his early thirties, clean-shaven. His dark hair was combed back. I knew instantly that he was the one to fear. He was the *zaabit*—officer of Aman al-Dawlah—and he didn't need a machine gun to assert his authority.

"Are you Maagid Nawaz?" he asked.

"I am," I replied.

The *zaabit* nodded. He knew this already.

"You need to come with us." The way he said "need" made me flinch.

"Look, I opened the door, I let you in, I've got nothing to hide. Can I please just wake my wife? You can follow me in if you like," I said as I was trying to calm Ammar.

"OK, let's go."

And he followed me to the bedroom door as I walked in and woke Rabia with a low, trembling voice.

"Rabia, wake up, it's me." It didn't take much, she was up immediately, wondering why Ammar was crying. "You have to get up, it's time, they're here." Knowing instantly what I meant, Rabia shot up, threw her long jilbab (gown) over her body, and quickly covered what modesty she could with her hijab.

"What, are they really here?"

"Yes, right by the door, you better wake up sister Zahra. Be strong for Allah's sake. I'm afraid I'll need to leave you shortly."

I could hear a slamming of drawers and cupboards as I tried to keep calm. They were ransacking the house. Rabia rushed to wake her friend Zahra in the guest room as I walked back out to the sitting room. As Ammar still clutched to me in terror, I asked one last favor from the *zaabit*.

"Can I take this small Qur'an with me?" I asked calmly.

"Sure," came the steady reply.

My immediate fear was not what they might find—I had no weapons of any sort—but what they might pretend to "find": the planting of evidence.

"Wait here," said the agent, as he left me guarded. Through the doorway, I could see that they were throwing my books into trash bags. I had HT literature in the house and plenty of it: enough to make my membership in the group incontrovertible. These soldiers, though, were just randomly taking handfuls of books off the shelves, normal books, available tomes about Islam and other subjects. That gave me a flicker of hope that these soldiers didn't know what they were looking for, and that maybe they might miss the most damning texts. They carried out trash bag after trash bag.

The *zaabit* spoke sharply, "You must come with us now, Maagid Nawaz."

I knew that traveling to Egypt as a member of Hizb al-Tahrir, and to actively participate in recruitment, was going to be a high-risk activity. It was a different situation from the one I'd come across in the UK or Denmark. Even in Pakistan the organization wasn't banned until 2003, after Musharraf's purge of my army friends. Before I went to Alexandria, I'd prepared myself psychologically for what might happen. I discussed with the UK leadership the possibility that I might be arrested and tortured, and what my response should be.

The HT policy was clear. I was to give my name and that I was a member of HT. It was important to state that—to show you had courage and principles. To deny your membership, even to save your skin, was an affront to your beliefs, cowardice in the face of tyranny. This was the only information you should give your interrogators: whatever they did to you, you were not to reveal any further details of the group's activities. As far as I am aware, this remains the group's policy even though it is a deeply unrealistic one.

To give an interrogator that carrot—to stand there and say *I'm in HT but I'm not going to tell you about it*—is asking for trouble. Everyone has a threshold when it comes to torture, and the HT line is simply impossible to sustain. It would have been better not to admit membership at all and hope the interrogation didn't go any further.

HT's policy was particularly absurd given the group's response to a member's arrest. While the arrested were told to stand tall, the group had an active policy *not* to support what they considered to be fallen soldiers. While the HT member is interrogated and tortured, HT would carry on as though that person was no longer their responsibility. Of course the group would make noises about its fallen members, but there would be no support officially provided by the group to the families. So while the HT member was under orders not to disown the group, the group would essentially disown the HT member.

The reason that I was willing to put myself in such a dangerous position was because of the elements of HT's teachings. In the numerous *halaqahs* I had attended over the years, the importance of sacrifice was drilled into me. Stories were told and retold about Prophets, companions, and martyrs who gave up everything in order to establish Islam. We were taught to believe that our struggle was so absolute that it was impossible to contemplate victory without blood being spilt. If that sacrifice was to be mine, I knew Allah would recompense me in the hereafter. I had considered the possibility of *shahadah* (martyrdom) and had reconciled myself to this outcome quite decisively. Never one to do things by halves, if the *shahadah* was in store for me, it would not only be Allah's will, it would be my honor.

The final part of my preparation was to discuss with Rabia what would happen if I got arrested. As a fellow member of HT, Rabia understood why I was doing what I was doing. We discussed all the consequences of my possible arrest, because the Aman al-Dawlah left no stone unturned when it came to extracting information. There were stories of wives and children being brought in front of arrested husbands, in order for him to watch them being tortured.

The one advantage that Rabia and Ammar had in such a situation was that they had British passports. We came up with a plan to follow if I was arrested: Rabia was to get herself to the British Embassy without delay and to make sure that she left the country at the first opportunity. My arrest would mean an uncertain future for Rabia and Ammar—we knew my family would be given no support from HT while I was incarcerated. My sacrifice would be hers as well as my own. And in a certain sense, I'm still unsure who suffered more.

———

As I was about to be taken away that night, I spoke to Rabia one last time, quietly and quickly, as they began tugging at my arms.

"Do as we agreed," I said, looking at her desperately straight in the eyes. "Do you understand?"

Rabia looked at me that final time, stricken with grief, and nodded. I knew she understood. She knew she had to get to the consul in Alexandria and then get herself and Ammar out of the country quickly.

"Where are you taking him?" Rabia suddenly asked the agent. "When are you bringing him back?"

The agent looked a little surprised at her questioning but took it in his stride. "In three days' time," he said calmly.

"And how do I get in contact with you?" she asked. "Who are you, anyway?"

The agent smiled a little patronizingly at my wife. *As if I carry a badge,* he seemed to say. He wrote down a number and handed it to her.

"Thank you," she said.

The number would turn out to be a false one. What she didn't know was that our phone socket had been ripped out. A number that wouldn't work, to be called on a phone she couldn't use. I later learned that she had to go out into the streets at 4 a.m., knowing no Arabic, begging people to let her use a phone to call the consul.

Rabia's questioning stirred up something within me.

"This is ridiculous," I said. "You can't just come in here in the middle of the night like this. You haven't told me what I am being arrested for. You haven't read me my rights. I haven't seen any ID. Do you even have a warrant to search my flat?"

The agent listened to my diatribe with a look of faint amusement. When I had finished, he laughed and shook his head, like I just didn't get it.

"Welcome to Egypt, Maagid. We do as we please," he said with a sneer.

The calmness of his demeanor then cracked. Ammar's crying, which had been incessant, was the last straw. He came over to me and wrenched Ammar from my arms. It was a flash of temper, all the more brutal for the fact that it was the little boy who bore the brunt of it. To have Ammar's hand ripped away from me like that in those final moments was the most painful thing. He looked me straight in the eyes, bawling, his arms outstretched as the *zaabit* shoved him toward Rabia. That image is still scorched in my memory. This was to be my parting image, and the last time I was to see him, or his mother, for a long time.

The *zaabit* then grabbed my arm, quite aggressively, and I remember thinking that this was the first time since the police had burst in that anyone had touched me.

"Right," he snapped. "Let's go."

There was no chance to say goodbye, not even a final glance back as he half pushed me through my front door, frog-marching me down the stairs to the police van below. She didn't know it yet, but that night Rabia was to lose her husband forever.

CHAPTER EIGHTEEN

The *Ghimamah* Has No Rules

The cold of the night air smacked me in the face. I could see that the whole area had been cordoned off: there were more armed police standing at the front of my building, further vans and cars sealing the road. The *zaabit* spat an instruction in Arabic to a *shaweesh*—police conscript. *Kalbishuh*—cuff him, he said, and my arms were duly shoved behind my back. I could feel the sharpness of the metal scoring my wrists as I was shoved into the van. A heavy hand pushed me forward on the back of my head, and it was a balancing act not to stumble on the steps as I got in. A horseshoe of wooden benches ran along the sides. *U'ad*—sit, someone barked. I sat in the middle as the benches filled up with *shaweeshiya*, the van swaying each time another jumped in.

The *zaabit* shouted another instruction as the back doors of the van slammed shut, "*Ihna mashiyeen, ghummimooh.*" I didn't understand this but soon found out. The *shaweesh* next to me pulled out a rag, a dark, dirty, stained piece of cloth, and motioned at me to lean forward. It was a blindfold, and now, for the first time, as the gift of sight was taken from me, I began to feel petrified, complete fear—the kind that cannot be described but only felt. The rag was wrapped tightly round my face, tied roughly at the back. I could feel the pressure of the cloth pushing against my eyeballs, the unpleasant odor battling the lingering traces of Ammar's baby talc.

Most of all, there was the unremitting blackness as the driver started the engine and began to pull away. It now dawned on me that in the back of this van, with heavily armed *shaweeshiya* surrounding me, I was powerless to use my hands to stop them if they attacked me, and I would not see it coming. This was helplessness. My remaining senses began to strain for any clues of sudden movement. The flicker of confidence I'd had in the flat seemed part of a different world. I was totally at their mercy, and I knew it.

The *ghimamah*, or blindfold, answered the question that the *zaabit* had ignored. I knew now that I was in the hands of Aman al-Dawlah. If they had been ordinary police, I'd have been starting down the civil jurisdiction route. I'd be processed and deported, my rights as a British citizen granting me some semblance of respect. Egypt, however, was a country with two parallel judicial systems; the second, the Emergency Law track, wasn't bound by any rules. The *ghimamah* told me this. You don't blindfold someone unless you're taking them to a place that's off the radar.

My mind, as always, began wondering about details:

The ghimamah. It's a filthy, torn piece of rag; it's not even a proper blindfold. That offends me. I'm worth more than a rag.

I wonder where it's been. I wonder how many other petrified souls have shared this yard of cloth. Their sweat and mine will now share a common foe.

Actually the fact that it's a rag frightens me. Rags are unofficial, unaccountable.

Real blindfolds have to be purchased and processed with receipts, in the cold light of day. Rags are free of rules.

My body began to tremble uncontrollably. As if the odor of my *ghimamah* had finally defeated Ammar's last act of defense for me, the scent of his baby talc on my neck, and the odor assaulted my brain, my nervous system. *I am in deep trouble.* Subhan Allah! *I am in serious deep trouble.* As it began beating its war drums my heart didn't want to surrender to the rag. Preparing to defend my body from whatever may come, I began breathing out, deeply, to try to calm myself.

I thought of how odd my twenty-four years of life had been. Essex, Newcastle, London, Lahore, Raheem Yar Khan, Copenhagen, Cairo, Alexandria, Amman, and al-Quds all flashed before me. I thought of *Tai Ammi* and her stories, Patrick, and the unintended path that his small act of racism had set that scared, lonely boy upon.

I thought of my first girlfriend Sarah crying on that first day at Cecil Jones after I told her there were too many new girls to choose from.

I thought of N.W.A, and "Fuck tha Police," and my stomach turned as it struck me that only those with the luxury to speak could afford to be so defiant, and to get rich out of being so.

I thought of the white friends I'd abandoned, my companionship with Sav and Marc, with Dan, who was stabbed for us.

I thought of my crew, Chill, Ricky, Ade, and Paul, and the mad times we'd had as every other girl wanted to get in on our scene. *Had I really ever been that youthful teenage B-boy bopping to those beats in Southend's clubs?*

Then I saw Abi beating her womb, pleading with me not to go, not to go, and I began to long for Abi's smile. I remembered Osman and Yasser, and how proud they were of my activism. I thought of Ed Husain at Newham, Uncle Qayyum in Raheem Yar Khan, Ash at SOAS, how are you all?

And now I wondered if Rabia had managed to call that number and knew instinctively that I would not be back in three days. And so I prayed, I prayed and felt close to Allah in my loneliness as I begged Him to protect me from these *zalimun* these tyrants: *Allahumm Inni aj'aluka fi nufurihim . . .*

We stopped. I assumed we were still in Alexandria, but I had no idea. It was the middle of the night. Everything was eerily quiet. I assumed, again, that we were at the Aman al Dawlah building. But we could have easily pulled up somewhere else: a disused factory, a deserted warehouse. My mind, now defeated by the odor of my *ghimamah*, was ready to suggest, in despair, any number of nightmare scenarios.

I was taken out of the van and guided into a building. Up we went, stumbling up some stairs that became impossible to navigate without the aid of sight. A door opened in front of me, and the cold slap of night struck me again. A second or two, and I worked out that I must be on the roof of a building. *Why had they brought me up here?* Pushed along, I was eventually guided to what felt like a precipice, the wind rushing against the front of my body, my feet sensing an edge that I dared not test. And then with rather more care than I had experienced until now, I was positioned into a spot and told to stand perfectly still. *Ya Allah*, the thought came to me as fast as the wind rushing past my hair: *They're going to push me off the top of the building.*

The *shaweeshiya* were laughing at me now. They'd done this before; they knew exactly what I was thinking. They could probably see my knees trembling as I struggled to stay perfectly still.

"Don't move," a *shaweesh* said, with a sneer. "You really don't want to move."

I could hear him retreat, his steps getting quieter as he crunched gravel behind me. I didn't dare move a muscle. I didn't dare feel anything. I didn't even dare to think. *Focus on keeping still. Focus on keeping still. Nothing else exists.* I willed time to move fast for me, I wanted this moment to be over, regardless of what came next, and as if to say, "Who are *you* to ask me anything?" time stretched out and took a yawn. It seemed to me that I was standing there for fifteen or twenty minutes, but it could just as easily have been two.

Eventually, I heard the gravel crunch behind me again. I tensed up, petrified that I might be about to get a shove. Instead, though, the *shaweesh* grabbed me and pulled me back. I tried not to buckle as he did so, the rush of relief loosening my limbs. Not that the relief lasted for long. When there are no procedures, there's no knowing what might happen next. They're softening me up, I thought to myself as I was dragged back across the roof, barely able to walk from the tremor in my legs. That's what this is all about. To make me more susceptible, more suggestible, to weaken me. *Come on, Maajid! You're not weak, you're never weak! Ya Allah, give me strength!*

I was taken up some more stairs, and back inside. Through the darkness of my *ghimamah* I caught the glimmer of a lamp. Positioned in front of what I assumed to be a desk, a *zaabit* began to address me. I assumed this was the same *zaabit* who'd led the raid on my flat, but he was speaking Arabic now; there was so much I was no longer sure of that it almost didn't matter. Everything was uncertain: where I was, whom I was talking to, what was going to happen next. Reality was starting to fray at the seams.

"Maagid Nawaz," my interrogator said.

"Yes," I replied in English. "That's my name." I wondered if he could see through my attempts at trying to sound strong and confident.

My Arabic wasn't bad. Having been in Egypt for seven months, I'd picked up the basics, but here I was struggling to understand every word of what my interrogator said.

"We know everything about you, Maagid. We know you are with Hizb al-Tahrir. We know you are attempting to revive this banned group in Egypt. We know you have tried to recruit people here, that your wish is to overthrow the Egyptian state." He reeled off each statement like he was flicking dirt from his jacket. "We know about your work in Pakistan, Maagid. It seems you think you're an important man." He said the word "important" with disdain. "You know what I think, Maagid? I think you should tell me everything you know. That way, this will all be a little easier on you."

There was a pause, as he allowed what he had just said to sink in. If it hadn't been for Ahmed's warning those few months earlier, I would have been terrified at the mention of Pakistan. That's what he wanted me to feel, that stomach-churning sensation that there's been intelligence gathered against me: Aman al-Dawlah, ISI, MI6—he'd leave me to fill in the gaps. But thanks to Ahmed, I already knew they had this information. My prior knowledge gave me that fractional advantage, just enough to steel myself and respond.

"My name is Maajid Nawaz," I said in English, sticking to my HT training. "I am a member of Hizb al-Tahrir in Britain. I am here in Egypt to study."

A fist came down on the table. The slam sounded close. "Don't you dare play games with us, Maagid!" he snapped in Arabic. "I know you can speak Arabic."

That flash of temper emboldened me. I felt in some small way that I had gotten under his skin. If I am to be defiant, it means I must stand ready for the consequences. *Ya Rabb, my Lord, help me now for I am your humble servant.*

"My name is Maajid Nawaz," I repeated in English. "I am a member of Hizb al-Tahrir in the UK. I have come from Britain to Egypt to study. I have nothing more to say."

My use of English was deliberate. It was to emphasize where I was from. I wanted to remind the interrogator at every opportunity that I was a British citizen. This was the strongest card I had to remind him that he couldn't just treat me like he would other Egyptians. Or at least that's what I hoped.

"Tell me about Pakistan!" he shouted in Arabic. "Tell me about your activities there."

"I have been to Pakistan, yes," I agreed in English. "I have family there. It is perfectly normal for British-Pakistanis to visit the country to see their relatives."

"Family," he spat. "What family?"

"Aunts, uncles, cousins . . ." I was careful not to mention my wife's family. I didn't want to give them any possible reason to arrest her as well.

"Yes, yes, yes," the interrogator swatted my answer away. "It's not family members I am interested in, it's members of Hizb al-Tahrir."

In retrospect, he was oddly interested in Pakistan, considering that it had nothing to do with Egypt. Later, when I had time to think things through, it did make me wonder about who exactly this was asking these questions, and for whom. As he snapped and shouted at me, I stuck to my line. I continued answering in English, politely and firmly, emphasizing my British citizenship.

"Tell me about Hizb al-Tahrir in Egypt," the interrogator changed tack.

"I am in Egypt to study. I am here in Alexandria as part of my university degree to study Arabic."

Here the interrogator snorted; it's called a *shakheer* and is considered extremely rude. To Egyptians this indicates that you no longer make any pretense of social etiquette. "Whom have you recruited?" he asked. "Whom are you in contact with? Who else is involved?"

"I am a member of Hizb al-Tahrir in Britain," I reiterated. "I have nothing to do with the organization in Egypt."

"We'll see about that, Maagid," the interrogator said. "We'll see about that." He sighed. "If that's how you want to play it." I heard a rustle behind me, from where another *shaweesh* must have been standing. "I said that you had the chance to make things easier for yourself." I felt the *shaweesh*'s hand grab my arm. "But I can't help you now," he said as I was led away.

Taken back down several flights of metal steps outside of the building, I began wondering if I was about to be driven off somewhere else.

But instead we went back inside the building, down some more steps, and into what I think was a basement. I heard the click of a key from behind me: my handcuffs were being taken off. Then the heavier clunk of a door opened and I was shoved forward, the door slamming shut behind me. Slowly, carefully, still blindfolded, I used my fingertips to take in my new surroundings. I felt cold bars on all sides and realized I was in a cell. As I finally sat down, legs aching for respite, I began to rub my wrists where the handcuffs had been.

I was kept in that holding cell for hours. Again, I can't be completely sure of timings: your perception of time melts away in such circumstances. And then I heard a shout, more like an appeal, someone in broken Arabic asking to be taken to the toilet. With pangs of rising guilt, I realized it was Hassan. Later on, another call: this time it was Hiroshi. Then I heard the voice of Yusuf el-Qadi, an Egyptian friend of ours, and a Muslim Brotherhood activist. Hearing their voices scared me in a way that the interrogator's questions had failed to do. *They have arrested my friends.* They have arrested my friends because of me. None of them had anything to with any of this. I had never raised the matter of HT with any of them. I sat there, too scared to call out to them, and wondered what they would think of me if they knew the truth.

Eventually, we were given some food to eat: one slice of bread and a small round blob of white, extremely salty cheese. A bottle of water was passed around the cells, from which we were allowed a swig. After what must have been the rest of the night, the guards were suddenly all action: the cell doors clanked open and one by one I could hear the shuffling of people being marched outside. It was my turn and the guard snapped at me to hold my hands out in front of me. Back on went the cuffs, and I was dragged out into the daylight.

The coldness of the night air was now a distant memory, and the heat from the sun washed over me. I was shown into the back of a van, only this time there were no benches, just a metal floor onto which I was shoved with Hassan, Hiroshi, and Yusuf. It was a closed van with metal on all sides except for a couple of tiny square windows, covered in a metal mesh. The door slammed shut and the van pulled away.

As there were no *shaweeshiya* in the back of the van, we were finally able to talk to each other. We had cautiously removed our blindfolds, keeping them round our necks.

"*Subhan Allah*, are you all right?"

"What have they done to you?"

"What did they say?"

It was Yusuf who was doing the apologizing. He was the Egyptian and we were the foreigners, and he felt that acutely. "I can't believe they are treating you like this," he said as the van sped along an unknown road to an unknown destination. "I am so sorry." Yusuf had naturally assumed that it was his membership in the Muslim Brotherhood that was to blame. I said nothing. This only made my guilt even worse. I knew from the questions that this was an HT case, and they were there because of me. But anything I told them would inevitably be used against them, forced out of them through torture. If my friends had mentioned that they knew I was with HT, it would only make matters far worse for them. The questions would keep coming: *so he has spoken to you about it, then? You have joined HT, too? Maagid has recruited you to his cause, has he?* Their best hope was to remain in blissful ignorance of my beliefs. The interrogators, I hoped, would soon realize that they knew nothing and just let them go. And so I suffocated my guilt and my overwhelming desire to apologize, in order to keep them safe.

The buzz of the Alexandria traffic began to disappear. It became clear that we were being taken out of the city, driven out into the desert. They shot people here, I knew. Took them out into the middle of nowhere and never brought them back. The van was getting hotter and hotter. The desert sun was baking down, turning the back of the van into an oven. Our clothes were soaked through with sweat—I could feel mine clinging to me with their wetness. Heat and sweat, heat and sweat. The saltiness of the cheese we'd had, and the fact that we were sweating so profusely, made us all desperate to urinate. The sheer pain in our bladders was reaching dangerous proportions, but where to go, and how? Soon we felt the van pull over to the side of the road. But it was for the driver to go, not us.

The van started up again. Yusuf banged on the partition wall.

"We need to go," he said. "We need to use the loo back here."

"Do it in the back," the *shaweesh* shouted back. "We're not stopping for you."

The van drove on. We were in that van for maybe four or five hours, and there was no way you could hold on in that heat. There was a spare tire opposite the doors, and we decided to take turns and just do it there. The urine went everywhere: all over the steel floor, where we were sitting and standing. The van stank with the putrid smell of sweat, urine, and heat. Degraded and humiliated, there was nothing we could do.

As the journey continued, we came to the conclusion that we were being taken to Cairo. From the distance we'd traveled, it seemed the most likely destination. Yusuf kept on apologizing, which just made the situation worse. In the heat of the van, I kept quiet and tried to pray: *Ya Allah, Ya Rabb al-'arsh al-'azeem*, Lord of the majestic throne, grant me the strength to pass this test of yours. I remembered my lessons back in London, about how our struggle would not be achieved without shedding blood. Sacrifice was an honor bestowed on a chosen few. I am thankful to Allah for this opportunity to be tested and counted as one of His true servants, for the chance to prove the depth of my *eeman*, my faith. Allah will never fail me: I must not fail Him in return.

There was the noise of a city now. The van stopped and started amid the hustle and bustle of busy streets. "Cairo. We're here," I thought. The driver pulled the vehicle over, and as I swallowed hard I heard the door of the van being opened.

"Where are we?" Yusuf asked.

"Don't you know?" the *shaweesh* laughed as he began guiding us out. "This is al-Gihaz."

Al-Gihaz. The name sent a shudder through me. Aman al-Dawlah headquarters in Cairo—"The Apparatus."

"My brothers, pray that Allah comes to your aid," Yusuf struggled to speak, while his face changed to a color just off yellow. "This place is a torture center."

A murmur. A groan. My arms were grabbed by a guard, my handcuffs roughly removed. A *ghimamah* was tightened over my eyes again and then, unceremoniously, my hands were pulled behind my back and tied together with another piece of rag. Another rag, another place of lawlessness. I winced as the cloth burned my wrists. Official procedures—like the handcuffs—were being left at the door. Manhandled down some steps, away from the sunshine and down into darkness, I was led into the underground cells of al-Gihaz to await my fate.

CHAPTER NINETEEN

Number Forty-Two

I will never forget al-Gihaz. It is the sort of place that remains etched on your memory forever. The sort of place that still, a decade later, I can recall with disturbing clarity as it wakes me up in the night, slipping insidiously into my dreams. The piling of the bodies. The heat and cold. The begging screams from the torture room at the end of the corridor. The waiting. It's the sort of place that when you first enter, you cannot quite believe it exists. Something from a film. But it's real all right. If only my mind could come to believe that it wasn't.

Itnain wa arba'een. Number forty-two. That was who—what—I'd become. My last vestige of identity and dignity was stripped from me as I was shoved down those stairs. I heard with mounting horror my fellow prisoners being called and taken down the corridor, the crackle of electricity. I heard the prisoners being dragged back, the "schlump" sound as their near-lifeless bodies were deposited back in line, the faintness of their whimpers and murmurs as they lay there, recovering.

I was only a number. This was the only order in that cretinous hellhole, the way the numbers called out moved up, ever closer to my own. Each individual torture session varied, but each must have been between thirty minutes and an hour. The wait for our own turn was over a drowsy, sleep-deprived day and night. I was at least sure of that, because I could hear the call to prayer, the *azan,* drifting in from outside the building: the morning *azan* is longer, with an extra line—"*al-salatu khayrun min al-nawm,* prayer is better than sleep." I thanked Allah for letting me live through another night, for being with me, for preventing me from losing my mind. I'd heard that call twice since arrival, so I knew I was into my third day of imprisonment. Even in the abyss of that building, my faith was giving me answers and keeping me strong.

The crackle of electricity was getting closer. So too were the beatings. The roll calls continued day and night, and anyone who didn't answer or forgot their number was beaten there and then. The sound of beating a helpless, crying man is sickening. Others were made to stand for hours on end for failing to answer to their number. If they didn't stand still, or if their legs gave way, they were punished again. Some prisoners, while their hands were still tied at their backs, would have their arms pulled back and lifted from behind, hung by the edge of a door from the rope on their wrists, until their will or their body gave way and their arms dislocated from their sockets.

In a cell behind me, within earshot, I heard a guard march in and order a prisoner to sit up. There was a scuffle.

"If I tell you to do it, you do it," the guard leered.

"Please," the prisoner begged. "Please not that."

"Did I say you could speak?" the guard snapped. The prisoner, by now, was whimpering. And with a snorting *shakheer*, the guard barked: "Put it in your mouth . . ."

"Number forty!" My moment was coming closer as I struggled to remember my prayers. But my attempts to focus were interrupted by the brother next to me, the brother I was leaning against, who by this point was gently beginning to cry.

"Brother," he whispered to me, "*akhi*, I'm next. I, I don't know what to do."

"Sssh," I said quietly, trying to listen for a guard was nearby. If anyone heard us talking to each other, we'd both be beaten.

"Help me, *akhi*," the prisoner whimpered. "They're going to torture me, I know they are and my number's next. Help me for Allah's sake."

But what could I say to this brother of mine to ease his pain while I couldn't even find a way to comfort my own soul? Poor man, he's next; at least I have another few minutes for myself. Let me try to help him.

"Calm yourself, my brother," I gently whispered. "You need to be strong now. Remember you are here *fee sabeelillah*. You will be justly rewarded for the sacrifice you are about to make."

The prisoner, number forty-one, continued, "But I don't know if I can do this. I don't know if I'll be able to get through."

It was heartbreaking to hear a proud man broken. His sobs were the sound of someone whom al-Gihaz had worked its twisted magic on. He was a wreck. The only thing I could think to do was to recite a passage from the Qur'an for him, in the hope that it would give him the courage he so desperately needed. Slowly, and ever so quietly, so low that only he and I could hear, I willed my voice to utter the sounds of Allah's words. It was a risk, I knew, especially as it was our turn next to be called. If we'd been caught speaking, we'd have been accused of collusion, and any punishment meted out would have been that much worse.

What I recited to him was a passage called *al-Burooj*: an ancient story about a boy and a king. It is especially pertinent for those who find their *eeman* being tested. The king demands that everyone in the village worship him. But a boy, who converted to believe in the one true God, refuses. The boy stands by his belief and is persecuted by the king for it. Like the others in the town who stand with the boy by the one true faith, he is thrown into a pit and burned alive. It took the use of all my energy to get my voice out.

I swear by the mansions of the stars,
And by the promised day,
And by the bearer of witness, and those against whom witness is borne,
Cursed be the makers of the pit,
Of the fire fueled, and by where they sat,
They will surely bear witness to what they did to the believers,
Persecuting them for no other cause, but that they believed in Allah, the
Mighty, the Praised,
Whose is the Kingdom of the heavens and earth, and Allah is a witness
unto all things . . .

I recited the entire passage to him in Arabic, in the low, rhythmic tones of recitation, or *qira'ah*. Swallowing after each line to catch my breath, control my palpitations, and calm my fear: hoping that my words would somehow summon the very angels of our Lord, descended by His command in a righteous rage to protect us from these animals. Like a child, his crying slowly stopped, his sobs drifted further and further apart as he listened intently to my voice, to Allah's words. The beauty of each *ayah*, each verse, seemed to me to sparkle ever more in the grit and grime of that dungeon.

"May Allah reward you, *akhi*," the prisoner said as soon I had finished. "I don't know who you are, but you are a good man. *Wallahi*, you are a good man."

"Number forty-one!" the guard shouted.

"And so are you," I whispered. And as I lay there, my *ghimamah* soaking up my tears and itching my eyes, the brother was hauled to his feet and taken to be tortured.

❧

Now I was alone. When the numbers had been lower down, I wondered if a phone call might come before they got to me. Perhaps the British Consul would have found out where I was. The guards would have been told to get number forty-two up and out of there, before anything happened. But as the roll call got higher, I knew that there would be no hope of escape.

But I still had my *eeman*. Helping number forty-one—I never learned his name nor saw him again—had stirred me. It showed to me that for all my fear, I still had my core strength. I was not yet a broken man. I was not weeping and begging number forty-three for help. And I had a plan, too. For while I was lying there, my hands had not been idle. Little by little, I had worked away at the rag behind my back. It was loose now. I was holding the knot in place with my fist: otherwise, my hands were free.

All my life, I had been in situations involving stabbings and assaults, but not once had I been the one beaten. I had never been forced into a humiliating position where I had no choice but to take a beating. It had happened in front of me but never *to* me. And I decided that I wasn't going to let it happen now. Somewhere in the vicinity, I could hear the tortured screams of number . . . brother forty-one.

If they try that with me, I thought to myself, they'll have to kill me for the wrath I intend to unleash upon them. They may have guns and torture machines, but I've got surprise on my side. My hands are free. I braced myself, and decided that at the moment of torture I would jump on my interrogator. I would jump on him and simply bite down into his neck, and bite and bite until they would have to shoot me dead to make me stop. I would die fighting, without pain, without suffering, with glory.

It sounds surreal now. But al-Gihaz is a surreal place, and listening to the screams of grown men pleading over forty-eight hours can do surreal things to one's mind. It's as if the outside world—the normal rules—no longer existed. The dehumanizing nature of the regime turns even the most rational minds to their animalistic instincts. Like a tiger in a corner, I was seriously prepared to fight viciously, ruthlessly—to sacrifice my own life rather than suffer the indignation the other prisoners had been put through.

The screaming suddenly stopped. I heard the guards drag brother forty-one back, body limp like a sack of potatoes, until they dumped him beside me. Stillness. My time had come. I was next. And I steadied myself in preparation for my number to be called. The anxiety at that moment is not something I will ever, ever wish upon my worst enemy. The seconds turned to minutes, and the minutes turned to irrelevance as time drifted out of the window, my mind running from the sheer inhumanity of my situation. The war drums of my heart began to gather pace, and I prepared myself for the last moments of my life. Be strong, Maajid, Allah is with you, be strong and embrace your martyrdom.

Itnain wa arba'een!

There it was. Number forty-two. My whole body literally shuddered. It is my turn. Number forty-two. Odd, I thought, as my mind wandered off into that all-too-familiar place of randomness. Forty-two is my age, twenty-four, but backward. How strange. I wonder if I'll ever reach forty-two years old. I gathered the strength to speak. My voice came out weaker than I would have liked:

"*Na'am*—Yes."

And I stood up.

CHAPTER TWENTY

Assalaamu Alaykum, You've Just Come out of Hell

To be asked to voluntarily walk toward your own torture is the cruelest of requests. Why can't they just carry me? Each step is a personal betrayal. My body is convulsing in revulsion against my commands. Every instinct is screaming at me to turn the other way, but I am expected to walk on. Try standing in the middle of a highway watching an oncoming bus without flinching—that's hard. Now try voluntarily walking *toward* that bus instead of stepping out of the way: impossible.

My legs are buckling under each step, but I force compliance and walk on. Guard, your chaperoning hand that helps me walk blindly to my own torture feels perversely merciful; for how could I avoid stepping on my brothers in the corridor were it not for you? Alas, without sight I cannot help but feel so disgustingly dependent on you. Now it is hard to breathe. Fighting to stay hidden away deep within me, even my breath fears coming out to face my torturer. My heart is attempting to escape the cage that is my chest, and my mind is beginning to shut down. I am in shock. Ya Allah, I need you right now. If any mercy I have ever shown to anyone has amounted to any value in your esteem, then send me your angels now to shield me from these monsters. I am trying to be brave for you, my Lord, but the truth is I am scared. Help me, my Lord, for I am very scared.

The interrogation room. I can hear my interrogator in front of me, his electrocution device crackling in anticipation. My whole adult life I've spent in preparation for this moment. This agony. Training my soul to accept what my body cannot. Now, I am so tense and tight that my jaw begins to ache. *What will happen next? Will he hit me hard to warm me up? Will he attack me without warning, as an indication that he is brazen?*

If I were him, if I had sold my soul to the devil in this way, if I was going to do unspeakable things to my helpless victims, that's how I would do it. In a terrible, unpredictable, twisted way. Why sell your soul only to be useless at being evil? My mind is racing. The possibilities are too many. Come on! Do it properly, man! I can't stand the wait any longer, just get it over with. But I waited, and waited, and it didn't come. Instead, I heard the shuffle of feet and the door close.

I had assumed that they would just attack you with the electricity there and then. What I learned later from other prisoners was that there was a whole *process* to electrocution. They stripped the brothers naked, pulled them down onto the floor, pinned a chair on top of them, and while someone sat on that chair to hold them down, they electrocuted them via their teeth or genitalia, or both. At the time though, I didn't know any of this, or else I'd have known I wasn't about to be electrocuted. But I didn't know, so I just stood there, waiting for the impact, my hands ready to be released, preparing to pounce on my interrogator's neck and bite it until death came to me.

I heard the squeak of a chair as someone sat down.

"Maagid Nawaz?" This was a different person from the one who had interrogated me back in Alexandria.

"Yes," I replied. The effort it took to make my voice audible was a battle in itself. At this moment, I felt brave just by being able to speak without breaking down.

"So tell me, Maagid. Tell me about Hizb al-Tahrir in Egypt."

I swallowed hard. Staying defiant in Alexandria, without forty-eight hours of listening to torture, was one thing. But now I saw, I heard, I *knew* what they were capable of. You will stand among the *Sahabah*, Maajid—the Companions of the Prophet, do not give up now. The *shaheed*—the martyr—will not die. Like a green bird flying beneath the 'arsh (the Throne of Almighty Allah), you will live under His shade. You will be that happy little boy once again. Do not give up.

"My name is Maajid Nawaz," I replied in English, in whatever level of voice I could muster, which probably wasn't very loud at all. I was still remembering my training, but barely.

"I am a member of Hizb al-Tahrir in Britain. I am in . . ."

A pause as I gasped for air.

". . . in Egypt to study."

I could hear the quality in my voice: though the words I was speaking were defiant in meaning, the way I was saying them was pleading. I scolded myself: *Be a man, what's wrong with you, is this how Yasir and Sumayyah, after whom you named your child, behaved? Stand strong, man!*

The interrogator said nothing. He let the silence unsettle me. Then, in Arabic: "OK, Maagid. I think you should listen to this." My interrogator got up and opened the door. As the door opened, the sound of screams flooded in from a nearby room. As I heard the screams and pleas, trying not to listen, a terrifying recognition dawned upon me. The person being tortured was pleading in English.

"*Kallim 'Arabi!*" the interrogator shouted back. "Speak Arabic!"

"I'm trying," the tortured soul replied, attempting through the shouts in badly broken, barely understandable sentences.

My God, I thought. *That sounds like Reza. They're torturing Reza Pankhurst.*

Subhan Allah! My last trump card, my British citizenship, really did mean nothing to these bastards. If they're torturing Reza, then there's no reason they won't torture me. Poor Reza, how on earth was a man supposed to speak in any language, let alone a foreign one, through the pain of electrocution!

The door to the interrogation room slammed shut again. The interrogator sensed from my reaction that I knew who was being tortured. Now he was right up to me, lowering his voice with menace.

"You hear that, Maagid? You hear what we are doing to your brother? Don't think we can't do that to you. For your own sake, stop these games and start speaking to me in Arabic." He was shouting at me now. "Start talking to me about Hizb al-Tahrir . . ." He spat the name of the group out in disgust. ". . . Everything! I want to know everything about your group in Egypt!"

The next thing I knew, I felt his fist in my stomach. A big, deep, powerful punch; it took all my strength for it not to knock me over. My mind went black and I struggled to breathe as the wind left my lungs. Somewhere in my distant memory, during more innocent days, I remembered that I hailed from a place where someone called Patrick had done this to me. But I had survived, I had lived to tell the tale and see Patrick cower in fear before me many years later. And that memory brought me back up with strength and a renewed *eeman*. Allah is with me. I see it now. This is His sign! Allah never abandoned me. He has been with me all along. And now I knew what I needed to say next to my enemy.

"I have nothing more to say to you. Do whatever you want."

And I loosened my hands in preparation for my attack. To this day, I find it hard to believe that I actually stood there and said this to him. There are many moments in my life, and in this story, I am ashamed of telling. But knowing that I uttered this one feeble sentence on that day fills me with pride. Ammar will surely be old enough one day to read these words, and right here he will know that his father tried with all his strength and all his might to be a noble, honorable man. Because he was named *Abu Ammar,* named after martyrs. And the rest is for the world to judge.

My enemy paused. I could hear him pacing. Then, to my surprise, almost as an anticlimax to what I had just embraced as the inevitable, he said in a dismayed tone, "I'm sending you back to your place. You have twelve hours to think about what you just said to me. And if, after those twelve hours, you still don't tell me the truth, be in absolutely no doubt that I will torture you in ways you have never imagined. Is that clear?"

I said nothing. The interrogator came close again, close enough that I felt his breath on me. Behind him I could hear the door being opened, and more footsteps entering the room. "You know, you've got such a nice face, Maagid," he hissed. "It would be a shame to have to ruin it."

With that, I was shoved and manhandled down the corridor. The guard was laughing.

"Such a nice face," he repeated. "He likes you. You know what we do to people we like, don't you?" The implication was clear as he dumped me back down on the floor. And he left me with that thought, to fester and rot in the darkest corners of my imagination.

The beatings continued. The numbers kept on being called, higher and higher: up into the hundreds.

I replayed in my head again and again the comments that the interrogator had said to me. *Such a nice face.* I remembered the pleas of the prisoner being assaulted in the cell behind me. What was going on? Why hadn't he just tortured me and got it over with? Why was I being spared in this way? I began to feel guilt, as if somehow I had escaped unfairly while all the others, even my brothers from the UK, were treated in the same, brutal way.

I had been in situations before where I had escaped by the skin of my teeth. Matt's stabbing by neo-Nazi hooligans in Southend was meant for me. The murder conviction in Newham was almost me. Somehow, I had always managed to get away with it. *Was Allah saving me for something else?* But as the night continued, punctuated by the sharp screams and sound of electricity ripping through the souls of men, it was a hope I was finding it increasingly difficult to cling to.

In my exhaustion, both mental and physical, I entered a sleep-deprived daze. I was in danger of losing it. The regular roll call prevented us from sleeping, and by this time it must have been three and a half days since my arrest in Alexandria. Alexandria, Rabia, Ammar, how long ago that all seemed now. How much had changed in these few days. I knew already that I would never be the same again, that Rabia had lost the Maajid who woke her gently from her slumber in order to spare her the ordeal of being woken by guns. Then it came. The phone rang. It was like civilization was calling to catch up on the denizens of some type of underworld. Like in a dream, I could hear it ringing down the corridor, fuzzy and out of focus at first. But when the guard started speaking I immediately zoomed in on what he was saying.

"*Aywa effandim*—yes, sir," he said with a sharp formality. "Correct, we have the five of them here . . . *Aywa*, I will, sir, right away."

The five of them. My alertness returned. My mind was light with the possibility. The five of them—he had to be talking about the foreigners.

I knew there was me, Reza, Hassan, and Hiroshi there. I'd figured that if Reza was there, then Ian Nisbet was probably there as well. He's the fifth! My heart leapt at the thought that we were the five. Rabia must have got hold of the consul.

"*Itnain wa arba'een.*"

My number was called again. Taken back to the interrogation room, I was positioned to stand in the same place as before. The interrogator arrived. This time, though, he didn't sound as aggressive as before. Disappointed, perhaps.

"Maagid, well, well, *hazzak sa'eed*—you are a very lucky man."

That was all he said. I was bundled out of the room again, and then, to my excitement, escorted the opposite way along the corridor. I could hear the screams from the torture rooms receding behind me, getting fainter and farther away.

A door opened in front of me.

Thank you, Door, you are my door to life, to civilization. I will owe you a great deal, Door. My apologies for stepping through you like this. Instead I should be garnishing you in celebration as my hero.

Then, that sweet smell, the taste of fresh night air. The real world. Life. Civilization.

Back in the police van, my new guard was an ordinary *shaweesh* again, rather than the state security *zaabit*. He spoke to me gently, "*Assalaamu alaykum,* you've just come out of hell," as he helped me up the steps into the van. There was no menace in what he was saying. It took me a second to recognize the tone. Then I realized. He was just being friendly.

CHAPTER TWENTY-ONE

The Luxury of an Audience

As I guessed, it was indeed the foreign prisoners who were being taken away: Hassan, Hiroshi, Ian, Reza, and me. Once the van pulled away, I broke the silence and started asking after the others. The relief of having just escaped hell itself overcame us. Each of us began thanking Allah to be alive and congratulating each other on getting out.

I quickly discovered that apart from Reza, the other foreigners had also escaped electrocution. Reza was in a different place from the rest of us and would remain there for the remainder of my days talking with him. Eventually, blindfolds and hand rags removed, we pulled up at the Public Prosecutor's Office. To be able to see again, after so many days, was a liberating experience. I found myself looking at anything and everything. How beautiful the world suddenly was when the ability to look upon it had been taken from you! And we were given food—something to eat that wasn't a hard lump of salted cheese. We had pita bread stuffed with *ful*, the sturdy staple bean mash of Egyptians; we wolfed them down, grateful for such small pleasures.

We were each assigned a public prosecutor. Mine was different from my previous interrogators. There's an Aesop's fable about the sun and the wind, in which the two weathers compete to see who can get a man to take his coat off: the wind uses brute force to try to blow it off and fails; the sun makes the man feel warm and relaxed and he removes his coat. The more the interrogators shouted at me, the more I buckled down and prepared for a fight. It was just how I had grown up in Essex; that's how we survived back in the day. But in the warmth and civility of that office I felt comfortable talking to the prosecutor. His name was Walid Minshawi, a suited, rather obese, educated man. Minshawi spoke about how he'd visited London on many occasions, and that his sister lived there. He played his "good cop" routine down to perfection.

"Do you know what they just did to us? They're torturing people down there!" I exclaimed.

"That's a shame," Minshawi said, "but if you don't cooperate with me, we'll have to send you back there. That decision is yours to make. If you refuse to cooperate, then I'll have little choice."

"I need a lawyer."

"Oh, that won't be necessary."

"What about the British Consul?" I asked. "When do I get to see him?"

"They know you're here," he said.

The consul should have been allowed to make contact with us within forty-eight hours. The Egyptians had been incompetent at best, mendacious at worst in getting back to them. But in the warmth of that office, and the relative civility of Minshawi's approach, I began to talk. I answered his questions in Arabic and in detail. I explained to him why I was in Egypt, discussed my studies in Alexandria, and emphasized at length that I simply wasn't there to propagate HT's message. Minshawi listened intently to my answers, then looked across to the scribe and told him which points he wanted written down.

"But that's not what I said," I would protest.

"It's OK, we're writing what you said, don't worry."

I found myself constantly correcting how my answers were being recorded, telling the scribe what he should write. But Minshawi would just laugh in his cheery, rotund way, and carry on. After four hours of questioning, each of our prosecutors wrapped things up, presumably at dawn. Without a chance to say goodbye, Hiroshi, my al-Quds companion, was released into the streets of Cairo that very morning. The prosecutors must have realized that his only misfortune was to have befriended me. I never saw him again.

For Reza, Ian, Hassan, and me, the situation was somewhat different. We were handcuffed—metal, not rags (it's strange the way that such small details make one feel relief)—and driven in a police van to what we later discovered was Mazrah Tora Prison. There we were placed in *habs infiradi* (solitary confinement) away from the main prison cell blocks.

After returning from hell itself, battered bodies lying over more battered bodies, the relief of having my own little space again was overwhelming. These cells were bare. They had no bed, no blanket, no light, no toilet, no sanitation, but this was my space, alone, where no one was questioning me any more, a place without screams and electrocution, a place where I could rest my weary head without fear of being beaten for oversleeping roll call, and so right now, in this moment, it was home. I had been awake for the best part of four or five days, and been put through the most extreme psychological distress. I was still in the same clothes I'd been wearing on my night out in Alexandria, and I was spent. I took my shoes off, used them as a pillow, and just slept on that concrete floor.

As the week dragged on, going back and forth to the prosecutor's office, I became hyperaware of my conditions. The fact that there was no toilet meant that I had to use a corner of my cell. I became aware of the cockroaches that covered the floor. And how hard the bare concrete floor was. And, having bitten on grit and insects in my food on more than one occasion, how tasteless the gruel being pushed through my cell door each day was. And how ever so lonely it was to be trapped in solitary confinement.

After seven days, the public prosecutor handed me a statement to sign. How much correlation it had to the answers I had given I had no idea. It was handwritten in impenetrable Arabic, and I could make nothing out of it. I literally had no idea what I was putting my name to. But the thought of being sent back to al-Gihaz was too much to contemplate refusing. Walid Minshawi had his way. I signed it.

Only after the questioning had finished were we allowed to see the British Consul. Gordon Brown[*] was a career civil servant in his late forties, well-meaning and sympathetic, but it was probably hard to offend his hosts without incurring diplomatic consequences. We were the first British political prisoners to be held in Egypt, and no one was quite sure what the rules of engagement were. In the post-9/11 world, it was unclear

---

[*] Not future UK prime minister Gordon Brown.

what was and wasn't permissible. From that initial meeting, it was clear that our case was of a different dimension from the ones that usually came across his desk.

Brown apologized for taking so long to see us. "We simply had no idea where you were being held," he said. This, it turned out, wasn't the only information the consul hadn't known about: Brown had no idea as to why we were being detained or what charges we faced. He was as lost as we were, and it was hugely dispiriting.

"What about our families?" I asked. Here, at least, there was a sliver of good news. Brown told me that Rabia and Ammar were safely back in the UK. But that was the only concrete answer we got. Cooperation between the British, American, and Egyptian intelligence authorities was clearly going on in the wake of September 11. A number of times in my interrogation with Minshawi, he had introduced details like, "We understand from the British that . . .", or "American sources tell us . . ." So even if the British Consul wanted to help us on a personal level, their instructions were probably not to upset an important ally in the War on Terror.

The night after Gordon Brown's visit, we were taken out of our cells and blindfolded and handcuffed again. As if to remind us of our place, we were frog-marched into the prison offices and interviewed again by Aman al-Dawlah. I recognized the interrogator immediately as the one who had questioned me back in Alexandria.

"We just want to be certain you're telling us the truth," the *zaabit* said. I asked him how long we were going to stay in prison.

"A week or two," he replied.

"That long?" I asked aghast.

The *zaabit* and his colleague burst into laughter. They must have known that a week was nothing inside Mazrah Tora. Some prisoners had been detained for years, even decades, under Egypt's Emergency Law, without so much as a charge. These were the *mu'taqaleen*. At the time of my arrest, 25,000 *mu'taqaleen* lined Egypt's prison system, all political detainees. I realized much later on, only after befriending some of these *mu'taqaleen* in Mazrah Tora, how green I must have sounded to the *zaabit*, fretting over a week in prison.

We were kept in solitary confinement, in those bare cells and sordid conditions, for over three months before we were ever charged. In the arid summer heat, it was difficult not to be overwhelmed by the sheer helplessness of my situation. The Aman al-Dawlah was the worst of both worlds: brutal and incredibly incompetent. I became consumed by this twisted combination of fear and boredom, which swirled around inside me until it became pure rage.

If driving to the African student's house that night of Ayotunde's murder had been my lowest moment, this was my darkest. With no one else to talk to and nothing to do, my mind began to wander. My cell had no lights, so once it was dark, it was dark. And as I tried to sleep at night on that hard concrete floor, I found myself flinching and flexing in case of cockroaches. I missed Rabia, I missed Ammar, I began to miss Southend; the life of that "Click"-suit-wearing B-boy seemed a distant dream now. I may have only been twenty-four years old, but from now on I would forever feel forty-two.

My mind began screaming out for activity, pleading with me for attention like Ammar used to. Boredom was on the verge of defeating me. I looked around, seeking anything to keep myself occupied, but all I had were the small stones on the floor. *Tai Ammi!* What did *Tai Ammi* do when I was unable to sleep, back in those days that seemed so distant now? That's it. She would make up stories. Those stories that sent my mind on adventures in magical lands of beautiful princesses and noble heroes. *Hey, stone, how are you, man? I name you Freddie-Fred, and you, stone, I name you Johnny-John, you know, after the old way, like Flavor Flav of Public Enemy. Yeeeeah, bwoyy! Freddie-Fred, can you beat Johnny-John in a race? Let's see. Ready, get-set . . . go!* And with a flick of my finger I would project the two stones, over and over again, across my cell floor, to see who won the most races.

And there were plenty of times in that dingy cell, during the darkest hour, when the only sounds in the still of night were the crickets somewhere far off in the reeds, that my mind turned to revenge. I wanted absolute, pure, and unadulterated vengeance upon Aman al-Dawlah. "My name is Maajid Nawaz, I am a member of Hizb al-Tahrir!" Rubbish! Did that stop Alaa' from having his teeth and testicles electrocuted for weeks and months till I could hear him pleading like a child? Did that stop Hisham from Kafr al-Shaikh being hanged by his arms till his joints gave way and he begged for mercy while his tormentors snorted *shakheer* at him like pigs? Did it stop the rape and electrocution of prisoners' wives right before their very eyes? Did any of it help Reza while he was tortured just for being unable to respond in Arabic? And why wasn't I tortured? Why was I spared this pain? Are they playing with my mind? Was Combat 18 playing with my mind? Where's Matt now? You took a stabbing for me. To protect me. *What did I ever do for you?*

Nonviolence? Nonviolence is only for those who have the luxury of an audience! An audience is an amazing thing. If people fear what you may do, if they fear the masses you may incite, they listen to you before you do it. What they really respect is your propensity to hurt them. The more you can hurt them, the more they respect you. But if people laugh at your pain, mock your suffering, goad you and prod you, knowing that you can do nothing, except sit back and say, "My name is Maajid Nawaz, Maajid, Maajid, Maajid Nawaz, I am a member of Hizb al-Tahrir" . . . Maajid! Maajid! Then what do we have left? Our own government couldn't even give a damn. *La'anatullahi 'alaykum*—May Allah curse you!

You preach nonviolence while you fund Mubarak and sell him arms. You train his men, and shake his hand with your bloodstained palms? Well, now I refuse to play by any rules. Let Nasim work for the *Khila-fah*—he doesn't need me. But Walid Minshawi, the thought of vengeance upon your ilk right now is what feeds me. How many years do you think you can keep me? I am but young and still so full of fire, it will take you many years to defeat me. You underestimated the flame that burns within me. And even as you catch me and eventually subdue me, I will kill as many of you as possible before you take me. And you will come to know how I went crazy, because of the poison that your own hands fed me.

And in the confines of that solitary cell, this all made perfect sense.

CHAPTER TWENTY-TWO

The Penguin Is Hit by Slippers

When we were finally charged, we came to hear about it second-hand. Some of the other prisoners had been listening to the radio, BBC Arabic, and they caught the announcement. Immediately they shouted the news over the wall, and the *shaweesh* guarding our cell told us what had happened. A few days later we received another visit from Gordon Brown, who confirmed the charges in detail. Hassan was not charged. He was released soon after and deported back to London. Reza, Ian, and I had been charged on two counts: first, for propagating in speech and writing the ideas of a banned organization called Hizb al-Tahrir; secondly, for possessing literature of said organization. Additionally, Reza also had a third charge: possession of a computer printer.

If our situation hadn't been so serious, the charges would have been laughable. Reza was facing a prison sentence for having a *printer*. None of us had been charged with what would have made sense, something that in our interviews we had all defiantly admitted to: being members of a banned organization. Instead, the charges were somehow more insidious: they were to do with discussing ideas and reading books—the right to free expression. This wasn't about HT or about Islamism; it was about something far more fundamental. It was about liberty, one of the basic tenets upon which civilized society is supposed to be based. Judge us by our Islam, and we will judge you by your freedoms.

The charges exposed Egypt, and the Emergency Laws of President Mubarak, for the police state that it was. We knew by now that our chances of getting off were nonexistent—they could make stick whatever they wanted to. We were looking at years in prison. By charging us in this way, it stripped them of any sense of moral authority. It made us prisoners of conscience. It meant that Amnesty International could take up our cause. And for Western leaders, it created uncomfortable questions for their entire Middle East strategy; they were supporting a regime that was torturing and imprisoning British citizens for "speech and writing."

Brown looked embarrassed as he discussed the charges with us. I could see him clearly for what he was: a career civil servant in an impossible position, the man in the bureaucratic chain who was seeing firsthand the human cost of the "price worth paying." There was a war on—the War on Terror. The first casualty, as the saying goes, is truth. I looked him in the eye and saw that he knew what we knew: Mubarak's Egypt was no great friend or ally. His state was built on the opposite of what the West was meant to hold most dear.

The trial, if one can call it something so legitimate, lasted the best part of two years. It would run for a week or two at a time, then there'd be a wait of another couple of months before the next session was called. There were twenty-six defendants being tried at the same time. In the courtroom, all dressed in white because we had not yet been convicted, we were held in a cage in the corner, like animals. The cage was so cramped that we would have to take turns sitting on the few benches provided, while the rest of us stood squashed round the sides.

Our group was taken to the courtroom each day in a convoy of blue police vans; the other defendants, all Egyptians, were being held in a mixture of other prisons. Each of us would be handcuffed to a guard for the journey. But rather than go in silence, we wanted to show Mubarak and his acolytes that he had not defeated us. We would not go quietly, we wanted the world to see us, and the world was watching. Each time we went in and out of that courtroom, we let off a huge cacophony of chants, rallying, and sloganizing. The TV cameras, BBC, al-Jazeera, and others, all of them loved the spectacle we were creating.

"*Usqut, usqut Mubarak!*"—"Down, down Mubarak!"

"*Laa nakhafu lawmata laa'im, al-Khilafatu fardun da'im*"—"We don't fear those who blame us, the *Khilafah* will forever be an obligation!"

We would shout these slogans in Arabic, all around Cairo's streets, as we were transported in those blue metal police vans in the scorching heat of summer, drenched in sweat. To speak so openly against Mubarak while under arrest was a shocking thing for Egyptians to hear at the time. Most would stand open-mouthed and gape as we passed, some would raise their fists in salute. Many broke down in tears of sympathy right there in the middle of the street. Anyone who caught a glimpse of our regular convoys in the streets of Cairo in 2002 will remember the sheer pandemonium we caused. After the total defeat of the jihadists in 1999, no one dared denounce Mubarak in public the way we did. Several years before the Egyptian people found the confidence to stand together in Tahrir Square, we were hoping to inspire the courage and confidence it would take for them to do exactly that. We wanted people in the streets to think: if they can do it from their prison vans, we can do it from our streets.

The miniature Qur'an I took from my flat, the last thing I took before leaving Ammar and Rabia behind, had somehow remained with me throughout my time in the torture cells. I would hold it up and wave it in full view while I shouted my slogans. It gave me strength and built my *eeman*. We were not criminals. We were proud political prisoners. We stood for Allah and His messenger, we stood for justice against tyranny and we were blessed to be chosen by Allah, as the ambassadors of *eeman*. Sure enough, our actions reached the world's media—TV, radio, print, and the rising Internet. The whole world was talking about the British political prisoners who claimed they had been tortured in Mubarak's dungeons.

The courtroom was packed. This was the first time that foreign nationals had been tried in a case involving torture. This created somewhat of a media frenzy. And it was in the courtroom that I discovered just how badly some of the other brothers had been treated. One of the brothers, Ahmed, described how his wife had been stripped and tortured before his eyes in order to force him to confess. Sadly his story was far from unique. We quickly used those moments in the cage to announce to the world how we had been treated. Journalists became fascinated with our case: liberals, Islamists, socialists, all began to sympathize with what had happened to us; news of our plight was spreading far and wide.

Everyone in that cage pleaded not guilty to the charges. But unlike our Egyptian brothers, we three Britons also admitted to our membership of Hizb al-Tahrir in the UK. As HT was legal there, we felt there was nothing to hide. In one of the subsequent court sessions, a letter was delivered from Jalaluddin Patel, the young HT leader in the UK who had tried to marginalize me after my return from Pakistan. The letter felt like a sofa-critique of how we had all carried ourselves. According to him we should have pleaded guilty, shown more defiance, and the Egyptian members should never have denied their affiliation to HT. We were disgusted. Jalaluddin, sitting in London, had the nerve to tell these men how to behave?

We wrote back immediately: you are no longer in our chain of command; we fall under the jurisdiction of HT Egypt. Its leader is in this very cage with us, having been tortured nonstop for three and a half months. These brothers have watched their wives tortured in front of them. You have not the right or moral claim to tell us what to do, and in doing so you presume to violate our channels of communication. Do not write to us again. Thankfully, he never did.

Right away, you could sense just how much the system was stacked against us. The judge, whose name was Ashmawi, would sit at the top of the bench, right next to the leading prosecutor, Walid Minshawi. As the case was to be tried under Emergency Law, both the judge and prosecutor were appointed by Aman al-Dawlah. The defense lawyers, meanwhile, were seated at the opposite end of the courtroom with the accused.

The three of us chose a brave man called Ahmed Saif as our lawyer. Saif's political views couldn't have been more different from ours. Saif was a communist, which under normal circumstances would have been anathema to our Islamism, but he had our respect. Saif had been imprisoned many times under Mubarak's regime, and yet he still continued to speak out fearlessly. We might have held different political views, but Saif was every bit as anti-regime as we were.[*]

---

[*] A couple of years later, Ahmed Saif would go on to become a key founding member of the *Kifayah*, or "Enough," movement, a liberal collective that decided to break the taboo of openly challenging Mubarak's authority in public. In those days, in Egypt, this was an absolute red line. Later on, while serving my sentence, I would read of Kifayah's brave anti-Mubarak protests. They would gather openly in the streets, attracting only around ten or twenty brave souls, surrounded by hundreds of riot police, and most people would laugh at their delusions of change. But Kifayah became the collective that ultimately snowballed into the Egypt uprising, led by liberal youth, in 2011. History, it would turn out, was on Ahmed Saif's side.

Almost two years after our arrest, on the day before we were due to be sentenced, Egypt's foreign minister, Ahmed Maher, was on a state visit to Jerusalem—*al-Quds*. Maher was a short, fat man with a huge bald head and a pointed nose. He looked like the Penguin from *Batman*, and we found this image of him comforting. As part of Maher's visit to al-Quds, he went to pray in the Al-Aqsa Mosque compound, the very same mosque where I had met all the HT brothers, and where I agreed with Issam Amireh that I would one day return. HT was founded in al-Quds, and we had a strong force of brothers all over Palestine. When Maher entered the mosque, to his utter horror, and the TV cameras' delight, he was met by a large group of HT protesters. They greeted him with a barrage of shoes and slippers hurled at him with abandon.

"Get out, you *kha'in*—traitor!" they shouted at him, as slippers rained down.

"*Zalim*—despot! Agent of America! You torture our brothers in Egypt, and think you can come into our mosque and pray? *La ahlan wa la sahlan*—you are not welcome in this mosque, out!"

Back at our prison, as the radio announced the humiliation of untouchable Ahmed Maher, the brothers, young and old, Islamist, jihadist, liberal, all whooped and rejoiced in spontaneous celebration. *Allahu akbar! Taste a fraction of what you have put us through, and see how you like it!*

The next day, Egypt's national papers were full of images of the Penguin being hit by slippers. It was a real day of victory for us. The Egyptian state would not let this one go, and sure enough, they took their revenge. In the wake of the assault, our sentencing date was delayed by another three months. When we were finally taken to court, the judge announced that he was dropping all the original charges against us, only to replace them with a single, new charge: *intimaa*—membership of a banned organization. After two years of a painfully slow trial, this time around there was to be no new discussion, no new defense. There and then, we were charged anew, convicted, and found guilty within the same session, on the same day.

"*Intimaa*" was a far more serious charge. Reza, Ian, and I were all sentenced to five years in prison: the other defendants got a mixture of between five and ten years for their membership of HT. As these sentences were read aloud in court, families began to cry, journalists began scurrying, and we rose up in defiance. Like lions roaring with pride, the courtroom was ablaze with our chants and slogans.

"*Allahu akbar! Allahu akbar!* We will never surrender!"

We began congratulating and embracing one another in the cage, and chanting and praying and prostrating in thanks to Allah for this opportunity to present our sacrifice for His cause. The judge rushed out of the courtroom in fear, and Walid Minshawi looked on in utter confusion: *How can they be celebrating? If I were in their place, I'd be crying.* And we did cry, tears of devotion to Allah, tears of love, tears of piety, the romanticism of struggle, and we knew we would go down in history. People would look to us and be inspired.

After two years, once the verdict was finally passed, in between frequent letters, we began receiving occasional family visits. How can I forget that day, Ammar, when you first came plodding along, by now a three-year-old, not knowing your *Abu* except for seeing him in chains on television screens? It's been two and a half years, my son. Two and a half years since these *zalimun* first tore you crying from my arms. And you came dressed in trousers, shirt, and tie, and extended your hand out to greet me, "*assalaamu alaykum, Abu,*" unsure of how formal I expected you to be. And I swept you up in my arms, not wanting you to see the tears welling in my eyes, and I held you close for all the years I was unable to hold you, for the days in the dungeons when I thought I might never see you again. I was so proud of your mother who had kept the memory of me alive within you.

Your mother approached me that day, her radiant face so happy, so proud and smiling at the visage of her man who had proven his sincerity to Allah's cause. And instantly, just by holding her in my embrace for the first time since my arrest, all my pain melted away, nothing mattered any more. My *ghimamah* of darkness had been lifted, and all I could see was the glow of your countenance. How happy I was on that day.

When Ash, my trusty HT protégé in SOAS days, came to visit me in Mazrah Tora, I was naturally excited.

"Ash, what's wrong?" I asked.

"I don't know how to tell you this," he said, "but I've left the group. I've left HT."

"Why, what happened?" I asked disappointedly.

"I don't believe in it anymore," he answered; and then in his typically irreverent way, "It's all bullshit, bro, the whole damn thing, they're a bunch of Muppets, clueless thick idiots, they're an embarrassment to Islam and Muslims."

Ash explained how he had become disillusioned with HT members, then with the group itself, and eventually with the ideology. Instead, he had become interested in Sufi mysticism.

"You're a bright person, Maajid," he said. "I know for a fact that you'll work all of this out and come to the same conclusions that I did."

My reaction was to laugh this off.

Ash was insistent though. "In Sufism, you have a sheikh, a spiritual guide," he continued. "My sheikh told me before I came here that he'd had a dream about you. He told me that not only are you going to leave Hizb al-Tahrir, but that you're going to become a great leader for Muslims."

"*Subhan Allah*—can you hear yourself, bro?" I said and laughed.

"It's true," Ash said, shaking his head. "That's what I came to tell you, and that's why I came."

I dismissed Ash's flattery as that of a friend overcome by emotion on seeing his one-time mentor in prison. But even so, there was something about the confidence with which Ash spoke that struck me.

Life doesn't stand still just because you are in prison. During those years my parents' relationship finally cracked, and they divorced. By the time Abi came to see me she had met a friend, who accompanied her to Egypt on prison visits. He was an Englishman, a non-Muslim, and they were not married. For the first time since my incarceration, my liberal upbringing was on public display in front of the top cadre of Egypt's hard-core jihadist scene, and I was torn: they're not married, he's a *kafir*, this is *haram*, prohibited. But he's come all this way to look after Abi, he's waiting outside the prison in the desert heat, from fear of offending me. This is a noble man, like Dave Gomer, like Mr. Moth. And so I found a solution.

"Can I conduct an Islamic rite, the *nikah* ceremony, to legitimize your relationship before Allah? It's just some prayers before two witnesses," I asked Abi.

"If it makes you happy."

"But he'll need to embrace Islam first—pronounce his *shahadah,* the testimony of faith. I can teach him what to say," I said.

"I just want you to be happy."

In this way, right there in the visiting area of Mazrah Tora prison, I supervised the conversion and Islamic *nikah* ceremony for Abi and her partner. I asked him to repeat after me, "*Laa ilaaha illa Allah* . . . There is no God but the One God, *Muhammad ar-rasool Allah* . . . and Muhammad is the Messenger of God." As my two witnesses I called over two of my prison friends, Omar, a Dagestani, and Hisham, a Dutch-Egyptian jihadist, famous for flying into momentous fits of rage against the prison authorities. I don't think Abi or her partner quite understood what the witnesses to their *nikah* were in jail for. Equally, I don't think Omar and Hisham quite understood Abi's and her partner's views. As far as my jihadist friends were concerned, I had just successfully converted someone to the Islamist cause. They were overjoyed, sharing a few sweets around the visiting area.

"Maajid's mother and her partner have just embraced Islam," they announced with warm smiles across the room. The implication being, of course, that, by virtue of being in this relationship, Abi had not already been a Muslim. Hisham, the Dutch-Egyptian jihadist, embraced Abi's partner in a long, tight hug. Hisham then explained how he must never compromise on his new faith, to always remain strong, and to remember to fight the enemies of Allah wherever he finds them. The Englishman nodded in sincere agreement, and Hisham hugged him again, believing he had just witnessed the creation of another martyr for Islam.

CHAPTER TWENTY-THREE

"Monocracy"

Mazrah Tora, where we would serve out the remainder of our sentence, was no ordinary prison. Originally built by the British in the days of the protectorate in order to hold political prisoners, it stayed ever true to its purpose. Over the years Mazrah Tora has held some of Islamism's most well-known ideologues. This was the prison where Sayyid Qutb, the ideological godfather of modern-day Jihadism, was held. It was at Mazrah Tora that Qutb wrote his seminal *Ma'alim fi al-Tariq* or *Milestones,* which led to his execution in 1966, instantly turning him into a flame that would light the sky for thousands of future Islamists.

The manuscript for *Milestones* was smuggled out of this prison by Mohammed al-Badei, a young devotee of Qutb's at the time and a member of Egypt's largest Islamist group, the Muslim Brotherhood. By the time I got to Mazrah Tora, Dr. Badei had again been imprisoned along with many of the Brotherhood's leadership in the case known as "The Professors," *Qadiyat al-Asaatiza.* By now he was a member of the leadership of the Brotherhood, serving on their Office of Guidance—*Maktab al-Irshad.* During those days we became close, exchanging many stories about his friendship with Qutb.

Badei would go on to become *Murshid al-'aam,* the Supreme Leader of the Muslim Brotherhood. After Mubarak's removal in 2011, the new Egypt is practically ruled by his group. Among other Muslim Brotherhood prisoners there were Dr. Essam el-Aryan, their spokesman at the time; and Abdul Monim Abul Fatouh, an Islamist presidential hopeful. The Brotherhood was not revolutionary or militant Islamists, and as such their members usually attracted shorter sentences, typically two or three years.

There were also many members of al-Gama'a al-Islamiyya, which until its ceasefire in 1999 had been Egypt's largest terrorist organization. This was the larger faction that broke away from Salim al-Rahhal's Tanzim al-Jihad after the assassination of President Sadat. Following their ceasefire, the majority of Gama'a's members signed up to what became known as the *muraja'aat* or "revisions," essentially renouncing their former militancy. However, they remained Salafists in doctrine and nonviolent Islamists in ideology. Among their number, with us throughout the holy month of Ramadan, was one of their founders, Sheikh Salah Hashim.

There were still prisoners at Mazrah Tora who had been involved in the assassination of Sadat back in 1981. The main assassins had been executed, but those involved in the plot who were still incarcerated included former Egyptian military intelligence officer Lieutenant Colonel Aboud al-Zommor and his cousin Tareq al-Zommor, who were held in our wider prison complex, and Dr. Tariq and Salah Bayoumi, who were held in our block.

Some of those executed in this case had been sent to their deaths back in 1982 by Maher el-Guindi, who was then the public prosecutor. As the years progressed, el-Guindi had gone on to become the governor of the province of Giza. One day the prison was alive with commotion. "What is it, what's going on?" I asked. Maher el-Guindi has been convicted for bribery and corruption, I was told. He would be joining us here in Mazrah Tora, to live among the remainder of the Sadat case, those still left alive after he sent their colleagues to the gallows. An extremely odd scenario unfolded that week in Mazrah, as some of the assassins of Sadat sat in conversation with the public prosecutor who had led the case for their convictions twenty-two years earlier.

"That man was a bloodhound, supervising interrogations over brutal torture, and I never stopped my *du'a*, my prayers, that one day he too would see justice as we have," Salah Bayoumi said to me that day. "Allah never raises anyone high except that he brings them down again. You watch, Maagid, one day my Lord will place Mubarak in here too, *bi iznillah*, with God's permission."

There were other jihadists too, like Akram, a British-Egyptian accused of supporting Islamic Jihad, Ayman Zawahiri's group before he joined bin Laden and started al-Qaeda. We befriended Akram and helped him to make consular contact after he told us tales of his brutal torture. Soon, a number of new foreign nationals began to arrive. They had all been convicted in the case known as *Qadiyat al-wa'ad*. These were a new breed of global jihadists, raised under the shadow of al-Qaeda. International, extreme, fully trained, and dangerous, they cut an intimidating specter. There were two Dagestanis, built like Russian bears: Omar Hajiyev and Ahmed. Omar was a professional bomb-maker. Having learned his trade in Chechnya and Afghanistan, he had been making his way to Gaza in an effort to train Hamas in his deadly skill. He had been sentenced to seventeen years in jail, but I often wonder what became of him after the mass prison breakouts during Egypt's uprising a few years ago.

Finally, at the other end of the political spectrum, there were leading liberal political prisoners and even those accused of homosexuality from Egypt's infamous "Queen Boat" case—where fifty-two men were arrested for being on a floating gay nightclub. A blue-eyed, well-off Egyptian named Sharif was the most visible prisoner accused in that case. Imagine if you can the dynamics between the jihadists and those from the Queen Boat case, being held in the same prison block.

Two of President Mubarak's more high-profile liberal rivals, heads of the Tomorrow Party, were there as well: presidential candidate Ayman Nour and sociology lecturer Sa'ad el-Din Ibrahim. Nour had stood against Mubarak for the presidency in 2005, finishing second. In other words, he won. As his reward, he was duly accused of fraudulently acquiring signatures to register his party, all one hundred of them, and sentenced to seven years' imprisonment. His criminal conviction meant that he was barred from standing for president again.

Dr. Ibrahim had written an article denouncing Mubarak's plans to groom his son Gemal as his successor. In the article, Ibrahim argued that Egypt must not become a "monocracy," a *jumlukia*, a hybrid phrase from the Arabic word *jumhouriya*, a republic, and *mulkiyya*, a monarchy. Ibrahim's was a seminal piece that shifted the liberal mood in Egypt against Gemal Mubarak ever taking the reins of power after his father. This infuriated Hosni Mubarak. Ibrahim's eventual conviction for "bringing Egypt into disrepute abroad" shocked the world, especially the Americans, and was crucial in shifting US policy toward pushing Egypt for more and faster reform.

Together with Ayman Nour's, the injustice Ibrahim faced went on to feed the growing liberal discontent that eventually led to Egypt's uprising, and Sa'ad el-Din Ibrahim became recognized as one of the liberal intellectual godfathers of this uprising. Many years later, as I addressed former president George W. Bush's conference in Dallas, I was to be reunited with Sa'ad el-Din over a video link; as the conference looked on, we conversed for the first time about our days together at Mazrah Tora prison.

All of these figures, like me, were imprisoned on one side of Mazrah Tora. In the same way that Egypt had a parallel judicial system—the official one, and the Aman al-Dawlah one—so this prison was split down the middle. On the opposite side of us was the criminal block, separated by guards. The split personality of the prison was emphasized by the dual command of the place: besides the prison governor, there was an Aman al-Dawlah *zaabit* assigned to our side. The name he used, probably fake, was Mohammed 'Ashwawi.

From time to time, Aman al-Dawlah would embark upon sporadic crackdowns against the Muslim Brotherhood, and because there were so many of them, the criminal blocks on the other side of the jail would have to be cleared out. We were all then stuffed, thirty or more at a time, into these group cells to make space. There'd just be row after row of beds with inches of space in between. These crackdowns would last for months, and while they went on, all the hard-fought-for privileges we'd gained would disappear.

The more people they shoved into those cells, the more the tension ramped up. Two or three prisoners had recently died before us in custody; one was Hisham, my cell-neighbor for a while. Whenever that happened, we would take to banging our cell doors all night in mourning. It was a macabre and eerie spectacle: loud metal clanging would echo throughout the prison, punctured sometimes by wailing and cries of mourning, tempered other times by the murmured sounds of desperate prayer.

Now, as the air was already thick with pent-up anger and the cells already overflowing, Aman al-Dawlah announced the arrival of yet more prisoners. Tempers boiled over. Over-crammed and frustrated, all of us swarmed out of our cells in a rage and, in a direct challenge to Aman al-Dawlah, refused to go back in. The prison sent in the riot police. The brothers, well-versed in prison rebellion, were skilled at causing a commotion, and had everyone whipped up into fervor. When they arrived, the riot police were an intimidating sight. Fully armored, they banged out a warning rhythm on their shields with their batons as they marched toward us in rows.

Focused fully on the approaching batons and shields, determined to stand my ground, I was too enraged to turn around and look at what was unfolding behind me.

"Enough! *Kifayah!* We've had enough! We're not animals, you cannot stuff more people into these cells!" I was shouting at the top of my voice.

But as I turned, to my surprise, I saw that all the Egyptian prisoners had retreated back into the cells! Their fervor had been nothing more than hot air. Or maybe it was experience: they'd been there before and didn't want to go there again. And now, outside alone, enraged, desperate, and just plain fatigued, I turned my anger away from the approaching batons and drumming shields and began shouting at the prisoners instead.

"Traitors, cowards! Where have you run to? Come and fight, you cowards!"

The brothers looked upon me pitifully. They saw me for what I was: a desperate and tired young man who just wanted to go home. Some of my friends came back out then, and gently held me close to calm me down, and guided me back to my cell before I was beaten black and blue.

"*Akhi* Maagid, there's no point. It's going to achieve nothing, we just have to exercise *sabr*—be patient. You cannot defeat Aman al-Dawlah like this."

Except for when we forced their hand, we didn't benefit from much British government intervention in that prison. In fact, "liberating" Iraq, rather than liberating tortured British prisoners in Egypt, seemed more of a priority for British politicians. Back in the UK, our local representatives David Amess and Stephen Timms kept the issue alive in Parliament, and our lawyer Sadiq Khan did whatever he could, including visiting us once in Mazrah Tora, but polite condemnations don't carry well across the oceans. These years marked the height of Bush's War on Terror: the Iraq War was unfolding during my incarceration, and the West needed Mubarak's support. Indeed, Prime Minister Tony Blair had accepted a succession of free holidays from Mubarak at the exclusive Sharm el-Sheikh resort while we Britons were tortured in Mubarak's jails. (Blair later stated he had made a charitable donation equal to the cost.)

But now and then, through acts of pure desperation, we were able to influence events. On one occasion, Ian got into an altercation with a prison guard. The guard complained to the warden, and Ian was duly thrown into solitary confinement. As the main conduit between us three and the warden, I went to see him to try to mediate on Ian's behalf.

"If I say Ian is in solitary, he's in solitary," the warden snarled. "And I suggest you back down immediately, Maagid. If you don't, I'll have you deported to another prison. I can set you up, have you killed by another prisoner, and no one will ever know. It's as easy as that."

This was simply too much. *You're threatening to kill me? You're threatening to do to me what Combat 18 never did, what Aman al-Dawlah never got round to? You, a prison warden in Mazrah Tora, are threatening to kill me?*

You obviously do not know my Lord, Creator of the universe, Master of the heavens and earth, for he has shielded me in the harshest of battles, and against the worst of all odds, and I would be grossly ungrateful to Him if I now cowered before your threat.

So I will resist you, like I resisted all those before you who tried to force me down, and I will win. Unified, we will all stand against you bi iznillah, *and we will fight you with all our might and all our bodies, and our Lord will see you fall. Mr. Warden, your time is up.*

⌒⌒

Immediately Ian, Reza, and I launched a hunger strike. For eleven days and nights we didn't eat, insisting that the warden be investigated and charged with threatening to murder me. As the media attention piled on, the prison was plunged into tension. By the seventh day, with extremely low blood pressure, I became bedridden and unable to stand. But unlike the riot-that-wasn't, this time it was just the three of us involved, and we were determined not to give in. It often amazes me at how men in positions of authority so often underestimate the willpower of the desperate.

There is an old tradition ascribed to the Prophet Muhammad, '*alayhi salam*—"The prayer of the oppressed is never rejected." Whether by divine intervention or sheer determination, in my experience, eventually, the oppressed always manage to turn the tables. On the eleventh day the authorities cracked. The British ambassador to Egypt came to the prison personally and explained that our demands had been met. (The warden was investigated and ultimately removed.) It was a rare, sweet victory in those harshest of years. But our most common prayer in prison during those years, which we shared with tens of thousands of other interned detainees, was to see Hosni Mubarak face justice during our lifetimes. My Lord does not fail me.

PART THREE

RADICAL

Start a huge, foolish project, like Noah . . . it makes absolutely no difference what people think of you.

—JALALUDDIN RUMI

CHAPTER TWENTY-FOUR

Where the Heart Leads,
the Mind Can Follow

In some ways, the most interesting story from my days in Mazrah Tora was the one unfolding inside my own head. Many political prisoners, and criminals alike, harden their beliefs and skills while incarcerated, and come out more committed than ever. With its rich mix of prisoners, from the assassins of Sadat all the way through to the liberals and even homosexuals, Mazrah Tora became a political and social education *par excellence* for me. The studies, conversations, and experiences I gained in Mazrah Tora, over months and years, were crucial in overcoming my dogmatic allegiance to the Islamist ideology. Having entered prison as an extremely idealistic twenty-four-year-old, full of rage against society, and having nothing else to do but study over the course of four years, I came to reevaluate everything I stood for.

My change of views wasn't an overnight process. Ideological dogma doesn't work like that: it's not like a tap you can just switch off. So ingrained was HT's cause in my very being that it would be a process of years for me to work my way out of it. First emotionally, and then intellectually, then politically, and finally socially, until piece by piece I had to reconstruct my entire personality from the inside out. This is not an easy thing to do.

Although I'd started this process by the time I left prison, I would return to the UK still a member of HT. It would be another year before I announced my departure from the leadership of my group, and more time still before I finally dropped the remnants of my Islamist baggage. That's five years to overturn the ideological convictions that had defined me for over a decade. This was the prism, the mind-set from within which I had viewed the world: to unpick that, in descending order, until I questioned all my fundamental convictions was nothing less than a paradigm shift, and in those days there was no one to guide me.

The starting point of my leaving had probably occurred back in Pakistan. My treatment out there had given me pause for thought about HT: not the ideas themselves, but the people who were in charge of the organization. A similar moment occurred at the trial, with Jalaluddin's "supreme command" that we should be more "defiant." I had plenty of time to think about these events, lying awake in my cell.

Each time, it had been me who had gone forward, sacrificed everything for the cause: in Pakistan, my degree and educational future, and in Egypt my body, yet each time there were idle hawks hounding me due to their own personal insecurities. This didn't challenge my faith in Islam, or initially my belief in the Islamist ideology, but it did make me question the capability, tactics, and strategy of these figures. This, I believe, is the beginning of the process of leaving an ideological movement, for those brave enough to see their thinking through to its logical conclusion. Like an onion, you have to continue to peel back each layer and expose the next one, no matter how painful that process may be. My disillusionment with HT leaders and their tactics meant that by the time I was sentenced, I was ready for some serious thinking about my ideology.

The behavior of HT members, though, was not the only factor that started me on this route. I believe that where the heart leads, the mind can follow. After our conviction, Amnesty International adopted us as "prisoners of conscience" and began campaigning openly and vigorously for our release. This came about through the tireless work of John Cornwall, who insisted at Amnesty that our case was worthy of the organization's support. Having been put away solely on the basis of our beliefs, we deserved to be adopted officially as prisoners of conscience. John, a frail Christian man in his eighties, campaigned for us with a passion not seen in most twenty-year-olds, and our story together eventually became the subject of an Amnesty video aired on television.

Not everyone within Amnesty agreed that they should be campaigning on our behalf. I later learned that the subject of whether the group should support us became quite a hot topic internally. The counterargu-ment was that, although we had committed no crimes ourselves, the ide-ology that we preached advocated a gross invasion of human rights. Once our version of "the *Khilafah*" was formed, we advocated an aggressive policy of foreign invasion and expansion, the death penalty for apostates, "rebels," and homosexuals, and a forced dress code for women. Thieves would be punished by having their hands cut off, and adulterous women would be stoned to death. Why should Amnesty campaign for our human rights, when given the opportunity we would deprive others of theirs?

There's no easy answer to this question. What if, prior to coming to power, Adolf Hitler had been detained for his not-yet-violent beliefs in national socialism? Or what if, closer to my own story, Mubarak came to be tortured as Gaddafi was? Amnesty resolved this controversy in the manner of Voltaire, best summarized using the words of Evelyn Beatrice Hall: "I disapprove of what you say, but I will defend to the death your right to say it."

Biases aside, that's the only possible answer for me to arrive at. Any other stance makes a mockery of the universality of human rights. Even now, as I spend my life campaigning against extremism, I would still want Amnesty to protect prisoners in a similar position to the one I was in. And I will defend people's right to read *Mein Kampf,* or Qutb's *Mile-stones,* even as I fight both far-right fascists and Islamists equally. But the devil is in the details. Where I disagree with not just Amnesty but also many human-rights groups is in their failure to highlight a clear and obvious distinction between a victim of human-rights abuses and a cham-pion of human-rights causes.

Any prisoner held solely for the nonviolent expression of their beliefs has an unconditional right to our support as a fellow human being. However, not every former prisoner should be automatically hailed as a champion of human rights and placed on platforms as a spokesperson for human-rights causes. I will campaign against anyone who would want to torture Mubarak, for he remains a human being, but I would never extend to any one of the Mubarak regime's men a human-rights platform from which to address an impressionable crowd of students. He may have been mistreated after the uprising, but he is not now some great champion of human rights. A human-rights platform, by virtue of what it is, must necessarily have a stricter tolerance threshold.

Many human-rights groups blur this distinction when it comes to propping up Islamist and jihadist speakers on their platforms. Life is more complicated than that. Islam, Islamism, and jihadists are more complicated than that. Just as the world is not a binary between Muslims against all others, it is also not a binary between America against all others. The long-term credibility of human-rights causes rests on the perception of principle, a perception damaged if populist causes are reduced to campaign binaries, whether during the War on Terror or recently during the Arab uprisings. In this, I gently agree with Gita Sahgal's principled critique from inside Amnesty's International Secretariat, for which she was suspended from Amnesty.

As a former Amnesty prisoner of conscience, and as someone forever indebted to the organization, my advice comes from someone who discovered Amnesty's principles the hard way. Amnesty's support was a fundamental part of my political journey. I am, in part, the person I am today because of their decision to campaign for me. It's because of this that I do not want to see anything dilute that message; their work on human rights is too important for that.

It was the unconditional nature of Amnesty's support that humbled me: *you're a human being, so you deserve our support.* There was something very powerful and very pure about that premise. Like many ideologies, Islamism derives part of its power from its dehumanization of "the other." It is easier to dismiss and do things to "the other" if you consider them as unworthy: the Nazis and the Jews; the jihadists and the infidels. Throughout my teenage and young adult life, I had been dehumanized by others and desensitized to violence. As I got sucked into the Islamist ideology, I in turn began to dehumanize others.

Amnesty's support challenged all that: instead of dehumanizing people, it *rehumanized* them. I thought now of Sav and Marc, of Matt and Dan—stabbed for their association with me, of Dave Gomer and Mr. Moth, of my mother's partner, bonds that were forged with non-Muslims who cared about my well-being. And instead of being fascinated with the afterlife and death, for the first time in many years I began to reconnect with life itself, and with humanity. This is not something you can teach; it is something you must live and feel. Where the heart leads, the mind can follow.

———

I began to see the other human interventions around me in a different light, too. At 8:50 on the morning of July 7, 2005, three bombs exploded on London Underground trains in a coordinated terrorist attack. Just under an hour later, a fourth bomb was detonated on the back of a double-decker bus in Tavistock Square, right by my university, SOAS. In total, fifty-two people were killed and many hundreds injured. Sa'eed Nur had become many Sa'eed Nurs. Jihadism had finally struck London. From the distant vantage point of Mazrah Tora at the time, I felt revulsion when I heard the news. In contrast to my reaction to 9/11, I immediately thought of the human cost involved. Gone were my ideological acrobatics and Machiavellian justifications. This time I saw the plain and simple death of innocents.

That wasn't the view of everyone in the prison. Many, including Omar Hajiyev, my Dagestani bomb-maker friend, were initially proud of the terrorists' action. Omar was still at war, and London was a legitimate target. Britain had taken part in the invasion and occupation of Iraq, where they had bombed and killed thousands of "our" civilians and occupied "our" lands. The government that led that action had been voted in by popular vote. Politically and theologically, Omar was convinced that "an eye for an eye" was the appropriate deterrent for these infidel *kuffar*. It was his job, after all, to train young jihadists in the fine arts of doing exactly that. Omar felt satisfaction that we Muslims were finally prepared and able to strike back. Here was a man fully and operationally capable of preparing such attacks himself.

Whereas before I would have either quietly scoffed at *kuffar* suffering as not my affair, or toed the HT line that such acts were simply a distraction from our real goal, this time I actually felt the human cost involved. Compassion now moved me where once only anger had. I turned to Omar and asked him: Do you know where the biggest demonstrations against the Iraq War took place? From news clippings in old newspapers,

I showed him pictures of the million-strong march of February 15, 2003, in London. The fact that the largest demonstration against the Iraq War was not in Egypt, Saudi Arabia, or Pakistan, but in the UK, touched me. These were human beings in London, campaigning for other human beings in Iraq. *Rehumanization. Where the heart leads, the mind can follow.*

I explained to Omar that just because a government goes to war doesn't mean that everyone supports it. Democracy is not the same as a referendum, and there was no referendum on Iraq. And even if there had been, it would not have endorsed willingly killing Iraqi civilians. "By your argument," I continued, "you should blow up Turkey before you detonate a bomb in London. Turkey's a member of NATO, which supported the war as well. Turkey's a democracy, too, and the protests there were nothing on the scale of those in London, so surely by your logic the Turks must have been more supportive of the war than the British."

Omar shook his head: "But the Turkish people are Muslims; we can't be killing our own people."

And I continued to push: "So whom you kill is less about principle and more about expediency? Human life for you is about political point-scoring? Then how is what you're fighting for any better than what you are fighting against? How can you feign disgust at Bush's war games when this is just a game to you, too? Don't you see, if the Turkish people aren't a legitimate target for attack, then neither are the British people. Look," I pointed to the placards being waved on the march, "here are Christian groups, Muslim groups, political groups, students, old-age pensioners, just people. *Ittaqillah, akhi,* fear Allah's judgment."

And we went on like this for an entire day, discussing theology, politics, and war, until eventually Omar began to rummage his hand through his hair and appear extremely uncomfortable. So I stopped pushing. For a moment, I thought he might turn on me. I'd seen him wrestle in the prison yard with bear-like Ahmed, and if he wanted to, he could settle this in an instant. But Omar was no fool, certainly not unintelligent, and he had grown very fond of me. A couple of days later, there was a knock on my cell door. Omar was back: "Maajid, I've been thinking about what you said. I've decided you're right. I agree. British civilians are not a legitimate target."

On that day I felt that I had saved many future lives from the hands of this bomb-maker friend of mine (who after Egypt's uprising is also likely roaming free). And I was proud for myself that I had achieved something small but worthy, proud for him that he was humble enough to change his mind, and proud for the British people, who despite not being able to "Stop the War," did not fail. Their campaigns, energies, and lobbying did not fall on deaf ears here, not in Mazrah Tora and not with Omar. For here the price was worth it.

The rehumanization process that Amnesty had helped kick-start within me was furthered by others in prison, too. Ayman Nour was one of the inmates in Mazrah Tora whose views were furthest away from my own at the time. He was a remarkably interesting figure to spend time with in jail. He was both ambitious and audacious. Nour had been prepared to put his head above the parapet and actually challenge Mubarak for the presidency when to do so was still a cardinal sin. That alone, regardless of any political disagreements, was worthy of respect.

Nour and I would spend time going for walks around the prison yard, and I would interrogate him about his thoughts, motives, and dreams. I wanted to understand what motivated people to sacrifice for a cause other than Islamism. That intrigued me. For me, it was Islamism that allowed us to finally stand up to Mickey, allowed me to challenge the African students at Newham, and allowed me to face my torturers with absolute conviction. But Nour and Sa'ad el Din Ibrahim were prepared to face jail for liberalism, a Godless cause and the bane of religion.

But there was something of himself that Nour recognized in me. Nour, it turned out, had not always espoused such liberal views. To my shock, and to his delight, Nour explained how in his younger days he too had been a supporter of HT. Our paths had even crossed back in London, when he attended the same Wembley Arena *Khilafah* conference that shook the country with thunderous roars of *Allahu akbar!*

"What? But . . . *subhan Allah!* So why did you leave the cause?" I asked, genuinely interested.

And as we walked across the desert sand of Mazrah Tora's prison yard, Nour looked at me and simply said, "I grew up."

The way he said it caught me completely off guard. *I grew up.* The phrase made me pause. I had been expecting a long pseudo-theological justification for why he had left, but Nour never tried that. Knowing my training would tear his arguments to shreds, he knew he'd lose. He was too smart to get into that. Instead, he just left that phrase hanging there, and me to think about it. Which I did.

While my heart led the way, through bonds with people like John Cornwall of Amnesty, Ayman Nour, and Sa'ad el-Din Ibrahim, I also decided to nourish my mind. I used my time in prison to study everything I could about Islam, the faith that I believed formed the basis of my Islamist ideology. And, as a nod to Abi's encouragement during my childhood, I decided to read as many English literature books as I could.

I became good friends with a brother called Mahmood. Mahmood was sentenced to fifteen years for being in the Cairo leadership of al-Gama'a al-Islamiyya, though he had since recanted his beliefs. Mahmood was a graduate in Arabic from Dar ul-Uloom, Egypt's most prestigious Arabic college. On top of brutal torture, Aman al-Dawlah used psychological warfare as well, intimidating Mahmood's wife into divorcing him. I spent many days perfecting my Arabic grammar, morphology, and vocabulary in Mahmood's cell. In return, I would try to help him learn some English.

One of the difficulties that Arabs have in speaking English is that Arabic doesn't contain the letter "p," and for some reason they manage to shorten the double-vowel sound "ee" to a single "i." A word like "please," therefore, typically comes out as "bliss." One day I was trying to teach Mahmood the difference in pronunciation between "peach," "beach," and "pitch." I said the words slowly and pronounced them heavily: "Peach . . . beach . . . pitch." Mahmood listened carefully, and then with all the sincerity a former jihadist could muster, proudly spoke my words back at the top of his voice: "Bitch, bitch, bitch!" He looked at me in bewilderment as I burst into fits of laughter.

I found other teachers for my studies, too. I befriended a reformed member of Islamic Jihad, Momin, and Abdul Hameed, arbitrarily interned for five years, who was a graduate of Sunni Islam's most prestigious theological university, al-Azhar, as well as Sheikh Nidal, an exceptionally bright theologian also arbitrarily interned for around three years. All three instructed me well in ancient Islamic jurisprudence. It might sound strange, given how committed I was to the Islamist ideology, but I had never properly studied Islam or the Qur'an. Islamism was a political movement before it was a religious one, and many of its followers came from irreligious backgrounds. This was something that the Salafists have always taken us to task for. Sure, I'd read excerpts over the years, discussed specific passages in HT *halaqahs* where scripture was deemed to back up our arguments. But I had never attempted to study the Qur'an properly for myself.

So in Mazrah Tora, I committed half of the Qur'an to memory at the hands of another reformed member of Islamic Jihad, Ali Fiqih—sentenced to twelve years—who had an *ijazah*, a qualification in the art of *qira'ah* recitation at the hands of a master. To fully appreciate the ancient text of the Qur'an, one needed an exegesis, and understanding the dense theological jargon of these exegetes is a Herculean task in itself. This is what my various teachers helped me with. I began to develop a deeper, fuller appreciation of Islam than I had ever experienced before. That dark period of solitary confinement, when I had vowed to become a suicide bomber, now seemed like the thoughts of a distant madman.

During my incarceration, al-Gama'a al-Islamiyya, formerly Egypt's largest terrorist group, had also been busy publishing their *muraja'aat* of jihadist thought. These *muraja'aat* deconstructed the violent ideology of Jihadism using traditional theology. Crucially, they were written and published by the leadership of Gama'a themselves. Here was, for the first time, an entire jihadist organization admitting that it had got it so very wrong. Book by book, I devoured these *muraja'aat*. Though I had never been a jihadist, it wasn't hard for me to start seeing how the basic arguments used here could be extended to the very ideology of Islamism itself. And my mind started joining dots that even Gama'a hadn't dared to connect.

Reading classic English literature did for me what studying Islamic theology couldn't; it forced my mind to grapple with moral dilemmas. Upon our request, the British Consul would regularly send us books from the embassy library. I devoured the classics but, in addition, focused on Tolkien's *Lord of the Rings* trilogy, reading it twice over. I couldn't shake the moral paradox that Gollum-Sméagol came to embody. Gollum was an evil creature prepared to do anything to get his One Ring back. Yet, as the story climaxed, it wasn't the hero Frodo who destroyed the ring. As "evil" Gollum had done before him, Frodo eventually succumbed to the lure of the ring, making a last-ditch attempt to keep it. It was in fact Gollum who pounced at the ring, biting it off Frodo's finger, before accidentally falling to his death in the lava of Mount Doom, destroying the ring with him. An evil character had thus inadvertently achieved the good that the story's hero failed at, and saved the world. This moral complexity began to fascinate me.

I also read and re-read Orwell's *Animal Farm* and Golding's *Lord of the Flies*. *Animal Farm* made me ponder on life under "the *Khilafah*" ruled by the likes of Imtiaz, Irfan, Abdul Wajid, Jalaluddin, and their ilk. *Lord of the Flies* served as a stark warning about the tyranny that could arise from the most innocent of souls with the best of intentions. Even the innocence of children was insufficient to guarantee against injustice, yet here we were working to set up a system that would install a ruler for life, run by people like Abdul Wajid, or Jalaluddin, and claiming to rule in God's name.

Over the years, I began to reexamine everything I knew and had been prepared to die for. Though we had placed establishing an "Islamic State" and "implementing" *shari'ah* as law above even the most religious of rituals, I couldn't help noticing that not once were the words "law," "state," or "constitution" mentioned in the Qur'an. When I thought about this further, it made historic sense. The Qur'an was an ancient text, while political ideas such as a "unitary legal system," "codified law," "statehood," and "constitution" were modern political concepts: they did not exist at the time the Qur'an was written.

I went back to look at what Islamists held as the last true example of legitimate government: the Turkish Caliphate or Ottoman Empire. Again, history was telling me a rather different story than HT had. This Caliphate never had the sort of unitary codified legal system that HT was proposing to "implement," with the *shari'ah* as law. Instead, justice was run under what was called the "Millet" system—a pluralistic legal structure where the interpretation of *shari'ah* was left to local community tribunals. These would hear evidence and interpret *shari'ah* as they saw fit. There was not even any law obliging people to go to these tribunals—it was a voluntary decision. The Ottomans offered general edicts on administrative matters, but these were different from any sort of legal system.

The idea of a unified, codified legal system, and of having a judiciary subservient to that legal system, and of having a constitution that frames this legal system, and a state that protects that constitution by monopolizing the use of force, all of these concepts emerged with the birth of the European nation state. These were modern, *Western* constructs. The Ottoman Caliphate, struggling to adjust, even initiated a reform process, known as the *Tanzimat* reforms, in an attempt to study how best to incorporate these new European ideas into their empire.

Throughout almost all of Islam's history, a single interpretation of *shari'ah* was never adopted and enforced over society as a codified system of law. In fact, unlike in its English rendition "Sharia Law," where we use *shari'ah* as an adjective describing the noun "law," in original Arabic *shari'ah* is simply a noun. The specific "adoption" of an interpretation of *shari'ah* as law by a ruler was not religiously mandatory, and it didn't happen in history. Unitary legal systems were a European idea, and worse, the desire to merge law with religious canons was specifically a Catholic pre-Reformation idea. This realization had profound implications for my beliefs. Rather than justice—legal consistency—being derived from Islamism, Islamism relied on *Western* concepts of justice to get off the ground. I buried my head in my hands as I slowly realized: we Islamists were the bastard children of colonialism.

I now thought about people like my trial lawyer, Ahmed Saif. He wasn't an Islamist; he was a communist. Yet there he was, fearlessly campaigning as a founding member of Kifayah—Egypt's first openly anti-Mubarak platform organized along non-Islamist lines. Ayman Nour and Sa'ad el-Din Ibrahim were liberals, from the opposite end of the spectrum, yet they too were passionate that Mubarak should go.

I also thought about Amnesty International, and their campaigns for prisoners of conscience like myself. In each of these instances, they were driven by the same principles as I was when I had joined HT: to fight for justice. Yet their causes and beliefs had nothing to do with Islamism.

I had always been taught—and had passionately believed—that the presence of Islamism meant justice, and the absence of it created injustice. But now I began seeing things differently. What Ahmed Saif and Ayman Nour were campaigning for—from their different viewpoints—was undeniably just. The freedoms that Amnesty International was championing were something I'd learned for myself to be manifestly just. Yet none of it was Islamism.

I came across a tradition of the Prophet, concerning Najashi, the Christian Habasha king who protected the Companions by providing them with shelter as they ran from the pagan Quraish. *Malikun 'adlun la yuzlamu 'indahu ahad*—"A just king under whom no one is oppressed," said the Prophet, *'alayhi salam*. Justice, from a Christian king, endorsed by the Prophet himself.

I'd only joined HT because of the fire that injustice had lit inside me. And as I started to decouple justice from Islamism in my mind, it was the beginning of the end of my belief in Islamism. If justice and Islamism were separated, then not only was it possible to have one without the other, it also meant that there were situations where *the two might come into conflict*.

It was an uncomfortable recognition, and not one that I swallowed immediately. I shied away from its implications for a long time, retreating back into the comfort of my Islamist beliefs. But as hard as I tried to bury them, I couldn't shift the nagging thoughts I had in my mind. And where the heart leads, the mind can follow.

CHAPTER TWENTY-FIVE
No Right to Silence

Like the desert scorpion, Aman al-Dawlah still had one final sting to deliver us before we were allowed to leave Egypt. The Egyptian prison system is supposed to release prisoners after serving three-quarters of their sentence. Our release date—the marker of three years and nine months—had come and gone. Paperwork, we were told. Bureaucracy. In Egypt, one could never be sure if it was incompetence or something more sinister behind things. One only had to look at the tens of thousands of white-clothed prisoners arbitrarily detained—the *mu'taqaleen*—to witness the elasticity of the Egyptian justice system.

Then one day, out of the blue, a *shaweesh* came running into my cell:

"Maagid, they've arrived! They've arrived! Start packing your things, *inta murawweh*—you're going home!"

But does anyone ever leave Egypt's jails? What of my friend Ashraf al-Nahri, who completed a ten-year sentence, only to be taken on a round-trip to al-Gihaz and interned again? I still remember the look of total sadness on his face. Have you ever seen total sadness? He left in the blue overalls of those with sentences, only to be processed and returned in the white clothes of a *mu'taqal*, arbitrarily imprisoned again with no respite. I went to him then to make him a cup of tea and to share words of comfort, perhaps a game of chess; al-Nahri was a master of chess, and he had always been kind to me.

Put aside cruelty, put aside violence, even put aside murder for a moment, and consider justice. Justice, if it means anything, must mean to adhere to your own confessed principles. If you claim to stand for the rule of law and democracy, then stick to what you claim and be judged by it. If you claim to stand for death, and violent revolution, and armed struggle, then stick to what you claim, and be judged by it.

These men stood by their ideology, they fought and in some cases killed for their cause, and they were judged by it. Killed, tortured, or locked away. Now they have recanted. They have not only served their time but they have also renounced their past because they trusted in your "rule of law." So will you now be judged by your principles? Or what else is left, but a return to lawlessness and vigilante vengeance? And so I didn't dare hope that I would be returning home. After all this was Egypt: "we do as we please."

As word rippled through the prison that we were leaving, a succession of people came up to say their farewells. Salah Bayoumi, convicted for the assassination of President Sadat, in prison since I was four years old, gave me a farewell present—a copy of the Qur'an with a dedication from him at the front. He began to cry as he embraced me and bade me farewell. His eyes carried the burdens of a tortured soul, confused about his own past and doubtful about his own future. As much as possible, I tried to keep my emotions in check out of respect for the many who had completed their sentences only to be re-interned as *mu'taqaleen*.

I had less respect for the prison authorities. We were taken in to see the prisoner governor, the one who had threatened to kill me. He had not yet been transferred but was clearly worried about what was to happen to him. He asked us three to sign a prepared statement about our stay in prison. I read through the document. What a complete travesty it was. It went into farcical detail about how well we had been looked after throughout our stay. Each of us refused. I handed the governor his pen back. *If you want to know what I think about Mazrah Tora*, we told him, *you'll have to watch it on al-Jazeera, with everybody else.*

The metal blue police vans came to pick us up. We were fully expecting a deportation order, to be escorted straight to the airport, put on a plane, and handed over at Heathrow Airport. Until we set foot on British soil, I refused to let myself believe that we were actually going home. As it turned out, Aman al-Dawlah didn't want to let us go without saying a special form of goodbye first. When the door to the van opened, I could see a guard holding my old nemesis, the *ghimamah*, a rag with which to blindfold my eyes, and my worst fears were realized.

This time, we were taken to Lazughli, the only Aman al-Dawlah building to match al-Gihaz for notoriety. We tried to protest. We explained to the guard that we had documentation, demanded to see a British representative, but he just laughed.

"No British here," he said. "Just Egypt. Now silence!"

Blindfolded again, and held in another torture center, day turned to night and my dreams to darkness, as the terrifying backdrop of tortured souls continued without let-up. Scream after scream began to echo through the building. Four years had passed since our ordeal in al-Gihaz, but Aman al-Dawlah had not changed. They were still practicing the systematic use of torture as their default interrogation device. Except this time with a sickening, macabre twist. Penetrating through wild screams of agony, we could hear the clear, distinct, rhythmic sound of the guards listening to a recorded recitation of the Qur'an as they tortured people. Such a flagrantly sacrilegious display could also be a twisted psychological trick—to say to the Islamist detainees, *your faith won't help you here.* Or perhaps in some sort of sociopathic way, they thought they were doing God's work.

After some hours I asked to go to the toilet. A guard picked me up and escorted me through the building.

My mind was playing tricks on me. *My name is Maajid Nawaz, I am a member of Hizb al-Tahrir. It's OK,* I said to myself as I tried to ward off the nightmares of al-Gihaz, *calm yourself, Allah is with you. You will get out of here.*

As I came out of the toilet, I heard a quiet sobbing in the bathroom area and turned to speak to a young man nursing his wounds.

"*Akhi,* what's wrong?" I asked, unable to see him through my *ghimamah.*

"I-I-I cannot stand," the man cried. "The pain. My feet, my legs feel like they are burning."

"What have they done to you?"

"The electricity," came his broken reply.

"You have been chosen to be tested by Allah for your faith in Him. Be proud of yourself, don't cry, *akhi,* you're a man now. You join the ranks of the heroes and martyrs of old."

And then the guard returned. "No talking! I'm warning you, we can do that to you too!" he shouted.

"I'm sorry, I'm sorry, I was just asking this brother where you had gone."

Eventually I heard the morning *azan.* We had been in Lazughli all night, sixteen hours before we were finally processed. This time the blue van made no more unscheduled stops. British officials were waiting for us at Cairo International Airport, our passports and travel documents ready. An Aman al-Dawlah *zaabit* was to escort us all the way back to Heathrow on our British Airways flight.

"Any trouble," the *zaabit* leaned over to tell us, "and I'll cuff you immediately."

That was the last threat the Egyptian authorities threw at me. It was an empty gesture, and a pointless one. I was so exhausted after that sleepless, horrendous night in Lazughli that, as the plane took off, I fell into a deep sleep for most of the journey.

❧

Egypt—after five years in your care, I bid you farewell. Despite all the pain we shared, I cannot forget you. How could I? Blood, sweat, and tears are not so easily removed from porous souls. I came to you a boy, those years ago, full of lofty ideals, my soul at peace with God, my ideas at war with man. I leave you now, my hair gray, full of confusion, my soul warring with God, my ideas finding peace with man. Don't cry, my love, *habibti,* for though together we were stranded on a barren floor in anguish, and though together we banished insanity by embracing pain, our Lord will see us through, as He always has. And the spring that you planted in my chest shall carve its path and ripple through your streets soon enough; like a river bursting its banks, it will flood your youth with hope. So prepare to rise again, for you are *Misr,* the land of the brave, *Ard al-Kinanah.*

As soon as we landed, the Aman al-Dawlah *zaabit* melted away as if he had never existed. We were met on the plane by officers from London's SO15, Special Branch.

We sat in the specially built interrogation room at the airport. "Are you going to read me my rights?" I asked wearily. Having just come from one police state, I wanted to feel reassured that I hadn't flown back into another. "You know, my right to remain silent and all that?"

The officer smiled at me thinly. "Not here, Mr. Nawaz," he said. "If you refuse to answer any of my questions, it's a criminal offense."

"What? I'm sorry, how's that possible? Don't tell me you've done away with the right to silence?"

"Mr. Nawaz, UK law no longer grants you the right to silence in any port of entry or exit in the UK. I'm afraid that I will need a sample of your DNA and you will need to answer my questions. If you do not, I will have to charge you with a criminal offense."

"Then I demand access to a lawyer, or is that a criminal offense now too?"

Fortunately, we had a lawyer waiting for us on the other side of the gate. Stephen Jackobi of the group Fair Trials Abroad had been active in campaigning for our release and was now with our families awaiting our return. Jackobi was friendly but clear about the law.

"The officer is correct, I'm afraid," he said. "Since September 11, the rules have changed: at any port of exit or entry into the UK, there is no right to silence. That's why they want to interview you now, rather than on the other side of the barrier."

"So what should I do?"

"My advice would be to cooperate for now," Jackobi said. "You'll have to answer their questions."

"And if I don't?"

Jackobi sighed. "They'll arrest you. There's nothing I can do about that, I'm afraid."

And so I answered their questions briefly and succinctly, desperate just to go home.

"If you hear anything, or come across any information that might be useful, would you mind keeping us informed?" the officer concluded.

"No," I replied. "I have no intention of doing anything of the sort."

After four hours of interrogation, we were finally released. Jackobi had stayed to advise us. And not just on the legal side of things. He'd dealt with prisoners returning from abroad before, and in the short space of time he had, he wanted to brief us as best he could.

"I've got to warn you," he said. "It's going to be difficult. Don't think for a second that once you walk through that gate that all of this is over. To readjust to normal life after what you've been through is going to be really hard. You need to realize that it is going to test your relationships to breaking point. I've seen so many people come back and for their marriages to fall apart. The statistics show that most people in your position end up getting divorced or abuse their spouses. I don't want that to happen to any of you, but you've got to be aware that you'll really have to work at your relationships. Otherwise, you'll end up the same way."

And as we stood at that airport gate, alive and alert, just about to be reunited with our families, I turned to Jackobi with a wide, warm smile. "Don't worry about me, Stephen. I'm married to a loyal wife whom I will embrace with all my heart. She's the mother of my child, and she kept me alive out there."

I walked out of that gate, oblivious to the forces that were about to tear my heart clean out of my chest.

CHAPTER TWENTY-SIX

How Many Years Did You Fail?

I see you, London. Heathrow, immune from change during long spells of absence, oblivious to the distance of lovers, you seem to welcome me back with no less warmth than when I left. I see you, London. How I despised you and loved you. How I hated everything you stood for, and yet when deprived of your familiarity, your openness, how I missed you miserably. At once head of the colonial snake that poisoned my people and snared my lands, yet also bastion of justice, the rule of law and fair play. And even now, as I rush to embrace you again, your boots stamp on my people in Iraq and Afghanistan, while I know that my boots are nowhere safer than resting in your green parks. Why do you confuse me so, beating me with one hand while drying my tears with the other? How I tried for thirteen years to rip you out of my soul, to deny you, to bury you, but how I've longed for you to claim me from the hell that I just returned from. London, I see you.

❧

The media interest in our return was huge. We were greeted from every angle by the flashing of bulbs and the shouts of journalists. I looked around and all I could see was a blur of people—*where shall I turn, where is my family?* Then I heard my dad's familiar voice rising above the din, shouting, "Maajid!" My mind instantly traveled back to when I was a boy. I would make these silly little gifts for my dad, from the spare materials in his garage, in anticipation of his return from Libya every month. How long a month would seem in those days! And Dad would walk in, Stetson on his head, jeans, belt, and boots on, and he would shout, "Maajid!"

He would scoop up my tiny little body and hold me in a huge bear hug. Instinctively, my body moved toward the voice I could hear, until I found myself embracing my dad with joy. Next to him, right there by his side, was Rabia. She was crying.

And there I saw Abi, the womb that bore me, whom I had hurt so much through the years. And I wanted to tell her everything, about the storm that was raging in my heart, about how I wanted to change, to make her proud again, about all the literature I had read. But there was no time. Then there was my childhood best friend, my protector and brother, Osman. I did you proud. I stood up for what we believed in, I fought them all the way, I didn't back down, just as you showed me. And Sorraiya! My God, you're all grown up, from nine to fourteen, what a difference! My sister, I'm sorry you had to grow up on a diet of torture, jails, and anger. No child deserves that. I will try to show you a better way now, to heal our hearts together. And John Cornwall, my friend, my humane friend. As I saw him for the first time, I felt like I knew him well.

But it wasn't just our friends and relatives at the gate. Elbowing and jostling for position were many members of Hizb al-Tahrir. No longer were we fallen soldiers who "hadn't been defiant enough": at a stroke, we were returning heroes, and the leadership wanted to bask in the glow of our media attention. Here was Jalaluddin, the man who had admonished me from the safety of his sofa, welcoming me back like he was my best friend. "You are our heroes, brothers!" he proclaimed as he shook my hand and offered me whatever help I needed to settle back into the group.

I desperately wanted to see my son Ammar, who was waiting for me at my in-laws' house. As quickly as I could, I greeted family, friends, and colleagues and got into a car with Rabia by my side. I remember holding her hand in that car, as I had done in the car journey home the day we were married. And she smiled at me now as she had smiled at me then. And we drove off together to see our son.

Ammar was now six years old, and had been running and messing around before I arrived. As soon as I opened the door and he saw me, he stopped. His expression completely froze: it was such a shock for him to see me there. For a moment, as when I had first seen him in prison, I was worried about his reaction. But as in prison, I needn't have been. He gave a little jump and ran over to hug me. I held him so tightly then and lifted him high into the air with a love that was deep and pure. We had a celebration meal, and then went back to Rabia's flat, our flat, which she had carefully arranged and decorated for my return. And that night, after I put Ammar to sleep, I slept awkwardly, not knowing how to express to Rabia the storm raging in my chest.

"Shhh, sleep now," she said, "there's no need to talk. We'll have plenty of time to talk."

It didn't take any time for Hizb al-Tahrir to start seeking my involvement in the group's UK leadership. The brothers had organized a press conference for the following day. My mind was haunted with thoughts of all the brothers we'd left behind, of Akram and so many Egyptians who were languishing in jails for years well beyond their sentences. I owed it to them, to the world, to get matters off my chest, and to speak of the atrocities of Mubarak's regime.

That day we addressed al-Jazeera, Al Arabiya, the BBC. As we had promised the warden, we told the world about Mazrah Tora prison and the brutal transgressions of Aman al-Dawlah. Later that week, I was interviewed for the BBC, toeing the party line, playing my role as an HT spokesman, desperately trying to cling on to anything familiar from my past to remind myself of who I was. During this period, I gave many talks for HT, spoke at rallies of thousands, and even shared a platform twice with "Napoleon," a member of the Outlawz, rapper Tupac Shakur's former group. After Tupac's death "Napoleon" had become a hard-core Salafi, disrespectfully declaring to all that Tupac was now burning in the fires of hell.

And throughout this period, Rabia looked on with that same wounded look in her eyes, while I focused on the only thing I knew best: galvanizing and rallying crowds.

In the weeks and months ahead, I took stock of my situation, and my self-esteem began to falter. I was twenty-eight years old, still an undergraduate, the father of a six-year-old I had to support, unemployed, and a recently released Islamist political prisoner in a post-9/11 world. I began to panic. For the first time in my life I began to feel old, old inside my heart and in the depths of my eyes. The burden of what I knew and what my conscience was telling me about Islamism was heavy on my mind. My doubts kept growing, but the more they screamed for my attention, the more I sought to bury them away. This is all I've known in my adult life: "My name is Maajid Nawaz. I am a member of Hizb al-Tahrir." *What was I if not this?* So I set myself some goals—if I could give myself something to aim for, then that might help lift me out of this trough.

My starting point was my degree. I went back to SOAS to see if they would allow me to continue my law and Arabic degree. They could quite easily have told me where to go. I'd done my first year and taken two years out, done my second year, and then was imprisoned for four years halfway through my placement abroad. Abi though, God bless her, had been persistent in persuading the university to keep my place open.

To my relief two of my old Arabic lecturers, Muaz Salih and Muhammad Sa'eed, were still at the university and had kept the doors open for me. SOAS let me back in. I'd been arrested a few months before I was due to take my third-year Arabic exams, so my faculty head said I'd have to pass those in order to be allowed back. As my one-year placement in Egypt had unexpectedly been extended by several years, my ability in Arabic was not in question. I took the exam and got 97 percent.

If I had just stuck to keeping my head down and getting my degree, things might have been fine. But HT asked me to join their leadership. There were two leadership committees by this point. After London's terrorist attacks in the summer of 2005 (7/7), Prime Minister Tony Blair had threatened to ban the group. In response to this, HT had created both a front leadership and a secret leadership committee. The "executive committee" was the publicly recognized leadership, but the real power lay behind the scenes, in a "*wilayah*" committee. Because of my media profile, I was given a place on the front committee. Because Nasim knew me well and trusted me completely, he put me on the secret ruling *wilayah* committee too. Again, I had my feet in two worlds.

I began trying to find a way to accommodate my changing views within HT. I felt the way forward was to hone my arguments and convince other members to come around to my revised position. In that BBC interview, the reporter, Sarah Montague, asked me what I stood for, and I replied that HT was calling for a "representative Caliphate." This led to a great deal of furious discussion inside the group. What did I mean by a "representative Caliphate"? The Caliphate was "*The* Caliphate." There should have been no argument about that: this was the imposition of Islam on society.

But I had seen how people could change in prison. I had seen how someone's certainty to the point of death could turn to regret and sorrow at lives lost. I'd seen how almost every facet of our ideology relied on modern European political philosophy, and that any Islamic legitimacy it had was at best debatable. I had seen how Islam could be abused to justify almost any political position, including torture. I remembered the character flaws of all the Islamists I'd come to know, both inside HT and others. It was fanciful, I felt, that just because someone was a committed Islamist, they would run things the right way. This came back to the decoupling of Islamism and justice in my mind. There needed to be some accountability, not only built into the system but also into the very formation of our ideology itself. Our ideology, ultimately, was a man-made construct.

Nasim, who was now running the *wilayah* committee, actually began to praise me. He applauded me for my new ideas, and for my ability to think outside the box. He told the others that this was how we were going to move the organization forward. But as the year went on, and the discussions continued, I became increasingly disillusioned at the slow response I was getting. My questions bore deep, to the very legitimacy of imposing *shari'ah* as law. After learning and studying how this had never been done before, I began to see such a goal as un-Islamic. How could I remain inside an organization that I now believed was striving for a goal that ran against the very spirit of Islam?

As my doubts grew, I increasingly began to consider my HT brothers as ignorant of Islam, politics, and history. My mind felt as if it was going to implode. One wrong word and I could be unceremoniously suspended from the group as a deviant. Then any legitimacy I would have to make reform arguments would be useless. I had to speak to someone. I turned to Rabia, whom I could trust with my secrets. But although Rabia was the more moderate, she was still an HT member. The reality now hit home to me like a blow to the head: my own wife would be a stranger to who I had become.

Whom was I fooling? I'd spent most of my life recruiting from her family, I'd been responsible for the recruitment of her Uncle Abdul Rauf, Dr. Qayyum's younger brother, who had been tortured in Pakistan's jails. Rabia's cousin, who had joined HT after my recruitment efforts, had also been arrested in Pakistan, and his mother had died while he was still incarcerated. I had argued a hard-line position to her entire family, bringing nothing but tribulation upon them. And here I was now, after she had just waited five years in the name of this cause, trying to convince her that my new ideas were correct instead. As the Prophet, *'alayhi salam,* had advised, "Indeed there is a kind of magic in eloquent speech." She was right. *Why should she listen to me now?*

"You were right then and you are right now," she scolded, "no one can argue with you, Maajid. You are always right. So what is the point of having this discussion?"

To my dismay, she was unprepared to even entertain the discussion. And so, miserable and lonely, I began seeking solace among new faces at SOAS, overly keen to make friends. I frantically searched for whatever "normality" was meant to feel like. I desperately sought out people, not to recruit, but who could remind me how to live my life again; I simply wanted friends I could call my own. And then, in the junior common room of SOAS, I met her.

Fatima Mullick was the opposite of everything I stood for. (Or was she everything that Abi stood for?) Proudly Pakistani, proudly female, her answer to the face veil was to brazenly wear her beauty, her answer to stoning the adulterers was to cite Rumi's "Let the Lovers Be," her reply to Qutb was Khayyam, the mystical Persian sage. She embraced life in all its splendor, whereas I had come to embrace the afterlife in all its austerity. She despised the madness of men who cared more about whether their position in prayer was correct than they did about spilling innocent blood.

Fatima was a political science post-graduate, and she approached me one day with the question, "So, are you a PhD student?" She must have seen my salt-and-pepper hair, or perhaps she saw the age in my eyes.

"No, I'm an undergraduate."

"Oh really, how many years did you fail?" she blurted out, laughing.

My pride was hurt. "None. I was imprisoned in Egypt after 9/11. I served four years. I've just got back."

Her face changed. "I, I'm sorry, I didn't mean to . . . where are you from in Pakistan?"

"Gujrat," I replied, smiling at her bluster.

"Oh, you mean Gujarat in India?" she asked, too flustered about whether she'd caused offense to think straight.

"No, there is another Gujrat, in Pakistan." And after having caused her further embarrassment, and quite enjoying it, I decided to befriend her.

I tried to recruit Fatima. Like the death throes of a dying body, I tried to project all my insecurities about my existential crisis onto her. I showed her my BBC interview and told her about how important it was that we Muslims know our identity properly.

And Fatima just looked at me square in the face as she said, "I may not be able to argue with you, or respond to your points, but I know what you are saying is simply bullshit. And you know what, Maajid? So do you!"

And that was it. My mouth froze as I struggled to speak. Fatima had no idea she had just become the proverbial butterfly that would unleash a hurricane. I had just found my new best friend, my rock of support among the confusion that was my life after leaving HT.

In the end, the timing of my decision was forced. While I had been in prison, Nasim had been in Bangladesh, setting up HT out there. He now needed to get back there to resume this work, which meant that—after Jalaluddin's inevitable fall from grace—HT UK would need a new leader. I had the media profile, the international experience, my Arabic and Islamic learning, I had cut my teeth the hard way, and I had the intellectual ability. For Nasim, I was the ideal candidate.

The ball dropped. I could go no further. It was one thing to be arguing for my views within the organization; it was another to be leading a group whose ideology I was beginning to question. The timing couldn't have been worse. I was in the middle of revising for my final exams, but I had to make a move before anything was formalized. I called Nasim, friend to friend, mentor to protégé, and asked to see him alone at a cafe in London's Brick Lane.

I was very nervous; this was to be one of the most stressful conversations of my life. I had been a member of Hizb al-Tahrir for over a decade. I had known Nasim since I was fifteen years old, and through that time he had been a friend and mentor to me through so much. But I owed it to him to tell him my decision, face to face.

"I know you are preparing me to take over the leadership of the group, but it's something I'm going to have to turn down. In fact, I'm . . . I no longer believe in HT and I need to leave the group immediately. Please consider this my resignation." I just blurted it out.

Nasim was completely astonished.

"We can work this out," he argued. "You have so much to give. Come to Bangladesh with me, we have a real chance of getting into power over there," he said. "We can run the country together, you and I."

We sat in the cafe, going back and forth. It never got heated. It was more about sadness, and regret, and resignation. Nasim knew that I wouldn't have come to this decision lightly. He knew that I'd thought through the consequences, and that it would be unlikely we'd see each other again. In the end, as a favor to him, I agreed that I wouldn't announce my resignation for two weeks. Maybe it was to give him the opportunity to tell the rest of the group himself, or maybe he wanted time to have another go at persuading me. If it was the latter, I didn't give him the chance. I had my phone switched off throughout those two weeks.

When the deadline had passed, I released an email to the media, rather than leaving it to the group to announce—and twist—the reasons for my departure. *"In the name of God the Compassionate, the Merciful,"* I began. *"Assalaamu alaykum."* I tried to keep my resignation as brief and as dignified as I could:

> *I have deemed it necessary to announce that, after serving in Hizb al-Tahrir for twelve years and since I was seventeen years old, I have decided to leave the party and resign my membership effective immediately. I humbly request that I do not discuss the reasons for my*

decision at this moment in time, and ask that I be left to complete my
much delayed final examinations. Forgive me for any offense caused.

I hit "send" and a dozen years of my life came to a close.

I called Osman during this time. I somehow felt that I needed his support. All those years earlier we had started on this journey together; he had left HT long before I did. "Good," he said. "Don't worry, Islam is more important than HT." He didn't yet know that it was precisely the modern *politicized* interpretation of Islam that I actually had a problem with. I didn't have the heart to tell him.

I then immediately called Abi. As I told her my news, she broke down in tears of joy right there on the phone. "Finally, finally, my son, I knew you would make the right decision. In my gut I could sense this was happening to you. I'm so proud of you, thank God, thank God!" She cried, "All these years I've waited to hear this news coming from your lips, I knew you would eventually see the truth. How could you not? You're my son, it was my womb that bore you, I'm so proud of you!"

But my situation with Rabia was deteriorating day by day. I desperately needed the space to learn who I was, to construct myself anew, piece by piece. Every time she asked me to spend more time indoors, I felt suffocated; I tried to remove myself from everything associated with HT and their ideology. It was a terrible situation to be in. Guilt riddled my insides, and I felt as cruel as Aman al-Dawlah, if not more so. But I needed to define myself again before letting anyone else in.

As much as my wife struggled to find the Maajid who was so suddenly taken from her that night in our Alexandria flat, there was no turning back for me. I had seen too much, learned too much to ever again be that same Maajid she had married. In many ways I think I was a nicer person then, and like so many nice people who seek power, I wanted to force everyone else to be nice. It's a form of totalitarianism.

Now I felt like a horrible person, full of guilt for what I could see was happening to my marriage; yet I no longer wanted the world to be nice. I just wanted everyone to leave everyone else alone. I just wanted to be left alone. And I began to stay at home less and less because I was desperate to escape the claustrophobia of Islamism, my new prison.

But I had nowhere to go, nowhere to sleep. I slept wrapped in a blanket, in the backseat of my beat-up Renault Clio, parked outside the university in Russell Square, while my final exams were going on. If those last days in Newham were my lowest, and if those spent in solitary confinement my darkest, then these were my loneliest days. Sad and confused, I needed help to find myself again but couldn't rely on anyone to help me; the only people who were there now saw me as a traitor. I needed Abi, I needed home. While sleeping in that car I became certain: I would not be able to purge myself of Islamism while living with Rabia.

I didn't have the heart to tell her face to face I was leaving her, as I had with Nasim. I knew it would only result in more futile debate. Instead, I left her a letter announcing my decision, and just left. After one of my final exams, Rabia turned up at SOAS with her two sisters and brother-in-law, trying urgently to reconcile. But I wouldn't speak to them. I didn't know who I was anymore, how could I speak to them?

It took all the willpower I've ever known to turn away and run from her that day. But run I did. I got into a friend's car to leave, and pulling away, I could see Rabia running after me in the middle of the road, calling out my name, pleading for me to stop. As we sped off, I caught the look of anguish on her face. I hated myself for what I had to do.

CHAPTER TWENTY-SEVEN

Civil-Democratic Intimidation

I spent thirteen years of my life supporting Hizb al-Tahrir. Thirteen years as a deeply committed Islamist ideologue totally prepared to sacrifice all for my cause. My journey from prison to my departure from the group was not an easy one to make. Rage was a powerful factor blurring my judgment. Pulling myself away from the anger at what was done to us in prison was mentally exhausting. *How would Tony Blair vacation in Egypt, paid for by the Egyptian State, while British citizens were being tortured there? How could the world protest at the atrocities of terrorists while governments behaved in a similar way?*

Wives had been stripped bare, tortured in front of husbands. Children had been electrocuted. People would occasionally drop dead in our prison, succumbing to wounds from torture. Thousands of men had been interned for over fifteen years without charge. From those interned, some had in desperation doused themselves in kerosene to set themselves on fire. I witnessed this all. Yet Egypt was the second-largest recipient of American aid, and an ally.

Thus, the Islamist narrative of a clash of civilizations—*kuffar* against Muslims—echoed ever stronger in my mind. This was a war with no rules. Neo-conservatives had sent the message out loud and clear. The only voice heard was the voice of power, all the more reason for Islamists to seize the reins of such power. *Abandon Islamism? And join what? Where was that counternarrative?* As an Islamist I enjoyed the backing of thousands of hardened men, many who had died for my cause. Where were the Muslim martyrs of pluralism? Why were the few who spoke out ridiculed or ignored?

I had married into Islamism; all my friends and many family members were Islamists. I would leave a global movement, having been a hero, to become an outcast. What would I say to Rabia? What would I say to her Uncle Abdul Rauf who—after I recruited him to HT—had his spine dislocated in Pakistan's jails? How would I face her cousin, whose mother died from shock because he was not released from prison at the end of his sentence? I would have to look at these people in the eyes and say: *It was all so wrong. I was so wrong.*

But so what? Why should I be the only one to admit his mistakes? Is not winning the war more important than truth? This maxim, I knew, was also subscribed to by some on the left, the regressive left. For them, winning against capitalism was far more important than it was to their allies. I watched as our ideology gained acceptance and we were granted airtime as Muslim political commentators. I watched as we were ignorantly pandered to by well-meaning liberals and ideologically driven leftists. How we Islamists laughed at their naïveté.

I was horrified to realize that I was abusing my faith for a mere political project. After learning in prison that Islamism was not the religion of Islam, but rather a political ideology dressed up as Islam, I no longer felt guilty for criticizing a political system inspired by modern European constructs, justified by seventh-century norms. And despite what was holding me back, my desire for justice spurred me on. Ever since I had been a child, I had found unfairness, injustice, and oppression intolerable. I now saw how we had used these grievances as a means of perpetrating our own injustice, not only against non-Muslims but against other Muslims too.

We had used, even abused, people's grievances to suit our ideological agenda. What did the invasion and occupation of lands have to do with enforcing dress codes upon Muslims? Why should the solution to secular Arab dictators be *Islamist* Arab dictators? Why did foreign intervention mean that we needed to silence critical thinking and open debate by labeling it as heresy and blasphemy? In reaction to our own insecurities about our identity and position in the world, *we*—not anyone else but us—had become the real obstacle to progress for our own people.

But what was the problem with Islamism so long as it remained nonviolent? Was it not the right of Muslims to adopt whatever ideology they
chose? Of course, it was the right of Muslims to believe that one version
of Islam must be imposed as law over their societies, just as it was the right
of racists to believe that all non-white people should be deported from
Europe. But the spread of either of these ideas would achieve nothing
but division. If the dangers of racism are apparent, even in a nonviolent
form, then it was the same for Islamism. Communalist identity politics,
self-segregation, and groupthink are far more damaging to societies in the
long run than the odd bomb going off here or there; it is such a milieu
that keeps breeding bomb-makers. It's odd that Hizb al-Tahrir in Arabic
means the Liberation Party. We had hijacked the minds of the Muslim
masses, and those minds needed to be liberated.

Slowly and alone, I began to unpick the last thirteen years of my
indoctrination, concept by concept. Ideas that I had once held sacrosanct
were unraveling in my mind, revealed as crude political deceptions. My
whole character would have to change. Every moral frame of reference
that I had built up in my mind required reevaluation. I was not merely
questioning jihadist terrorism as the Gama'a had done in their *muraja'aat*
recantations. That was easy. No one really deserves a thank-you for promising not to randomly kill you. No, I needed to go further. I needed to
question the very basis of the ideology itself. The idea that an interpretation of Islam must be imposed as state law now seemed to me un-Islamic,
counterproductive, and anathema to what was fundamentally just.

This ideology of victimhood had taken the responsibility for reform
away from our people, and taken satisfaction in blaming everyone else for
our ills. My political grievances were still there, but I saw now that we no
longer required Islamism in order to campaign against them. *Islamism
itself had in fact become one of the grievances that needed challenging.*

As I began to formulate this idea, the sheer scale of what we needed
to do hit me. By now, Western governments, Muslim-majority governments, media outlets, and hundreds of thousands of Muslim youth world-
wide had all come to assume that Islamism was Islam. Leaving Islamism
was one thing, but outrightly challenging it was another. Who better to
do it than someone who knew the ideology inside out?

My head felt heavy as I took in the enormity of the task ahead. Most Muslims are not Islamists; yet the organized minority dominates the discourse. Islamism had been creeping upon Muslims for over eighty years now, and little had been organized to directly challenge it. Yes, certain Muslim associations have been stressing a tolerant Islam, but this was not sufficient. The good Islamist will merely co-opt that message into his political ideology, as we did. We tolerated the different strands of Muslim theology, and we were well-disciplined when engaging with non-Muslims. By doing this, our aim was to co-opt everyone into our political goal.

Unless Muslim communities stood together to reclaim the faith, we would have no chance of challenging this ideology that had grown among us. It also meant that certain leftists and well-meaning liberals needed to stop pandering to a global totalitarian project. It meant, crucially, that normal Muslims needed to take a stand by closing their doors to Islamism.

Most importantly, Muslim leaders and theologians needed to be firm in the face of this ideological onslaught against our faith. And while theologians are especially responsible for leading the Muslim resistance against Islamism, Muslims could not be expected to do this if Islamism's twin, Islamophobia, was not also challenged. There are those out there who harbor an irrational fear of Islam. Islamophobes and Islamists have this much in common: both groups insist that Islam is a totalitarian political ideology at odds with liberal democracy, and hence both insist that the two will inevitably clash. One extreme calls for the Qur'an to be banned, the other calls to ban everything but the Qur'an. Together, they form the negative and the positive of a bomb fuse.

A counternarrative needed to be created out of these ideals: a respect for basic human rights, pluralism, individual freedoms, faith, and democracy had to be reconciled with Islam not in the ivory towers of academics but out there in the hearts of the masses. To do that, we needed to permeate all elements of society with the counternarrative: politics and policy, media, the arts, social media, academia, and public opinion. We needed the backing of states, parties, coalitions, and movements, and we needed ideas, narratives, leaders, and symbols, all pooled together, just as Islamism had been doing since the 1920s.

For decades Islamists had spread their ideology at the grassroots, while Muslim liberals either detached themselves in their mansions or embroiled themselves in the corrupt politics of their regimes. As Islamists, we would look upon these elite Muslim liberals as completely out of touch and detached from the sentiments of their people.

Was it any wonder then that Islamism had become the most effective social phenomenon among Muslims in the world, in dictatorships and democracies alike? Dictators would either try to co-opt it or brutally suppress it. Both tactics inevitably aided its growth. In democracies, electoral politics could only react to votes, and if the most organized bloc is the Islamist bloc, they will have their way, intimidating government after government with their opportunistic use of Islam to influence policy. Why were governments everywhere scared of upsetting the sleeping giant of Islamism? Why had they gradually succumbed to the Islamisation of their societies? Why did they not fear a similar internal democratic lobby? *Where was the democratic intimidation?*

What I saw clearly now was the need for a radical new social movement, a Muslim Brotherhood equivalent, sitting above short-term party-political goals. It would advocate the democratic culture among Muslim grass roots: a civic-democratic intimidation pushing for democratization. Sitting in the seclusion of Abi's home in Southend, I realized that my quest for justice that began here was far from over.

I knew now what had to be done, and I knew the cost of doing it

CHAPTER TWENTY-EIGHT

The Decade-Late Apology

It was on the site of the 7/7 attacks in London, appropriately enough, that Quilliam came into being. Two years after the bombings, London life had moved on, and apart from the commemorative plaque in Tavistock Square, much had returned to normal. The London bus with its top ripped open had long been taken away, and its image was now a memory of history. Another number 30 continued the journey that bus should have completed, driving past a parked, clapped-out blue Renault Clio. Inside, an exhausted student was trying to sleep, curled up under a blanket on the backseat.

In the weeks after leaving HT and during my estrangement from Rabia, my car had become my home. I had my final exams to take and had to be in London rather than with Abi back in Southend. When I left HT, I also left my friends behind. My life had been so entwined with the organization that my entire social circle had gone with it. I didn't have a job or any money, and so the car became where I went at the end of the day. I'd drive around until I found a space in one of the streets near SOAS—Tavistock Square, Russell Square, usually—and that would be where I spent the night.

But it wasn't all bad. My final graduation ceremony, ten years after initially enrolling, was quite a sight to behold. SOAS had run out of seats in the main hall so some of us would receive our certificates and proceed to an overspill room to watch our own graduation ceremony via video link. I had waited ten years for this moment; my family was proudly in the main hall expecting me, and they had no idea that we would be denied seats alongside them. SOAS had just kicked the wrong guy out of his own graduation ceremony.

Quickly, I rallied and organized the by-now extremely distressed students. We were outraged, and I spread word that I would refuse to receive my certificate unless they made space for us all in the main hall. The majority of students followed my suggestion, and others wouldn't argue against my reasoning: if prison couldn't stop me from graduating, I'd be damned if this would. We announced our refusal to cooperate, declaring a sit-in. The management had no choice but to cave. A hasty compromise was suggested: we were told that we could sit on the stairs in the main hall, and we readily agreed.

It was a peculiar twist of fate that on that day Irene Khan, then secretary general of Amnesty, was to receive her honorary doctorate from SOAS. Irene was onstage to witness what happened next. As my name was called, I rushed onto the stage, and overcome with joy, I hugged the university president and raised my hands in celebration. To my surprise, the students started cheering my name, and they rose in a standing ovation. As I embraced her, the university president asked, "What did you do to get a standing ovation?"

"Oh you really don't want to know," I replied, laughing.

Earlier that year, I had one of those moments when the universe seems to align itself perfectly. At just the time when all my HT friends were viciously turning on me—Traitor! Sell-out! Agent!—I bumped into someone from my old days.

"Maajid! *Subhan Allah! Habib*—my dear friend, you're back from Egypt. I saw your news on TV. How are you?" Standing on the SOAS steps, exactly where I had last left him, still wearing his trademark blazer, was none other than Ed Husain, now studying for his PhD.

It had been ten years, but the bond between us remained as strong as ever. Ed was in the process of writing his acclaimed book, *The Islamist*, which would end up being published around the same week I left HT. Sensing that my thoughts had moved on considerably, he asked me to look through and comment on the Newham sections, which served as a reminder, if I needed one, of how far I had come. By this point I knew that I was going to leave HT but hadn't broken the news to the world yet. In fact, the first version of *The Islamist* concludes with the speculation: "Which direction will HT go in, the moderate direction of Maajid Nawaz, or the hard-line one of Jalaluddin Patel?"

The conversations and debates Ed and I shared in the back of my clapped-out car during those days were critical to informing our joint direction for years to come. For both of us, it wasn't enough just to leave HT behind.

"We need to reform the way we Muslims see politics, and revive knowledge of our traditional jurisprudence through the Sufi path," Ed suggested.

"No, *habib*, trust me, everything, absolutely everything needs to be reformed, and that includes traditional . . . what I call medieval, jurisprudence. It simply doesn't address our contemporary problems."

"But, that's . . . that's nothing short of a complete overhaul of the *deen*," Ed exclaimed.

"Exactly. I'm talking about enshrining absolute freedoms, human rights, a respect for individual liberty, women's rights, and reconciling modern scientific facts with Islamic interpretation. And I don't just mean in the lofty circles of academia or theology, that's all been done before, but actually out there, in the real world, just as we did for Islamism back in the day."

"Yes, we can start doing *da'wah* for these values, just as we did back at Newham for HT." The glitter in Ed's eye began to betray his excitement.

"Indeed! *Da'wah* for a religion-neutral space in the public sphere, *dhormo niropekhota*, I think it's called in Bangla. You know, it's so bad that in Pakistan's Urdu there is no appropriate word for secularism? They use *laa-deeniyat*, which implies no-religion. With such a translation, obviously Islamism will have a head start."

"You do realize there is a mammoth task ahead, Maajid, we will be roundly attacked," Ed said rather too eagerly. "But I have just the idea for how to begin. Let's start it all with a think tank, to lay the seeds for this idea globally, and let's call it after the Englishman who opened England's first mosque, to make the point that Islam doesn't always have to clash with society. His name was William Quilliam!"

And so it was, in that old Renault Clio, parked somewhere on Russell Square in London, the idea for Quilliam was born.

What Islamism had done in Europe was to set Muslim communities back an entire generation. It created a separatist agenda that became self-fulfilling. In an effort to protest discrimination, all it achieved was further segregation. Further social immobility created more discrimination, not less. When Omar Bakri Mohammed had left HT, he had founded al-Muhajiroun, which had protested against the bodies of soldiers returning from Afghanistan. In response to this, the English Defense League had been formed. Islamism was in danger of making the situation worse, repeating the cycle of racism: Islamist extremism, more racism, and more Islamist extremism. It is no wonder then that Omar Bakri's own daughter grew so disillusioned with her father's rhetoric that in one monumental act of defiance she left home and became a stripper, proudly declaring her profession to the tabloid press with glee.

What exacerbated the situation was a lack of understanding about what Islamism was. Governments were allowing the Islamist narrative to drive the debate, accepting it as the majority Muslim voice. This simply wasn't true: Islamism was a modern political phenomenon with opinions that could be every bit as offensive as those held by far-right organizations—its anti-Semitism and homophobia, for example. But government and society instinctively resisted challenging this for fear of coming across as racist.

Official policy lumped all Muslims together as "one community," the so-called Muslim vote, which required a "native-chief" to speak on its behalf. Instead of being represented by their Member of Parliament, like everyone else, Muslims were encouraged to seek separate representation via an exclusively Muslim political umbrella. In a "poor natives" sort of way there was the arrogant assumption that Islamism was a true expression of our authenticity, even if the so-called moderates tried to distance themselves from it. In a form of reverse racism, liberal values were expected of the civilized white person, but the brown Muslim could not be held to those same standards and should be judged by his or her own "authentic" culture. This was a colonial "poverty of expectation," which inevitably leads to segregation, low aspirations, patronizing expectations, and cultural glass ceilings, practically stalling Muslim social mobility and progress across Europe.

Ed and I wanted to expose all this. We wanted less separation of communities and more involvement of Muslims in every aspect of society: to focus less on the differences and more on the similarities of cultures. Mainstream society, not just Muslims, bore a great deal of the responsibility to make this happen. The state could help here, but it could never drive the process: imposing ideas like democracy and human rights would only lead to resistance. Instead, the change had to come from within communities themselves—the flowering of more liberal ideas through civic debate and discussion. To be successful, our initiative had to be the exact opposite of neo-conservatism: a "ground up," not a "top down" process.

The shaping of these ideas into what would become Quilliam wasn't an overnight event. Ed and I had many discussions, and disagreed at times too, while fretting over where and how to begin. We weren't the first people ever to want to change the world. Coming up with ideas, in a way, was the easy part. The difficult bit was how to take them forward: how to turn our excited talk into action. What would the process actually involve? Where would the money to fund it come from? Where would we even start?

Right from the start we were encouraged by the reaction to our ideas. Ours was the most visible and credible insight mainstream society had ever gleaned from inside Islamist organizations and the prisons that held them. Ed's book, *The Islamist*, was published to a lot of media attention and discussion. In the wake of that, when I finally announced my resignation from HT, we went to meet Peter Barron, then editor of the BBC's flagship news program *Newsnight*, who agreed to do an extended piece about my departure from HT. In late 2007, my story headlined the program; they were so keen for me to speak that they allowed me to tell my story directly to camera, rather than via an interview with a journalist.

But it wasn't just the media who were interested in my story; the government was, too. On the day the *Newsnight* piece was due to air, Ed and I were invited into the Communities and Local Government department to brief them about Islamism. As we entered the room, we realized just how senior the meeting was: as well as Hazel Blears, then Communities secretary, also present were Foreign Secretary David Miliband, Home Secretary Jacqui Smith, and Charles Farr, the director general of the Office for Security and Counter-Terrorism.

The last time an official had asked me about my political views, I was fingerprinted and had my DNA taken in the interrogation rooms at Heathrow Airport. Here we now were, offering our opinions to three of the UK's seniormost cabinet members. Later that week, I received a rather bemused call from Abi. "You'll never guess who came to see me after your story was aired on *Newsnight*," she said between laughs. "It was the Essex Police. They came to offer an apology for having arrested you at gunpoint all those years ago when you were fifteen. They saw it on TV and felt bad." I burst into laughter. This was my "green backpack" moment with the police. My message was reaching people, but this time it was a democratic one, and I was encouraged.

Quilliam was to be the world's first counter-extremism hub for activism. We would create a platform from which we could directly challenge the dominant discourse of Islamism. We would speak, debate, lobby, brief, mobilize, galvanize, write, publish, and organize in order to spread a counternarrative to Islamism, hoping to inspire the mushrooming of our cause anywhere and everywhere.

The problem was money. Starting up something like this wasn't a cheap thing to do: there was the expense of running an office and hiring staff, the cost of traveling to conferences and countries to spread our message. We would travel around the country meeting with religious figures, former Islamists, and government officials, trying to create a base for our organization. We wanted to get enough people on board to create a critical mass.

But we still had no idea where the money would come from. We were both still students. Ed was still completing his PhD at SOAS; I—having completed my law degree at SOAS—had now enrolled for an MSc in political theory at the London School of Economics. And so, to begin with, Ed and I simply used our credit cards and student overdrafts to pay for everything, a sure way of accumulating thousands of pounds of debt. But this was our baby, and we desperately wanted it to work.

Eventually, Ed's book led the way. Someone who had read *The Islamist* and had been impressed by our ideas gave us an introduction to a Kuwaiti organization called the Babtain Foundation. We met their representatives in London and explained our vision for Quilliam. To our delight, they agreed to give us the seed money to get the organization up and running. We were able to set up an office and to hire a couple of other former Islamists, Dawud and Rashad, who joined us to form Quilliam's first office team.

In January 2008, right behind Russell Square at the British Museum, to a great deal of media fanfare and public anticipation, Ed Husain and I launched Quilliam, the world's first counter-extremism organization. I'm still amazed at the speed with which we managed to pull it all off—to go from a discussion in the back of my car, to a full-fledged and funded organization in less than a year. I was most moved by the speech given by 7/7 survivor Rachel North, who stirred the audience to tears recounting her ordeal of being caught up in London's bombings and the work she has done since to reconcile both herself and communities.

Not everyone from within Muslim communities, however, wanted to congratulate us for our work. Though he had long since left HT, and disagreed with them on many counts, my brother Osman, my childhood friend and protector, completely disagreed with my decision to make our fight against Islamism public. As did my cousin Yasser, who also had left HT by now; he took Osman's view that challenging the ideology itself was one step too far. Our relationships inevitably suffered.

Very few of my childhood friends who had previously held me in such high regard for my commitment to Islamism agreed with my work. The most vindictive attacks came from Nas, the Greek, who began what seemed a personal campaign against me online, in the mosque that my *Nana Abu* founded, and in the local community. The only one who stood by me from the old converts to our cause was our British-Kenyan friend Moe, who back in the day had been attacked by skinheads with a hammer. A particularly touching moment was when my non-Muslim school friends, led by Sav and including the likes of Marc, Jamie, Katrina, and others, organized a welcome home gathering for me in Southend. Despite all that I had done during my Islamist years, and the distance I'd tried to place between us, they still cared. Indeed, Sav had continued to write to me in prison, offering me his moral support. Such deep loyalty spurred me on further; faced with a friendship like that, I knew was doing the right thing.

Among Muslim communities across the UK, my name was dragged through the dirt. Ed and I were both targeted in a highly personal and organized smear campaign. Where Islamist rappers had once sampled my voice on their songs, their supporters were now declaring me an apostate. Such declarations are a necessary prelude for any attempt on a Muslim's life to be "legal." Islamist teams of agitators toured the UK with information packs about why my colleagues and I were heretics.

As all of this unfolded, I was still officially married to—albeit separated from—Rabia. Any chance we had of reconciling matters was destroyed with the founding of Quilliam. I had left her home as an emotionally vulnerable ex-prisoner going through a second identity crisis. I wanted to rediscover who I was and needed the clarity of thought that seclusion could bring. Once I started the painful journey of my mental and emotional realignment, I felt that I was ready to begin working with Rabia to fix our marriage.

Rabia had married an ardent, fiery, passionate Islamist, but she was now getting a liberal Muslim, intent on standing up to challenge everything he had once held sacrosanct. Despite our best efforts, and much heartache both ways, there was no putting the relationship back together again.

Rabia's reaction to my work was not atypical. We hadn't just made enemies of HT but of most Islamist organizations from all branches of Islamism. Ed and I were accused of apostasy, of heresy, and far worse. Nowadays, a few years after founding Quilliam, such a reaction is harder to imagine. With the rise and spread of counter-extremism initiatives globally, with the debate being so much better informed, and with increased visibility for the liberal Arab youth behind many of the Arab uprisings, challenging Islamism is becoming increasingly common. But back then death threats and bomb warnings at our office were a frequent occurrence, even directly from al-Qaeda sources. We had to install blast shields in the office, and went to great lengths not to advertise our location. Even now, we keep the office address off our literature and website; even now I continue to be cautious about my movements.

A month or so after the launch of Quilliam, Ed and I were in Denmark. Many years earlier, I had been a regular visitor to Copenhagen, actively recruiting to build an HT chapter there. Now I was back, giving a speech in the town hall about the very organization I had helped to set up. The raw recruits I had persuaded to join had been different from the typical HT supporters in the UK: many of them hailed from the criminal fringe—drug dealers and gang members. After my speech Ed and I went to Friday prayers at a nearby mosque. As prayers concluded, Fathi, our host, approached me inside the mosque looking very worried.

"Brother Maajid, there is a very dangerous man outside the mosque asking for you, please do not leave." Naturally, being me, I went out to talk to him.

"Are you Maajid Nawaz?" he asked.

"Who are you?"

"Yes, you are Maajid Nawaz," he said, nodding, and cycled off.

The man was a well-known local drug dealer. As soon as he'd seen me, he put a call through. The next thing we knew, there were three cars full of young Islamist sympathizers, parked at the end of the road, waiting to attack us.

"Fathi, let me talk to them," I argued.

"No, brother Maajid, I'm afraid you don't understand. These men, I know them, they have guns. You must leave immediately."

Ed and I had to take shelter in the back room of an Islamic bookshop, and there we hid until a car came to collect us and evacuate us. This was Copenhagen in 2008, not Kabul in 2000.

Things got worse. While we were hiding from the Danish thugs, Ed's phone rang. It was our contact from the Babtain Foundation, telling us that they had decided to withdraw our funding. I felt they were unhappy with some of the public statements we had made. At a stroke all our financial support had vanished—we had a huge bill to pay the British Museum for hosting our launch, and now we had no way of paying for it. Assuming we got out of Denmark alive, Quilliam was in danger of being closed down before it had even started.

CHAPTER TWENTY-NINE

Monkeys in a Zoo

Ed and I coined a phrase in that hideout in Copenhagen: "We don't do fail." That became our mantra, our unofficial slogan. We weren't going to be intimidated from speaking by violent threats, nor financial ones. Ours would not be the sort of organization that tailored its message to suit its sponsors. If that was the sort of influence people thought their money would buy, then we were better off without their support.

We hit the same problem again with the next person to fund us, an Egyptian businessman who wanted to use Quilliam to promote a socially conservative version of Islam. We were a nonreligiously aligned organization with its focus on political rights; our backer wanted to become the public face of a conservative form of Sufi Islam. There were elements of our message he wanted adjusting, for example over civil rights for minorities and homosexuals. We accepted a goodwill donation from him, which cleared our debts, but we did not take the relationship forward. Again, the funding ceased.

The other source of potential funding was through the government. This, in its own way, brought as many potential problems as private donors: it can make people suspicious of your message and lead to accusations that you are little more than government agents. However, we had maintained good relations with the British government after our initial meeting; we had briefed them where requested, and they had continued to support us. If the various Islamist groups in the UK, the Salafists all over the world, and the "Afghan Jihad" could receive funding from the British, Saudi, and Pakistani governments respectively, why couldn't our cause benefit from this sort of boost?

It did not seem unreasonable to try to formalize the relationship a little and see if any funding was available. We went back to the Office for Security and Counter-Terrorism and spoke to their head, Charles Farr. Farr kindly agreed to support us via the government's Preventing Extremism program. We met various ministers and were granted government funding, until such a time as we could find alternative sources of financial support. Farr deserves credit for helping to get Quilliam onto its feet during these early days.

From these touch-and-go beginnings, Quilliam started to gain real momentum. We were able to start speaking publicly, debating, commissioning reports, lobbying politicians, traveling to conferences, working the media, offering policy advice and consultancy. But very early on, we saw that it was not just Islamism we would need to tackle. Away from Muslim circles, the two dominant trends we would most often come up against were polar opposites, either that of the patronizing "Orientalism" or an anti-Muslim form of conservatism.

Both sets of people attempted to use Ed or myself to grind their own ideological axes. In their own way, neither group was happy with half of our message. When we were critical of Islamism, the "Orientalists" got upset. When we raised the grievances in society that acted to fuel the Islamist narrative, the conservatives objected. Both sides wanted to keep us as their pet monkeys in a zoo: to come to us for entertainment and benefit when it suited them, and ignore us when our ideas went against their established ideological bent.

On many occasions after my talks, people—usually white liberals—would stand up and declare that I had no idea what it was like to suffer as a victim of society. They would assert that there was no way someone like me, an educated, articulate English-speaker in a suit and tie, could ever understand people who felt so desperate that suicide bombing was their "only" option. I was told that terrorists' reactions cannot be separated from their social causes and the blame lies squarely on society. I had invariably just spent half an hour telling my entire story, of violent racism and police harassment in Essex, and of torture and solitary confinement in Egypt, but because my conclusions didn't align with the angry "monkey" they were expecting to see, it was as if they hadn't heard any of it.

"I am a pure product of these grievances you keep harping on about," I would declare, "now deal with my conclusions."

Our aim would be to criticize Islamophobia and Islamist extremism as openly as possible. We would defend the right of Muslims to practice their faith, even those who were conservative, while vehemently challenging the idea that any one version of Islam—even a "moderate" one—should ever be imposed in any society as law. This position placed me on interesting sides of various motions. I argued on a panel that "Political Islam"—the desire to impose a version of Islam as law—was a threat, while I defended the religion of Islam itself as essentially one of peace, against Islamic-critic and author Ayaan Hirsi Ali.

Word soon spread, and from my appearances on *Larry King Live* to being interviewed on al-Jazeera, Quilliam was fast becoming the recognized authority on challenging both anti-Islam and Islamist extremism globally. Our work now started to attract a critical mass of support across society. Among the media, *60 Minutes* profiled our work and my story. In the arts, people like Jane Rosenthal, founder of the Tribeca Film Festival, helped to introduce our work at the Festival and to her friend Robert De Niro (or Bob, as she calls him). On the technology side, when learning how best to use social media in order to galvanize support, my work on Facebook benefited from the early advice of people like Facebook co-founder Dustin Moscovitz. My use of Twitter to spread our message was a task personally assigned to me by its founder, Jack Dorsey.

The corridors of political power were also beginning to show immense interest. Soon after setting up Quilliam, I received an invitation to address the US Senate about our work. The invitation came from Senator Joe Lieberman, chair of the Senate Committee for Homeland Security. I would become the first former Islamist ever to testify in the US Senate.

Being a senior former Islamist, however, is not without its problems. The State Department had sorted out all my travel arrangements, but a week before I was due to go, my visa had still not come through. At this point, I received a worried phone call from the Department of Homeland Security. There are problems with your visa, I was told. We're not sure we'll be able to get you one because of your conviction in Egypt. My conviction in Egypt, I replied, is exactly why the Senate has invited me to come over and talk! Back and forth we went, between Homeland Security and the State Department, with nobody sure exactly where the visa was stuck. Eventually, word got back to Senator Lieberman, who rang up the US Embassy in London, shouting as he instructed them not to embarrass him.

The night before I was due to fly, my visa still hadn't come through, and by now I was resigned to the fact that it wouldn't happen. Suddenly, I received a call.

"Mr. Nawaz? I'm calling from the US Embassy. I have your visa here."

"Great. I've got to be at Heathrow early in the morning: should I get a cab and pick it up on the way?" I replied with relief.

"Actually," the man said, "I'm not at the US Embassy."

I was confused. "But I thought you said you were."

"I'm with the US Embassy, but I'm based somewhere else."

"OK, where are you based? I'll come to you," I asked in bewilderment.

"Here's what we're going to do," he said. "I'll meet you myself at Heathrow tomorrow morning. I'll be waiting for you at the information desk of your terminal."

"How will I know what you look like?"

"I'll be wearing a blue raincoat." And with that, he hung up.

The following morning, I went to the information desk as arranged. There, sure enough, was a man in a blue raincoat.

"Good morning, Mr. Nawaz," he said, and handed me three brown envelopes.

"Is this my visa?" I asked.

"Sort of," Blue Raincoat replied. "We couldn't get you a normal visa, I'm afraid, but we are very keen for you to come and speak. Do you know about the Mafia?"

"What about them?"

"Sometimes we have court cases where we need to bring people over to testify. But these people are convicted criminals and technically aren't allowed into the country. So what we do is to arrange for a parole visa. This allows them into the US under the aegis of federal agents. From a legal point of view, they're under arrest for the duration of their stay."

"Right," I said, taking the envelopes. "So I'm on a parole visa, like a Mafia boss? I'm under arrest?"

"Technically," Blue Raincoat was keen to assure me. "Please don't be offended by that. We're not implying anything, it's just the only way that we could get you into the country to speak at the Senate."

"Are there any conditions to being technically under arrest?" I asked.

"Yes," Blue Raincoat admitted. "You will have a twenty-four-hour federal detail following you for the duration of your stay. But please, consider them your chauffeur service, rather than your arresting officers!"

It was one of those moments where my former and current lives slammed against each other. Phrases like "agents" and "detail" and "technically under arrest" were enough to give me a flashback or two from my time in Egypt. Heathrow was also where I'd been interrogated by Mr. Blue Raincoat's British equivalents. But I took the envelopes and handed them over as directed. I was escorted off at the other end, fingerprinted and interviewed, before being handed over to my federal detail.

The federal agents, from Immigration Customs Enforcement, took the hotel room next to mine. I had to inform them of my movements at all times. They were armed, and we were tailed by two more cars wherever we went. The agents were quite suspicious of me. It was only after I'd spoken at the Senate that their attitude changed.

The speech itself was a defining moment, as it allowed us the opportunity to define Islamism, explain its causes, and present the doctrine of civic challenge to the world. It all went out live on C-SPAN and hit the news globally. "I'm sorry, sir," the lead agent, Bryan, said as he offered me his hand. "Up until now, I had been under the impression that our job was to protect America from you. Now I realize that we are here to protect you *from* America!" That visit was the first time I'd been to the United States, and I was determined to make the most of it, federal detail or otherwise. Sayyid Qutb, Jihadism's ideological godfather, had visited the United States back in the 1940s. Qutb's trip inspired him to write a book about his experiences, *The America that I Saw*, in which he was heavily critical of the "licentiousness" of America. I wanted to challenge this, and created a rival version. I posted my "The America that I Saw" as a video blog on YouTube, and argued for the positives I'd seen. Without those same freedoms Qutb had been critical of, I argued, Muslims would not have been allowed to ever build mosques in this country. Having spent some years in the same prison that held Qutb before his execution, I felt somehow connected to his radicalism. The radical message for the Middle East of his time was Islamism.

How odd it was that now the truly radical idea for the Middle East, which was straddling dictatorships and extremism, had become grass-roots democratic activism.

CHAPTER THIRTY

Visiting No. 10

As with our initial Muslim donors, it didn't take too long for our policies to differ from our backers. The problem was a report we wrote on the UK government's prisons policy, run by the National Offender Management Service. This detailed the problem of rising extremism in prisons and what we believed was the disorientated response from NOMS. Our critical report really didn't go down well with the UK government, NOMS in particular reacted very badly, and a question began to circulate across certain government departments: why are we giving money to this organization for them to be critical about us?

It wasn't long before another flashpoint occurred. This time we had written a report reviewing the government's entire "PREVENT" strategy toward extremism. We had broken down, department by department, where we felt the failures were, but we were very careful how we presented it. We sent a hard copy to the government as a confidential briefing, to ensure that an electronic version didn't end up on the Internet.

In the end, though, that's exactly what happened. The report was leaked, scanned, and uploaded online from within a government department. That department was Farr's Office for Security and Counter-Terrorism, the very department giving us our funding. We had criticized some policies in the OSCT but had praised others. We were particularly critical of the view that government partnerships with nonviolent yet otherwise extreme Islamists were the best way to fend off Jihadism. This was meant to be constructive feedback. The OSCT begged to differ. We were caught up in the political storm of a general election, with the political parties taking potshots at each other on such issues, as well as the economic downturn.

Soon after, I received a call; the prime minister wanted to see me. David Cameron was due to give an important speech in Munich, distinguishing Islam from Islamism and extremism, and was requesting my advice. It felt strange indeed. Here I was, someone who had previously fought with all his might against everything this country stood for, and now I was called upon by the prime minister to provide expert advice on matters of critical national importance. I agreed to go.

Inside, 10 Downing Street felt quaint: a traditional terraced townhouse, a very nice one obviously, but a house nonetheless, with creaky staircases and all those quirks. The mahogany leather waiting-room sofa was the same as the one we grew up with in our front room—my dad used to ban us from sitting on it in our jeans in case we scratched the leather. There wasn't the sense of grandeur or pomp that you associate with places like the White House; it had an almost eccentric English charm all its own.

The other person called in for the private meeting was Paul Goodman, a former MP and shadow Communities minister. The prime minister came in: he was taller in real life than he seemed on television. It was a relaxed setup—we were seated on sofas, rather than at a formal roundtable. Alongside Cameron, Goodman, and myself, there were various aides in the room as well: Ameet Gill, then the prime minister's speechwriter, Jeremy Heywood, the cabinet secretary, and others.

Cameron was warm and engaging. His people skills were unexceptionally exceptional. By which I mean: you don't get to be in a position of power like that without an exceptional level of people skills. I have met enough political leaders—George Bush, Tony Blair, Gordon Brown—to know that this is the norm. It would have been more of a surprise, in a way, if he didn't have these attributes. He was bright and well briefed. He didn't come across as someone who was "winging" his way through the meeting.

I felt the policy that the government was pursuing was heading in the right direction. They were flipping Bush-era neo-conservatism on its head and restoring lost ground on civil liberties, while increasing the pressure on the civic challenge against extremism. Some time after this meeting, Parliament looked into many of these reforms, and they asked me to testify. In this hearing I directly challenged Congressman King and reaffirmed my stance that the excesses of the US neo-conservative era must be reined in. Cameron's government had the same idea. They weren't interested in pursuing ID cards, for example, and had begun to curtail the process of detention without trial.

Cameron then asked what I thought should be done about Hizb al-Tahrir. When he had been leader of the opposition, he had asked Gordon Brown why he had not banned my old organization as Tony Blair had promised after 7/7. Brown's response had been to quote me from my first *Newsnight* interview, arguing that rather than banning HT, a civic challenge should be presented instead. Cameron now asked me directly whether the group should be banned. Again, I explained my reasoning. Banning was not only illiberal, it wasn't the solution. It was far better to create a scenario where joining the group became a social taboo. An actual ban would only give the organization the publicity they were seeking.

Cameron was also interested in an idea that I had been espousing about the comparison between extremism and racism. I had argued that the two should be analogous in terms of public response. Why should extremist views, which went against basic liberties, be any more acceptable than racist or homophobic ones? I told Cameron that he shouldn't be afraid to criticize Muslims who were putting forward extremist views in the name of faith. Those views were not the same as religious piety. Finally, we spoke about the Arab world. I stressed that the old dichotomy pitting dictatorships against Islamism had to be abandoned or else extremism would be the inevitable outcome.

David Cameron seemed genuinely impressed by what I had to say. When he eventually gave his Munich speech, it included almost all of my suggestions. I then got another call from Cabinet Secretary Heywood, sounding me out about taking a government job as a special adviser to the prime minister on extremism matters. I went back in for another meeting, and we discussed the idea at some length. In a typically civil-servant way, they wanted to first hear whether I was interested in the job before making me a formal offer. Their condition was that I leave Quilliam, but that's something I wouldn't even do for Rabia.

Sure enough, when our funding came up for renewal, it was withdrawn. We lobbied hard to have it reinstated. Tony Blair stepped in, personally encouraging people to help us; we even got supportive MPs to force an emergency debate in the Parliament on the subject. They agreed to give us the outstanding money we were still due, but not any more than this. The government was battling with bringing down the deficit, and this was a bad time to get on the wrong side of the civil service.

The week before Christmas 2010, I had to make seven painful redundancies at Quilliam. At our lowest point we were reduced from a staff of twenty-five to just four. Ed had to leave, too; he took an opportunity to work for the Council on Foreign Relations in New York. Being left alone at Quilliam as co-founding chairman, with four staff members and a revival to orchestrate, I set to work to shape the organization more in my own personal mold.

It was an extremely difficult task, but "we don't do fail." Peaks and troughs in life have made me who I am. Losing our government funding came with a silver lining; we were able to reassert our independence. Cutting costs made us a leaner, more viable organization. We know now that we have the strength to survive, even in the most difficult financial climate. We've come out of the worst of that, and for the first time we found reliable donors who don't demand favors or want punches pulled.

The peculiarity of the situation wasn't lost on me. It seemed that here was a government that had cut the funding for my organization, primarily caused by our disagreement with the Office for Security and Counter-Terrorism, while they also appeared to want to hire me to give them essentially the same advice. It was a position of real influence, where my ideas could be put into practice and make a serious difference. But the advantage didn't outweigh losing my independence and my ability to speak out. Also, if I left, then the organization would most likely fold without me.

I didn't want to see that happen. I felt the work Quilliam was set up to do, despite all our success on the media and policy front, hadn't really begun. Lyndon Johnson once famously quipped, "It is better to have him inside the tent pissing out, than outside the tent pissing in." But in Muslim-majority countries there was no tent, and that's what I needed to help build.

CHAPTER THIRTY-ONE

Khudi Pakistan

Quilliam had paved the way for a global counternarrative and had captured the imagination and attention of the world, from heads of state to artists and technology leaders. But I wasn't satisfied. I wanted to show how it was possible to turn our ideas into practice on a grassroots level.

I wanted to create a counter-extremism social movement for Muslim youth that would actually carry our ideas, brand our ideas, popularize our ideas, just as we had done with HT. Ideas, narratives, symbols, and leaders: grassroots democratic culture needed what Islamism had. I wanted to create a radical civic force in society that would intimidate politicians into democratizing society, just as Islamism had intimidated them into Islamizing society. And I wanted to seed this work in a country that by 2010 everyone had given up on: Pakistan.

Pakistan, my old country of wandering Sufi mystics, where every woman is a *Sohni* and every man her hero, my old country of technicolored food and beautiful literature, my old country of original folk music, *qawwals*, and the most majestic voice, my old country of sharp wit, industrial ambition, and intense passion. Despite all your trials and tribulations, your people soldier on though they are told by all that they will fail, they soldier on against disaster, war, corruption, and poverty, because within them is a resilient spirit, an innovative flair and a fierce desire to live, to survive, and to prove to the world that they will stand up and be counted. Forgive me. Forgive me for I once went to weaken you even more, but through all your resilience I can now help with the cure. And so I went. I went to do what I could; fighting the very virus I had helped to sow deep within your veins. Fatima had inflamed within me a desire to discover you once more.

Since the US invasion of Afghanistan, Pakistan's troubles with extremism had gone from bad to worse. The Taliban had taken over vast swaths of the country in the north, suicide bombings were a daily occurrence, and the Islamist ideology was fast overtaking its rivals in gaining the attention of the country's youth. This sad state of affairs is best exemplified by the ruthless assassination of Punjab's governor Salmaan Taseer in 2011, followed shortly after by the killing of minorities minister Shahbaz Bhatti. Thousands of people came out onto the streets in celebration of Salmaan Taseer's murder, merely because he dared to suggest reform to the country's colonial-era blasphemy laws. As a final crippling wound, Salmaan Taseer's son was kidnapped by Islamist extremists seeking to exchange him for his father's convicted assassin. The true depth of Pakistan's problem finally began to be witnessed by all.

Throughout this period, Hizb al-Tahrir had been busy recruiting inside Pakistan's army. The army had made a series of HT-related arrests. In August 2011, friendly Uncle Qayyum, now a committed HT ideologue, was picked up by Pakistan's military intelligence and was held for nine months during which, he states, he was severely beaten. Dr. Qayyum has since released a statement. Like me, he claims that regardless of the consequences he openly admitted to his interrogators that he was a member of Hizb al-Tahrir. Ammar had been visiting with Rabia when Uncle Qayyum was picked up, and I couldn't help but blame myself for once again exposing my son to the brutal side of the "War on Terror." Matters were getting out of control; the country desperately needed a counternarrative.

Fatima had always tried hard to show me the other side of Pakistan, the side that I had either tried to destroy for so long or had never seen within my hard-core of Islamist circles. She reintroduced me to Pakistani music, indigenous poetry, literature, and history. As she spoke, memories of the days before it all went so horribly wrong would flicker in my mind: memories of *Tai Ammi* sitting by my bed reading those enigmatic stories, memories of my dad's devotion to Nusrat Fateh Ali Khan's legendary *qawwali* music, and memories of a distressed young Abi drying her bullied child's tears: "*They're calling you a Paki, so what? Tell them you're proud to be a Paki.*" Through Fatima's words it finally all began to make sense: Abi had been telling me to proudly reclaim my identity.

All those years earlier, Abi was trying to guide me to do exactly what the early American rappers had done: *Yeah, we're Niggaz With Attitude, and if you don't like it, fuck all y'all! Is my culture British, Pakistani, Arab, Muslim? It's all of those, and none of the above. I am what the hell I want to be, I will reclaim as mine whatever I feel like, and if you don't like it, fuck all y'all!*

Fatima and I decided that everyday Pakistanis needed to reclaim Pakistan and Islam as their own. They needed to reintroduce a brave new Pakistan to the world, the Pakistan of survivors, the Pakistan of fighters, and we would do what we could to help the country achieve this. In doing so, our fight was with those who had hijacked both our religion and our country. As always, the romanticism of struggle.

So it was that we founded "Khudi" Pakistan: a Muslim Brotherhood equivalent for democratic culture. I launched the idea from one of the world's most prestigious global platforms for thought leaders, TED-Global in Edinburgh. The starting point for Khudi was the work I had done in Pakistan with HT. I had seen for myself, and through my own efforts, how ideas and groups could flourish and set the intellectual standard for young people. The message was wrong, I knew that now, but maybe the *tactics* were right. Perhaps we could use the methods of the Islamist groups to create a counter-Islamist movement, to do *da'wah* for the democratic culture?

Since its inception, Pakistan has never had a *social* movement (outside of politics) to champion democratic culture. When I say outside of politics, I mean it's never given voice to the values that underpin democracy on a *non-partisan* basis. Democracy is more than just an electoral process: it's about the culture associated with it. Without freedom of belief one cannot set up whichever party one so chooses. Without freedom of association one cannot join that party. Without freedom of speech, one cannot campaign for that party. Without human rights one cannot run opposition parties without fear of imprisonment. Democracy must, by necessity, be more than just elections. These ideas need to be embedded within any democracy for it to function properly: there needs to be a democratic culture to tie everything together.

Groups like HT chipped away at this culture. Among the young population in particular, there was no appetite for these democratic values.

There were plenty of people out there promoting the opposite—and those extreme beliefs carried a certain caché. Being a young democrat, by contrast, wasn't trendy. It was in danger of becoming an outdated brand that no one wanted to be associated with. If that process continued, then as these generations got older and took power, democracy in countries like Pakistan was in danger of eroding away.

This was a bold new idea that no one had ever attempted before. No one had considered turning the tables on Islamist groups by using their methods for democratic ends. It sounds strange, but I looked at organizations such as Hamas in Gaza and the West Bank for inspiration. In the space of less than a decade, Hamas had managed to overtake the Palestine Liberation Organization as the main source of power in Palestine. They had put down roots in the younger population in a way that the PLO was unable to counter.

The basis of Hamas's rise to power was in their clear and powerful message. They also promoted this message through values-based welfare work, providing services like schooling and social relief. They were able to instill their ideas not just through sloganeering and campaigning but also through getting involved in the very fabric of society. What I wanted to achieve with Khudi in Pakistan was this, but for democratic culture. As the wise poet Rumi said: "Like Noah, my thoughts turned to starting a huge, foolish project, and it made absolutely no difference what people would think of me."

Khudi is an Urdu word originating from Persia. Used in the poetry of the famous South Asian poet Allama Iqbal and popularized by Pakistan's first major celebrity rock band, Junoon, the word roughly translates as self-empowerment or self-esteem. Using Islamist tactics again, I designed Khudi, ironically like al-Qaeda, to be an umbrella organization, under which existing groups and campaigners could coalesce and pool resources. I knew we needed a powerful and committed leadership to kick-start the group. My choice was obvious; by now I was convinced it was the reason God worked to make her approach me that day: Fatima Mullick became the first national coordinator of Khudi. We now needed to identify the best youth activists, recruit them, and form our first leadership committee.

In 2009, with a BBC camera crew in tow, and a security team watching out for attempts on my life, I embarked on a national counter-extremism tour of Pakistan, speaking at over twenty-two universities from Islamabad to Karachi, from Quetta to Kashmir. I used this tour to identify and recruit the leaders for Khudi. Across Pakistan, Fatima and I met thousands of frustrated young students, and through our interaction with them we carefully selected those who we saw could lead the way. This team manages two offices inside Pakistan, a network of thousands of volunteers, and has attracted tens of thousands of online subscribers to Khudi.

Fatima and I began to travel as frequently as possible to Pakistan to train this core group in building a movement. We laid out the basic idea and ethos with them, gave them the vision, set up the structure, and began to organize activities: student debates, a nationwide student magazine, democratic interventions with student wings of the various political parties, clean-up initiatives, media interviews, academic and political lobbying. Soon the name of Khudi began to spread across Pakistan.

Still focused on the need to reclaim Pakistan, we helped to set up the first International Youth Conference and Festival (IYCF) in the country. At this time, fewer and fewer people were willing to travel to Pakistan. Our aim was to try to help reintroduce Pakistan to the world, and to reintroduce the world to Pakistan. Having previously spoken at Google's Zeitgeist annual thought-leaders conference, I called some friends at Google and we managed to persuade Google's leadership to come to Pakistan and address our IYCF conference. This was the first time Google had ever sent an official delegation to Pakistan, including YouTube's then head of news and politics, Steve Grove, and from Google's philanthropy side, Jay Boren.

We also managed to bring in speakers such as Susan Gordon from the Facebook platform "Causes" and Marc Koska. Marc had invented the non-reusable disposable syringe, saving many lives in the process. At the top of our list, and to introduce Pakistan to her, I called in my friend, the godmother to activists, Stephanie Rudat. For a while, Stephanie had been working to coordinate and train democracy movements globally. She had been involved in the founding of the Alliance of Youth

Movements and now ran a similar platform called *Think*Consortium. We wanted Pakistani youth to feel part of the global picture: the more plugged in they felt to that, the less isolated and susceptible to Islamism they would be. The conference was a major success.

As was expected, some people weren't so receptive. Islamist groups in particular didn't take kindly to what they perceived as a traitor coming in to campaign against them. The threat that Ed and I had encountered in Denmark is just as real in Pakistan. Right from the word go, we had to be extremely careful about our security.

The importance of this hit home, literally, during one of my trips. I was in Lahore, on the second leg of my national universities tour. After a long day of campaigning, I had slipped out on my own to a cafe for a coffee and shisha. I happened to pick one that was a meeting point for Pakistani members of HT.

As I was drinking my coffee, an HT enthusiast came to sit down next to me, uninvited, and started talking about "the *Khilafah*." I humored the guy for a while, but he didn't take the hint and leave.

"Look," I said, "you're clearly from Hizb al-Tahrir. I'm afraid I am not interested. I am just here to drink my coffee."

At this point, the guy started staring at me. "Hang on," he said, "you're Maajid Nawaz, aren't you? You're that guy who is going round the universities, shouting his mouth off about us."

"Yes," I admitted, "I am. But I'm really not here to cause trouble. All I want to do is have a coffee."

By this point, two others came to sit at my table.

"This is him," the first one explained. "The one I was telling you about."

"OK," I said. "I'm really just here to have a coffee. It's eleven at night, and I've been working all day . . ."

"Yeah," one of the men said. "Working to spread your lies about us."

This wasn't good. "Who is the person in charge here?" I asked. The trio indicated another man, on his own in a corner. "All right," I said. "I'm going to go over and say '*assalaamu alaykum*' to him, and then I'm going to leave. I don't want to offend anyone here."

I walked over to the man in the corner. His name was Tayyab Muqeem, a British Pakistani who, like me all those years ago, had come to Pakistan to help recruit for HT. His inroad into Pakistan was through teaching English via the British Council—a common HT technique that Nasim used to set up HT in Bangladesh. Muqeem had managed to get himself appointed as head of English at a private university called Superior College.

I held out my hand to him. He refused to take it, saying instead, "If you don't get the fuck out of here right now, I am going to knock you out."

Startled, I persisted, "I'm just trying to shake your hand. I only came over to tell you that I'm not here to cause any trouble."

I heard a scraping of chairs behind me, and looked around to see those same three men get up and walk over. Everything happened so fast. Before I could work out what was going on, Muqeem took advantage of the fact that I had turned away. He stood up and hit me on the side of the face. Caught completely off guard, I found myself falling to the floor. As I went over, I caught a glass, which shattered in shards all around me. Ever the stubborn one, I stood up again immediately to face Muqeem, extending my hand a second time. "I'm not here to fight," I said. At that point, before it could go any further, the cafe owner stepped in and ushered Muqeem out.

Since that incident, I have been far more careful in Pakistan. So far no similar attacks have occurred. But the fact that the menace is there shows how threatened the Islamists feel about our campaign. It is still early days in the country, but we now have an organization that boasts two permanent offices, chapters in every major city, and a network of volunteers across the country. In the short time Khudi has been up and running, we have already taken some great strides. Changing a culture is not an overnight process.

CHAPTER THIRTY-TWO

I Will See Your Day When It Comes

In London we had founded Quilliam as a hub to inspire the counternarrative globally. In Pakistan we had founded Khudi as a practical example of what can be done; but ever restless, I wasn't satisfied. If the inspiration for Khudi was the franchise model of the Muslim Brotherhood, then I would need to franchise it to other countries. Just as Islamism had spread across the Arab world and throughout Muslim-majority societies, we needed the democratic culture to be oblivious to borders. As word began to spread, emails requesting guidance from young democratic activists in war-torn countries who had seen my TED talk began to arrive. Youth began to reach out to us from Yemen, Iraq, and Somalia; I traveled to Nigeria, India, and Bangladesh, where our advice was needed to prevent further HT infiltration of their military.

It felt odd, even surreal, to be going to Bangladesh—the country where I knew Nasim had founded HT—and to be working directly against the fruits of his labor. I was now using everything I had learned from Nasim against him. Even Europe, after England's youth riots of 2011 and widespread unrest in Greece, looked as if it could do with such a movement. But I knew we couldn't expand too fast. We had to take it slowly, carefully, and strategically. What mattered most was to instill clarity in the idea and set up a strong, experienced team. Our answer to how and where to set up next was looking clearer, as with Pakistan, due to another childhood association in my mind, my father's work in Libya.

One of the senior activists and analysts at Quilliam is Noman Benotman. Noman is a former leader of the Libyan Islamic Fighting Group (LIFG), and back in the 1980s he fought alongside Osama bin Laden against the Soviet invasion of Afghanistan. When the Soviets withdrew, bin Laden called a meeting of his Arab generals to discuss what to do next. It was at this meeting that bin Laden declared his wishes to turn the war against the West. Most of the generals agreed to follow him. The exception was Noman; he told bin Laden that this was crazy. He said that he'd come to fight the Russians, not to kill civilians. He felt they should be focusing on rebuilding the country they'd fought for, not attacking the West.

Noman and his troops returned to Libya. He then entered a process of demilitarizing the group and acted as the conduit between the LIFG and the Gaddafi government. He struck a deal with Saif Gaddafi whereby the group would renounce violence in return for their members being released *en masse* from Libya's prisons. He worked to guide his former group through their own process of de-radicalization, eventually encouraging them to write books recanting their old jihadist philosophy. In many ways, Noman was a kindred spirit.

When the Arab Spring swept into Libya, Noman was in Tripoli and in a difficult position. Here was someone who had been working to disarm the LIFG and had made promises to Saif Gaddafi to do so; now, however, there was an urgent need for the same people to re-arm. Would they return to their old jihadist ways, or would they fall into place under a popular leadership? Noman knew that the right place to be was on the people's side, and Quilliam lent our weight to the people's campaign in Libya.

As Gaddafi's forces were marching to crush Benghazi, Noman rushed back to London and opened Quilliam's front against Gaddafi's regime. In back-to-back media interviews we exposed Gaddafi's crimes and urged Western support for the Libyan people. We used the contacts we had made through Quilliam's work with the government to put Noman in touch with the air campaign. Noman had access to information on the ground in Libya, which he was able to pass on, and senior members of the RAF would call upon us for advice and analysis as the campaign progressed. Noman was one of the key figures behind encouraging the former head of Libyan intelligence, Moussa Koussa, to defect, and was the first to break the news.

Understandably, our activities attracted the wrath of Gaddafi's regime; they even hacked our computer system in an effort to stop us. Following the fall of Gaddafi, Noman has been working with Libyans to help them shape their new government. He is close to his former comrades in the Islamist militia and is crucial as a stabilizing force between these competing factions. Keen to continue his post-conflict work, Noman maintains ties with Libyan jihadists globally, even those currently held in Iraq's jails, in an effort to convince as many as he can about the need to democratize Libya.

But for any new government to succeed, what is eventually needed in Libya is an injection of civic ideals and democratic culture. Libya has been under a dictatorship for so long that it is completely lacking in any experience of democracy. It is tough for civic values to flower in such arid conditions, and the danger of sliding back toward the familiarity of a more autocratic regime is a real one. True to the Islamist model that inspired me, I began dreaming of franchising our Khudi-style movement to Arab nations. Pakistan was once again beginning to export positive political ideas. The months and years ahead will tell how far we can push this model globally, but the romanticism of struggle remains ever alive in our hearts.

And then there was Egypt. Out of all the countries where the Arab uprisings occurred in 2011, it is Egypt, perhaps unsurprisingly, that I took closest interest in. From my time in prison I have kept my unusual mix of contacts. My lawyer during the trial, Ahmed Saif, had been a founding member of Kifayah. He was there at the beginning, when you could count the number of protesters on one hand, and their protests were seen as a laughingstock. In my work for Quilliam, I had come across the leaders of the April 6 Youth Movement, the group that first sparked Egypt's anti-Mubarak protests. Again, no one had taken them seriously when they announced at a 2010 Alliance of Youth Movements conference in New York that they would lead a revolution against Mubarak.

So when everything began to come together on January 25, 2011, and the protests started to spiral, I was on the edge of my seat in anticipation.

I was quick to do what I could to help the revolution. A crucial factor in how things developed was going to be the reaction of the West. President Mubarak had always enjoyed support from being a close ally of the United States and its allies. If Mubarak received their support now, it would be that much more difficult to dislodge him. If the West stood back however, then his position would become untenable.

We helped get the protesters' message out and into the Western media. I wanted people to know that this was a movement led by liberal, young Egyptians. They were not instigated by the Muslim Brotherhood, and it was important that Mubarak wasn't portrayed as the lesser of two evils: for too long the argument had been that yes, he was autocratic and unpleasant, but rather that than the extremist alternative. What the Egyptian protests showed was something new and exciting—a third way of genuine people power: radical democracy. It's what we'd been arguing was possible for a long time. That was why it was so important that they succeeded: at a stroke it undermined the old dichotomy of secular dictatorship or Islamist rule.

I was quick to reconnect with the likes of Ayman Nour, the liberal leader who had told me to "grow up" in Mazrah Tora prison. I arranged for him to appear live with me on al-Jazeera to make the protesters' case.

I coordinated with the April 6 revolutionaries with their message for Western media. Quilliam sent out a number of press releases, endorsing the protesters' demands, and reminding the media of my own story, and how despotic the Mubarak regime could be. Mubarak, beware the prayer of the oppressed! For the first time I really understood the potential of Twitter. Every time I tweeted a link or a comment, I got calls from journalists who were following me, wanting an interview.

I then got in touch with Mona el-Tewahy, a US-based Egyptian American, a former journalist turned activist. Both of us were in contact with protesters in Tahrir Square, and I felt a consistent voice in the Western media was needed to put forward their cause; we began trying to coordinate our response. What followed was a nonstop cycle of media appearances and newspaper interviews, phone conversations and articles. I was delivering body blow after body blow to Mubarak through the press, the corridors of government, and in the court of public opinion.

I became a regular face on CNN, Bloomberg, Sky News, and the BBC; I wrote opinion pieces for *The Times* and the *Wall Street Journal*. And I tweeted, of course, relentlessly.

The success of our campaign had not gone amiss; former President Bush eventually invited me to his home in Texas to share my thoughts on the future of Egypt. We had that delicate conversation about the definition of torture that opens this book. My green backpack moment had finally come for Hosni Mubarak, and this time it was through our democratic advocacy that we were bringing down the bully.

I wasn't naive enough to believe that a liberal regime would take power when the post-Mubarak elections were held. It was always clear that the Muslim Brotherhood was going to capitalize on the uprising. It takes time for new political ideas to filter through, and in the meantime democracy means respecting the choice of the people. It would be wrong to see this as an endorsement of Islamism. The Muslim Brotherhood's success is a bit like how many analysts see the American invasions of Afghanistan and Iraq—not so much a reasserting of US power but an overstretch; and in Egypt, it's the beginning of the end of its fascination with Islamism. In the long term, now with room to breathe, the younger generation who began this uprising will move on to create other movements and inspire new trends, beyond Islamism. Already, reform wings and breakaway youth factions from the larger Islamist groups are emerging. Islamism is not the future. In time, people will realize how it is part of the past, the old order.

My prayers, our prayers, in Mazrah Tora that Mubarak see justice were finally answered. *Ya Muharak hashoof feeka yawm*, "I will see your day when it comes," was a regularly invoked phrase by many of those oppressed prisoners. It was a dream that kept us alive in the desert heat. For Mubarak to be swept from power was one thing; for him to be arrested was another. But for him to be put on trial, wearing those same white clothes, sitting in the same cage we were held in, and sent to the same prison that we were jailed in: that was something else. Mubarak, his two sons Alaa' and Gemal, and his interior minister Habib al-Adly, all ended up in Mazrah Tora prison. Divine intervention, call it what you will. But my Lord is just. He never fails me.

Seeing Mubarak in that cage was a cathartic moment. It brought it all back—the torture, the injustice, the wasted years of my early twenties. It was hard not to be moved. I felt a whirl of emotions: delight and sadness, victory and closure, vengeance and inner peace, all at the same time. I'd be lying if I said there wasn't an element of revenge in there, but it was revenge of a righteous variety: a just one. Mubarak's defeat had not come about through violence, not like Gaddafi. The supposed "strongman" of Egypt had not been taken down in a hail of bullets, or by a suicide bombing, or by an HT-inspired military coup. It had been achieved by peaceful, democratic means. By people pouring out onto the streets and having the courage to stand together. And I had played my part.

I remembered, too, how the Islamists reacted when I left HT: the way that the ideas I had been espousing through Quilliam and then Khudi had been criticized and ridiculed. At once, all my friends had turned on me, and I lost so much. Apostate, I was called. Hypocrite. Traitor. Sell-out. The people will rise up to prove how wrong you are, I was told. I looked at Mubarak facing justice and thought: the people did rise up, just not for Islamism. The small democratic spark that ignited our hearts all those years back in Mazrah Tora, with Ahmed Saif and the Kifayah movement, with Sa'ad el-Din Ibrahim and Ayman Nour, had finally engulfed the streets of Egypt. The radical alternative is here to stay, and whenever I think about it, a small smile flickers across my face.

POSTSCRIPT

On July 23, 2011, the day after the Norwegian right-wing terrorist Anders Breivik had committed his appalling massacre, I was waiting for my train home after work. On the platform, a man was racially abusing a helpless old grandmother in a hijab, walking with her young grandchildren. "Go back to your own country! This is England, we don't want you Muslims here!" he shouted at the terrified family. England had been tense. The anti-Muslim English Defense League had been on the rise, and Breivik had just taken their reasoning a step further. Now there was this man terrifying Muslim children in front of me on the train platform. Perhaps it was the freshness of what Breivik had done, perhaps it was the visage of cowering children in headscarves and the memories of Bosnia, perhaps it was everything—my entire life—that flashed before me then. Whatever it was, I found myself instantly transported back to the Essex of my teenage years. Memories of "Paki-bashings" came flooding back, and I saw nothing but Mickey standing before me. I hurtled toward this man in a rage, my voice bellowing out expletives and my eyes a tale of fury. In an instant the racist bully was transformed into a spectacle of fear. I didn't even need to lift a hand—he teetered away meekly in the hope that all could be forgotten. The family thanked me graciously, but as I started walking home, my hands began to tremble.

After all that's happened, this is not over. The cycle of hatred is coming back around. Time hadn't healed me. Somewhere deep inside me lurked a menace, and it took a trivial racist incident to bring it all back out. That scared me, and it took me awhile sitting alone at home to resume my composure. "Much remains to be done," I thought. But the question of what was playing on my mind.

As I pondered my next move, my thoughts turned to my son Ammar. I try to teach him what basic football skills I can offer whenever I manage to get access from his mother to see him. I smile every time he cheers on Liverpool FC, just as his father had done over two decades earlier. *You can be whatever you want to be, Ammar. Don't ever let anyone tell you otherwise.*

Returning again to the world he would be raised in, I thought of the work that lay ahead.

"But how much more can I do before I'm too old to be running around like this?" I asked.

"Maajid, you're only thirty-four. You have a whole life ahead of you to consider such things," Fatima laughingly reassured me. "Right now the movement you're building needs your support. It won't grow just like that."

"Yes, perhaps you're right," I said. "Maybe my next move can wait till I hit forty-two."

Here I am, back in Mecca. I am still travelling, trying to broaden my mind, for I've seen too much of the damage narrow-mindedness can make of things, and when I return home . . . I will devote what energies I have to repairing the damage.

—MALCOLM X (1925–65)
LETTER TO JAMES FARMER

Epilogue

2013: IDEAS ARE BULLETPROOF

Following the release of the UK version of *Radical*, I wrote this letter to a former leadership member of *Hizb al-Tahrir* who had left the group after extensive discussions with me:

Dear _____

I wanted to tell you something: you often ask how I have time to do so much and make sure all the loose ends are met. Please know, I don't have time. I am forced to prioritize. And I have prioritized you above other things in my life, as I did that day when you came to see me in London, and when I was meant to see my son.

I'm telling you this because I want you to know the reason I prioritize you. It's simple. I believe. I believe in what we must do together to make Europe, and the world, a better place. I believe in redemption. I believe that change is the only possible hope for Muslims in Europe to advance, and progress, and the only way for Muslims in Muslim-majority countries to become unstuck and to advance along with the world's nations, is to debunk this Islamist deadweight that has dragged us Muslims down to the status of the world's problem, rather than examples for mankind.

I wanted to thank you, for having the sincerity to pursue my arguments to the end, and for having the courage to take a bold and brave step and allow yourself space to discover new thoughts. Your country, and hopefully your region, will be a far better place with you in it.

Wassalam,

Maajid Nawaz

There is something more compelling than state power, more intimidating than all the bullets, all the torture, and all the chains that a brutal dictatorship can muster. It is fiercer than the iron fist of a despot and stronger than the stench of death. Since time immemorial, kings, rulers, and generals have feared the power of an idea.

An idea can outlive a demigod, outpace armies, and outlast censorship. And something that's even leaner, swifter, and more potent than an idea is a narrative. If an idea is a belief, its narrative is the propaganda used to spread that belief. The narrative, the story used to "sell" an idea, is the engine that gives an idea its power and influence. If an idea is nebulous, its narrative acts like a vortex, driving the idea forward. To control a narrative is to frame events and, ultimately, to shape history.

The Islamist narrative—that "the West" is engaged in a war against Islam—is a quintessential one. It has taken root and gained power. It has done what narratives are supposed to do—give ideas a way to spread. Those who fail to shape narratives face a lose/lose scenario: intervention in foreign countries is spun as "far too little, too late" in the case of Bosnia, yet spun as "illegal invasion" in the case of Syria.

True mastery over the destiny of nations comes by creating a vehicle that can carry the idea and narrative across time and space: enter the social movement. Social movements bring an idea to life, imbuing entire generations with a sense of emotional attachment to a cause or belief.

Ideas are like water: they take a while to reach boiling point, but as soon as they do, they erupt. We are still at the heating stage of our ideas; we require patience for our work to embed itself into society. Ever so slowly, we will start to see the boil.

—◦—

Soon after the UK version of *Radical* was released, I was contacted by a stranger. His name was Nick Jode, a self-confessed former racist and supporter of the right-wing British street movement, the English Defence League (EDL). He reached out to me after having read my book and said that it had changed his life. His letter said, in part:

I started to read lots on the internet about race issues and about the terrorist attacks of 9/11 and 7/7. . . . I looked at the problems the world was facing and saw that they too were caused by Muslims. It's no wonder then that I started seeing Islam as a destructive force, believing that Muslims were the cause of not only my own but also all the world's problems. I began shouting for and fighting for anyone who spoke out against Islam, eventually becoming a supporter of the English Defence League (EDL). . . .

[O]ne night, while I was browsing the web, looking for websites and information against Islam, I happened to come across a link on Twitter to Maajid Nawaz of Quilliam debating with Anjem Choudary of Islam4UK on Newsnight. As I watched the video, in which Anjem was advocating Islamic law in Britain and Maajid was opposing it, with interest, I found myself mesmerized by how Maajid beat Anjem in the debate.

At the same time, I began to investigate the future of EDL. Many of the people I met in the EDL were extreme and weren't interested in seeing another side to their issues, and I started to realize that I had been as closed-minded as the extremist Muslims I was against. Many of my so-called friends who were still EDL supporters stopped contact with me. . . .

When I came across Maajid's book Radical, I decided I really needed to read it. I wanted to learn more about Maajid and Quilliam, and I wanted to learn more about how Islam and Islamism are distinct. Over the past month I have seen so many of Maajid's speeches and have enormous respect for what he has achieved. I can finally say that I too have changed—I think we are all the same and can live alongside each other in peace.

Feeling proud that I could have a hand in pushing back not only Islamist extremism, but the racism that I spent my teenage years fighting, I tweeted about Nick Jode's turnaround. Soon after, and to my delight, another former EDL supporter replied saying that he knew of at least five others who had stopped supporting the EDL after being influenced by our work at Quilliam. We were carving out that middle ground, a united nations of democrats opposed to extremism in all its forms. It seemed like our efforts were beginning to find a place, even among British street politics. The vortex pushing our ideas forward was clearly working.

But, of course, ideas can be bad as well as good, and there is no guarantee that a popular idea will be a good one. In fact, sometimes those two things are diametrically opposed. In the twentieth century, communists realized the potency that is latent in ideas and began planting the seeds for their doctrine across the world through a series of social movements committed to spreading communism. In the Middle East, the communist idea was halted only by another: Islamism.

Islamists also realized that setting up social movements over generations to spread their idea (and by extension, their narrative) helps to create an unstoppable momentum. And so it was that they comfortably stepped into the vacuum created by young democratic Arabs who so passionately revolted against their dictators, but had failed to organize their own idea over decades. What despots have learned to fear, democrats are yet to master.

In perceiving the potency of ideas, Islamists vehemently oppose the rise of any intellectual alternative. They realize that if another idea were to take root in Muslim-majority nations, it would spell the beginning of the end for their own ideological stranglehold. This is why in October 2012 the world spun in shock as it woke to the news that the Taliban had shot fourteen-year-old schoolgirl Malala Yusufzai in the head at point-blank range simply for advocating that young girls should have the right to go to school. I went to Pakistan that month, working as usual to spread our own ideas and to build our own social movement, Khudi. We felt the need to respond with urgency.

The Khudi team had been preparing the ground for a weekly TV show that eventually aired as the *Khudi Debates* on Pakistan's Express TV every Saturday evening. We decided to film an episode of our show in Mingora, Swat, where the Taliban had shot that brave little schoolgirl as a gesture of solidarity with Malala and a protest to the Taliban. Our message to Pakistan was clear: the Taliban does not own Swat, nor does it own Pakistan. That same week *Newsweek* featured my profile in the global edition of its magazine, and *Newsweek Pakistan* placed this story on its cover. I had been worried that such prominent coverage might attract unwelcome attention to Khudi in Swat during a period as tense as this, but any cautionary hesitation I faced was dwarfed by the shame I felt that a schoolgirl had stood where a nation should have. We pressed ahead, and the episode in Mingora, debating who bears responsibility for extremism in Pakistan, became the first episode aired from our weekly series.

Since her shooting and her miraculous survival, Malala has been nominated for the Nobel Peace Prize and has fast become an international symbol of courage. In my 2011 TEDGlobal talk, I had argued that any counternarrative to Islamism in Muslim-majority societies needed to generate its own ideas, narratives, leaders, and symbols. Perhaps finally, in the tragedy and shock of Malala's shooting, democratic activists could find inspiration in a symbol of resistance. Perhaps, at long last, Pakistan could seize the moment and turn the tide of public opinion irreversibly against extremism. Alas, the window of opportunity was there, but it was brief. Again, lacking the machinery of social movements to make their case, democratic activists started off on a huge offensive, only to see their efforts eclipsed by the ubiquitous Islamist messaging machinery. Once again, the Islamist narrative had won.

Pictures of Malala sitting with the late US diplomat Richard Holbrooke fast began to circulate, first on the Internet and then in Urdu newspapers and on TV. Slowly, and with dread, we watched as the Urdu media of Pakistan started to entertain the despicable notion that, by sitting with Holbrooke, Malala may have been complicit in a US conspiracy to brainwash youngsters. Counteroffensives were launched, drawing attention away from Malala and instead to the innocent victims of foreign wars and US drone strikes. Without a preexisting and decades-old social movement in place, the basic fact that the Taliban had killed more Pakistanis than the US, Israel, or India simply would not be heard. Those who control the narrative control the nation.

On that same trip we took our counter-extremism movement to the streets, organizing a protest directly against the Taliban at Liberty roundabout in the city of Lahore. A few other civil society organizations had also held such protests, but none of us attracted anywhere near the throngs that come out whenever Islamists rallied the masses. More was needed— we had to continue to push the boundaries if our call had any chance of taking root. Our message was clear: the Taliban are child-killers; they can attack us, shoot us, blow us up, but they cannot silence us: our ideas will live on, they will continue to inspire people to stare down Taliban gunmen in defiance. You can't kill an idea. Ideas are bulletproof.

A year and a half before Malala's shooting, a symbol for a much different cause was also shot in the head at point-blank range. In May 2011 Osama bin Laden was found and executed by US Navy SEALs in Abottabad, Pakistan. Scenes of jubilation erupted in cities all over the United States. President Obama addressed the nation in what looked to me like a repeat of Bush's "mission accomplished" faux pas. Analysts clamored to hail the demise of al-Qaeda in sheer glee. I looked on anxiously. In this case, it was time for the Islamist idea to assert its own buoyancy beyond the life of any one person.

I knew that al-Qaeda would continue to grow long after bin Laden. With nothing but narratives as ammunition to hold the ideological frontlines against groups that believe in summary execution as a means for change, I couldn't help but feel that execution, as a method, had just received a huge boost from the United States itself. An inconvenient fact, often overlooked by we who presume to fight the "good fight," is that bad ideas are just as bulletproof as good ones. They wear the same flak jackets, dodge the same bullets, and erect the same blast shields. You can't kill an idea.

In December 2012 I was invited to Orange County, California, by some of Quilliam's supporters to celebrate Christmas as their guest. During my stay another of their guests turned up, and I was excitedly ushered forward by my hosts to meet the man. I soon realized why. The question pervaded the air without anyone needing to utter the words: How would this former Islamist greet one of the Navy SEALs team who had gone into Abbottabad that night to kill bin Laden? Back straight, eyes firm, I suddenly found myself face to face with this elite soldier, over a surreal brunch at the Ritz-Carlton in Laguna Beach.

I felt my body becoming unreasonably tense. I had spent years of my life evading men such as this, and I had no idea he was going to be there that day. In a past life, we would have been mortal enemies. In any life, he could kill me in a split second. And though we were now essentially working for the same overall goals, I didn't believe in executing my enemies and felt uneasy about meeting someone who had just done so.

He greeted me with a gentle demeanor befitting a true professional. "I've heard a lot about you and was told we should meet," he said, smiling. "Your work on the ground is crucial." With this endorsement, a hardened soldier had ironically disarmed me with his words before I could even fire a shot. I quickly checked myself. My disagreement is with those who give the orders, not with a soldier who risks his life to carry them out. I let this be just a brunch at the Ritz with my American friends.

In my humble view, it would have been far more consistent to bring bin Laden to justice, as had been attempted with Saddam Hussein, who, due to fears that he was able and willing to unleash chemical warfare, was certainly deemed no less dangerous. Except there was an election on the horizon for an already embattled president, and President Obama would not take the risk of anything going wrong. Forgive me for being cynical, but I found myself agreeing with the sentiments of schoolteacher Jessica Dovey:

I will mourn the loss of thousands of precious lives, but I will not rejoice in the death of one, not even an enemy.

In light of Jessica's words, which spread around the world and were erroneously attributed to Dr. Martin Luther King Jr., the street celebrations after bin Laden's execution seemed to me rather brash. As I had expected, al-Qaeda continued to go from strength to strength. Ayman al-Zawahiri, an Egyptian who, like me, had spent time in Egypt's jails, was quickly appointed the head of al-Qaeda. Even George W. Bush, despite all the mistakes of his militarized neo-conservatism, had come to realize the importance of inverting his model and working to bolster grassroots initiatives during the last two years of his administration. Frustratingly, the Obama administration took its eye completely off this crucial ideas debate. Amid a policy of targeted drone killings at a frequency far higher than Bush's—including the controversial targeted killing of an American citizen, al-Awlaki, in Yemen—Obama's administration turned toward a crude, results-driven desire to secure body bags.

When tactics become the strategy, you lose sight of the overall aim. And this is how the heirs of Osama bin Laden strategically blindsided the Obama administration. Al-Qaeda deftly utilized the security vacuum created in North Africa after the Arab uprisings and moved in with the dexterity of a surgeon's hand. Soon, under their new Egyptian leader's command, the group had achieved what it had never done under bin Laden himself: control of a territory the size of France directly by al-Qaeda in sub-Saharan Mali, as the ancient city of Timbuktu was seized and razed by jihadist militants. In Yemen, the Abyan province and then chunks of land in the southwest of the country came under direct al-Qaeda control as well. In Syria, the uprising to remove that country's brutal dictator was all but hijacked by Jabhat al-Nusra, a group formed of al-Qaeda veterans who descended upon this new battlefield from neighboring Iraq.

By April 2013 al-Qaeda in Iraq had announced its merger with Jabhat al-Nusra in Syria, under orders from Zawahiri himself. The simple fact was that since bin Laden's death, al-Qaeda had gone from being a terrorist group to a full-blown insurgency in at least Mali, Yemen, and the Levant. You can't kill an idea. Ideas are bulletproof.

And then there was Libya. In September 2012, Noman and I were sitting in the Quilliam office in London gaping at our news screens. An unknown had uploaded a "film" to YouTube that was gratuitously insulting to the Prophet of Islam. Some hooligans across various Muslim-majority countries seized on this event to incite riots and looting. The Islamist narrative that there was a full-blown war against Islam had just received a huge boost.

Symbiotically, the right-wing narrative that Muslims were uncivilized, ungovernable thugs had also just received reaffirmation. But that was not what we were gaping at. The news was reporting that US ambassador to Libya Chris Stevens had just been killed amid mob riots in the city of Benghazi. The accepted view across all media outlets was that this death was a result of the film, and the US government confirmed this version of events.

After some brief and tense calls to our network on the ground in Benghazi, Noman turned to me and said grimly, "Maajid, this was not a spontaneous attack."

"What are you saying, Noman?" I asked.

The reply came with Noman's characteristic confidence: "It is my belief, from the information that I have gathered, that Ambassador Chris Stevens was assassinated in a preplanned al-Qaeda terrorist attack in revenge for the US drone killing of al-Qaeda's number two, abu Yahya al-Libi."

I stared blankly at Noman, taking in what he had just said.

"I think we should make a statement," he continued.

"But, Noman, the entire world, the US government, CNN, the BBC, everyone is saying this was a spontaneous attack. Are they all wrong? How can we be so sure?"

Noman looked at me with steely determination and the sigh of someone who has been too much in life. "This attack was timed to coincide with the anniversary of 9/11, and a warning had already been given by al-Zawahiri in a pre-released video. The attack was orchestrated with military precision in two waves, using RPGs, which are not found randomly among mere angry mobs. Let me draft something, and you can see if you agree."

Instinctively knowing he was right, I let him put something together.

By the next day, while the world was still focused on the "film" and the deaths resulting from the furor surrounding it, the obvious seemed to be staring at me from a piece of paper on my desk. No doubt about it, the killing of Stevens was an al-Qaeda operation.

"Noman, if we release this, you do realize that we're putting our reputation on the line? If we're wrong, governments, the media, and especially Muslims will ridicule us." I continued, "They'll say, 'Here's Quilliam trying to resurrect the terrorism debate after terrorism is dead along with bin Laden.'"

Noman looked me square in the eyes. "But we're right, Maajid."

"And if we're right, we severely embarrass the Obama administration and people lose their jobs. No one is saying what we are about to claim," I said.

"It's the right thing to do," he said simply. He was correct, of course.

What was happening was nothing short of a scandal. Whether deliberately contrived or negligently missed, the world's greatest power had turned away from the terrorism agenda. It was as if with a killing here or a drone strike there—all the while seeing no evil, hearing no evil—Obama had hoped that the problem would simply cease to exist. But al-Qaeda continued to spread, maturing into an insurrection with deep roots in some of the world's most troubled countries. *You can't kill an idea.* Somebody needed to shake things up.

After we sent out the press release, our phones and email accounts came alive. The allegation we had made was initially reported with skepticism and credited to Quilliam. As the East Coast of the United States awoke, the rate of press queries we were receiving started rising to fever pitch, and our phones began dancing to their own tune. Pundits who we knew for a fact had received our press release—they are on our mailing list—started repeating our words verbatim across US media outlets without crediting their source.

Eventually, experts and news outlets began realizing that they might have all made a mistake. Received wisdom had shifted; what had happened in Benghazi was now deemed a terrorist attack. It took the US government another week to finally accept the truth. The CIA eventually conceded that it had arrived at the same conclusion, and the White House issued a public admission.

The family of Chris Stevens and other victims would now know the truth and could better seek justice. "Uncivilized" Muslim mobs in Libya would no longer be made the scapegoat for a preplanned terrorist attack. Obama's administration had learned the hard way not to neglect the terrorism agenda.

From our office in central London, Quilliam had just forced the world's only superpower to change its course. That's the power of an idea.

Glossary of Arabic Terms

(Except where indicated: Urdu/Punjabi)

Akhi (my brother)

'Alayhi salam (shortened Muslim prayer for Prophets: upon him be peace)

Al-Jabbar (The Compeller—one of the ninety-nine names of Allah)

Allahu akbar (God is great)

Allahu mustu'un (prayer: help is sought from Allah)

Assalaamu alaykum (greeting: Peace be upon you)

Amir (leader)

Azan (call to prayer)

Beta (Urdu: son)

Bhai (Urdu: brother)

Bi iznillah (with Allah's permission)

Da'i (missionary)

Daris (student)

Dariseen (students)

Da'wah (mission)

Deen (religion)

Eeman (faith)

Fee sabeelillah (in the path of Allah)

Ghimamah (blindfold)

Habib (dear friend, beloved)

Halal (permissible)

Halaqah (private study circle)

Hizbi (a partisan)

Itnain (two)

Itnain wa arba'een (forty-two)

Kafir (infidel)

Khilafah (caliphate)

Kuffar (infidels)

Kufr (disbelief)

Muhajir (immigrants, plural *muhajiroon*. Also the name of a banned extremist group in London founded by Omar Bakri Muhammad)
Muraja'aat (revisions)
Mu'taqal (the arbitrarily detained, plural *mu'taqaleen*)
Nana Abu (Urdu: maternal grandfather)
Nani Ammi (Urdu: maternal grandmother)
Nikah (marriage ceremony)
Qiyadah (leadership)
Raqam (number)
Sall Allahu alayhi wa-salam (longer Muslim prayer for the Prophet: May Allah's peace and blessings be upon him)
Shahadah (martyrdom, testimony of faith)
Shaikh (learned man, religious scholar, old man)
Shari'ah (body of Islamic edicts)
Shaweesh (conscripted Egyptian guard)
Sohni (Punjabi: beautiful)
Subhan Allah (Muslim invocation: Exalted be Allah)
Tai Ammi (Urdu: wife to eldest paternal uncle)
Wahid (one)
Wilayah (province)
Wallahi (oath: by Allah)
Ya Allah (O Allah)
Zaabit (officer)
Zalim (tyrant, plural—*zalimun*)

Resources

1. Maajid Nawaz debating Anjem Choudary on BBC *Newsnight*, www
.youtube.com/watch?v=2BrueU4xd2w.
2. *Telegraph* article about the arrested coup-plotters in the Pakistan army,
www.telegraph.co.uk/news/worldnews/asia/pakistan/1440284/Pakistan
-army-officers-arrested-in-terror-swoop.html.
3. Transcript of an exchange between Maajid Nawaz and Dr. Sa'ad al-Din
Ibrahim after the former's release from prison, www.bushcenter.com/down
loads/theInstitute/human-freedom/wave-of-freedom/A_Conversation
_with_Dr_Ibrahim.pdf.
4. Maajid Nawaz and John Cornwall Amnesty International promotional
video, www.youtube.com/watch?v=GpNzOBhvtoA.
5. Profile of Gita Sahgal, http://en.wikipedia.org/wiki/Gita_Sahgal.
6. Maajid Nawaz's BBC *HARDtalk* interview with Sarah Montague,
during the last of his HT days, http://news.bbc.co.uk/1/hi/programmes/
hardtalk/4931416.stm.
7. Quilliam website, www.quilliamfoundation.org/.
8. BBC *Newsnight* featuring Maajid Nawaz's journey from HT and Islamism,
part 1: www.youtube.com/watch?v=HYtP-4r4OE8
part 2: www.youtube.com/watch?v=2yLZRONdIa0
part 3: www.youtube.com/watch?v=CM4pkRqL0c0.
9. Lord Ashdown's remarks at the Quilliam launch, www.youtube.com/
watch?v=5KfLQ6olnwA.
10. Jemima Khan's remarks at the Quilliam launch, www.youtube.com/
watch?v=oN0QBNXMjxQ.
11. Survivor of 7/7 Rachel North's remarks at the Quilliam launch, www
.youtube.com/watch?v=5BbXckInd8Q&list=UU7fkP6rdeoTbrzlr7oXK
3Vw&index=77&feature=plcp.
12. Seumas Milne's far-left criticism of Quilliam, www.guardian.co.uk/
commentisfree/2008/jul/17/islam.race.
13. Glenn Beck's right-wing criticism of Maajid Nawaz and Quilliam,
www.youtube.com/watch?v=O_gr6FOBwOg.

14. BBC *Doha Debate*, Maajid Nawaz hosted by Tim Sebastian arguing against politicized Islam, www.thedohadebates.com/debates/player.asp?d=42.

15. Intelligence Squared debate, Maajid Nawaz and Zeba Khan defending the faith of Islam from anti-Islam rhetoric against Ayan Hirsi Ali and Douglas Murray, www.intelligencesquared.com/events/islam-is-a-religion-of-peace.

16. Maajid Nawaz interviewed on *Larry King Live*, www.youtube.com/watch?v=IF_A02IF4Bc.

17. Maajid Nawaz interviewed in-depth by al-Jazeera's Riz Khan, www.youtube.com/watch?v=4z1Eps1wJjQ.

18. Maajid Nawaz profiled on CBS *60 Minutes*, www.cbsnews.com/video/watch/?id=6711907n.

19. Maajid Nawaz's Facebook public page, www.facebook.com/MaajidNawazFanPage.

20. Maajid Nawaz's Twitter page, https://twitter.com/#!/MaajidNawaz.

21. Maajid Nawaz testifies in the US Senate,
part 1: www.youtube.com/watch?v=4XJLkdCgHQc
part 2: www.youtube.com/watch?v=HCF2dhtfy7k&feature=related.

22. Maajid Nawaz's video blog response to Sayyid Qutb's *The America that I Saw*,
part 1: www.youtube.com/watch?v=Q0qdURg4Qz0
part 2: www.youtube.com/watch?v=7mX6A27D5g0
part 3: www.youtube.com/watch?v=y3JqAKi2FTU.

23. Maajid Nawaz testifies in UK parliament, www.publications.parliament.uk/pa/cm201012/cmselect/cmhaff/uc1446-i/uc144601.htm.

24. Prime Minister Brown cites Maajid Nawaz among reasons for not banning HT in the UK, www.publications.parliament.uk/pa/cm200708/cmhansrd/cm071114/debtext/71114-0005.htm.

25. Analysis of HT activity within the Pakistani army, www.ctc.usma.edu/posts/hizb-al-tahrir-a-new-threat-to-the-pakistan-army.

26. Khudi website, www.khudipakistan.com/.

27. Maajid Nawaz on the TED stage launching the idea for a counter-extremism social movement, www.ted.com/talks/maajid_nawaz_a_global_culture_to_fight_extremism.html.

28. BBC *Newsnight* tour of Maajid Nawaz to Pakistan,
part 1: www.youtube.com/watch?v=yixGca6zZg4
part 2: www.youtube.com/watch?v=3unCtnLVZ-4.
29. Pakistan Lawyer's Movement, http://en.wikipedia.org/wiki/Lawyers%27_Movement.
30. Khudi youth magazine *Laaltain*'s website, www.laaltain.com.
31. Maajid Nawaz at Google Zeitgeist, www.zeitgeistminds.com/videos/impact-of-ideology.
32. Maajid Nawaz interviewed by *Newsweek*'s Christopher Dickey at Goa's THINKFest, www.youtube.com/watch?v=rKBE9Bm8aCI.
33. News on Bangladeshi military thwarting an HT coup attempt, http://newagebd.com/newspaper1/frontpage/49718.html.

ACKNOWLEDGMENTS

This book would not have been possible without the help of the key people who made it happen. Firstly, I would like to thank my agent and friend Neil Blair and his colleague Zoe King at The Blair Partnership. Neil, despite us initially meeting for an entirely unrelated purpose, you immediately saw the importance of my work and supported me above and beyond the call of duty. Thank you. Thanks also go to Jonathan Blair for suggesting that I abandon the large, corporate US agencies and consider instead his twin brother. It worked. I am indebted to the UK publishing director of the Virgin and WH Allen imprints at Ebury, Ed Faulkner, a visionary who saw me on the TED stage and instantly became enthused about the need to get my story out there. I'd also like to thank Yvonne Jacob at Ebury for being so proactive in spotting my story in the first instance, and Caroline Newbury, Sarah Bennie, and the entire publishing team for their support and backing. From the US publishing team at the Lyons Press imprint of Globe Pequot Press, I would like to particularly thank Jon Sternfeld. Jon, who would have guessed that you would go from being my prospective agent to my publisher! I should also mention Sharon Kunz, Meredith Dias, and the rest of the sterling team at Globe Pequot. Thanks to my co-writer, Tom Bromley, for the hours spent conducting interviews, transcribing my words, and picking my brain so that he could provide the structure I could build upon for this book. Thank you to Faye Husain, wife of Ed Husain, for fearlessly telling me to get more emotionally engaged with my rather stoic first draft, despite her husband's belief that "It would do." Thanks to Fatima Mullick for reading through my words so diligently, and putting me in my place when I was sounding too grandiose. Thanks to my son Ammar for reading the prologue and telling me it sounded really "cool." Ammar, now you can read on. Thank you to my family for being so patient while I worked endlessly on this book. A special mention for my mum, who ensured that the facts about my family history were correct, and for my little niece

Nusaybah, whom I didn't see enough of while I was busy writing, but at least you have now been joined by your little brother Burhaan.

This story would not be complete were it not for my many early supporters: Iqbal Wahhab, Jemima Khan, Ruth Turner, Evelyn Rothschild, Hazel Blears, Dougie Smith, Dean Godson, Catherine Fieschi, Jonty Feldman, Michael Gove, and Yonca Brunini, and my main man, Rich. From the United States, I would particularly like to thank Michael Davidson, Bailey Cuzner and the GenNext team, Darren Henderson, Courtney La Bau, Frank K, Chad Sweet, Farah Pandith, Juan Zarate, Jared Cohen, Dan Sutherland, Tim C, Paul D'Agostino, Truman Anderson, Mauro Lorenzo, and Michael Murray.

My thanks to the tireless staff at Quilliam, especially Noman, Harriet, and Milly, who expertly handled things for me while I was away compiling this story, and the brave team at Khudi Pakistan: Imran, Ali, Shabbir, Rab Nawaz, and Umair, for building the dream. Finally, to Rachel I send my love.